The Ark of Yahweh
in Redemptive History

The Ark of Yahweh in Redemptive History

A Revelatory Instrument of Divine Attributes

Deuk-il Shin

WIPF & STOCK · Eugene, Oregon

THE ARK OF YAHWEH IN REDEMPTIVE HISTORY
A Revelatory Instrument of Divine Attributes

Copyright © 2012 Deuk-il Shin. All rights reserved. Except for brief quotations in critical publications or reviews, no part of this book may be reproduced in any manner without prior written permission from the publisher. Write: Permissions, Wipf and Stock Publishers, 199 W. 8th Ave., Suite 3, Eugene, OR 97401.

Wipf & Stock
An Imprint of Wipf and Stock Publishers
199 W. 8th Ave., Suite 3
Eugene, OR 97401
www.wipfandstock.com

ISBN 13: 978-1-61097-329-8
Manufactured in the U.S.A.

Bible translation: The author does not follow a specific English translation of the Bible. Instead he translated the Hebrew texts by consulting different translations, such as KJV, NASB, NIV, and ESV to arrive at the proper English expression.

*To my wife, Jeongsook Park
and two sons, Sangdoo and Sanghwa*

Contents

Acknowledgments / ix

Abbreviations List / xi

Introduction / xv

1. The Origin of the Ark / 1
2. The "Constituents" of the Ark / 14
3. The Appellations for the Ark / 27
4. The Suggested Functions of the Ark / 32
5. The Ark in the Pentateuch / 45
6. The Ark in the Book of Joshua / 52
7. The Ark in the Book of 1 Samuel / 69
8. The Ark in the Book of 2 Samuel / 84
9. The Ark in the Book of 1 Kings / 105
10. The Ark in the Poetic and Prophetic Books / 114
11. Some Theological Considerations / 127

Bibliography / 151

Scripture index / 165

Author Index / 179

Acknowledgments

This book is a concise and largely revised version of my dissertation at North West University in Potchefstroom, South Africa (2004). I am forever grateful to Dr. F. N. Lion-Cachet, my supervisor. Gratitude is also expressed to Professor Philip H. Eveson of London Theological Seminary for his encouragement and recommendation, and also to his wife, Jenny, who read proofs with care. I would like to thank Dr. John Currid at Reformed Theological Seminary in Charlotte, NC, who recommended that this book be published. My thanks also go to the library of Tyndale House in Cambridge, UK, where I have researched almost every winter since 1999, as well as to the library of Reformed Theological Seminary in Jackson, MS, where I was privileged to stay as a visiting scholar (2004). Appreciation is also extended to Dr. Woudstra's work as it offered many insights for this study on the basis of Reformed view of the Bible. Finally, I wish to thank the staff at Wipf and Stock Publishers and my professional copyeditor, Nancy Shoptaw.

D. I. Shin (Duke)
Busan, 2012, Feb.

Abbreviations

AB	Anchor Bible
ABD	*Anchor Bible Dictionary*. Edited by D. N. Freedman. 6 vols. New York: Doubleday, 1992.
AEL	*Arabic-English Lexicon: derived from the best and the most copious eastern sources*. Edward William Lane. Beirut: Librairie du Liban, 1968.
AHw	*Akkadisches Handwörterbuch*. W. von Soden. 3 vols. Wiesbaden: Harrassowitz, 1965.1981.
AJSL	American *Journal of Semitic Languages and Literature*
ANET	*Ancient Near Eastern Texts Relating to the Old Testament*. 3rd ed. Edited by J. B. Pritchard. Princeton: Princeton University Press, 1969.
AOAT	Alter Orient und Altes Testament
AOTC	Apollos Old Testament Commentary
ATD	Das Alte Testament Deutsch
BAR	*Biblical Archaeology Review*
BBR	*Bulletin for Biblical Research*
BJS	Brown Judaic Studies
BKAT	Biblischer Kommentar Altes Testament.
BN	*Biblische Notizen*
BuK	*Bibel und Kirche*
BWA(N)T	Beiträge zur Wissenschaft vom Alten (und Neuen) Testament
BZ	*Biblische Zeitschrift*
BZAW	Beihefte zur Zeitschrift fur die altestamentliche Wissenschaft.

Abbreviations

CAD	The Assyrian Dictionary of the Oriental Institute of the University of Chicago. Edited by A. L. Oppenheim et al. Chicago: Oriental Institute, 1956.
CAT	Commentaire de l'Ancien Testament
CB	Century Bible
CBC	Cambridge Bible Commentary
CBQ	*Catholic Biblical Quarterly*
COT	Commentaar op het Oude Testament
DBI	*Dictionary of Biblical Imagery*
DCH	*Dictionary of Classical Hebrew*. Edited by W. Smith and H. Wace. 4 vols. London, 1877–1887.
DDD	*Dictionary of Deities and Demons in the Bible*. Edited by K. van der Toorn, B. Becking, and P. W. van der Horst. Leiden: Brill, 1995.
DISO	*Dictionnaire des inscriptions sémitiques de l'ouest*. Edited by Ch. F. Jean and J. Hoftijzer. Leiden, 1965.
ErIsrI	Eretz-Israel
EdF	Erträge der Forschung
EH	Europäische Hochschulschriften
ÉTR	*Études theologiques et religieuses*
EvT	Evangelische Theologie
FRLANT	Forschungen zur Religion und Literatur des Alten und Neuen Testaments
GK	*Gesenius' Hebräische Grammatik*. Edited by E. Kautzsch. Leipzig: Vogel, 1909.
HALAT	Koehler, Ludwig, and Walter Baumgartner, *Hebräisches und Aramäisches Lexikon Supplement zum Alten Testament*. Leiden: Brill, 1996.
HAR	Hebrew Annual Review
HAT	Handbuch zum Alten Testament
HCOT	Historical Commentary Old Testament
IB	*Interpreter's Bible*. Edited by G. A. Buttrick et al. 12 vols. New York: Abingdon, 1951–1957.

ICC	International Critical Commentary
IDB	*The Interpreter's Dictionary of the Bible*. Edited by G. A. Buttrick. 4 vols. Nashville: Abingdon, 1962.
IEJ	*Israel Exploration Journal*
IVP	InterVarsity Press
JBL	*Journal of Biblical Literature*
JNES	*Journal of Near Eastern Studies*
JNSL	*Journal of Northwest Semitic Languages*
Joüon	Joüon, P. A *Grammar of Biblical Hebrew*. Translated and revised by T. Muraoka. 2 vols. Subsidia biblica 14/1.2. Rome, 1991.
JPS	Jewish Publication Society
JSOT	*Journal for the Study of the Old Testament*
JSOTSup	*Journal for the Study of the Old Testament Supplement Series*
JTS	*Journal of Theological Studies*
KAT	Kommentar zum Alten Testament
KHC	Kurzer Hand-Commentar zum Alten Testament
KTU	*Die Keilalphabetischen Texte aus Ugarit*. Edited by M. Dietrich, O. Loretz, and J. Sanmartin. AOAT 24/1. Neukirchen-Vluyn, 1976. 2d enlarged ed. of KTU: *The Cuneiform Alphabetic Texts from Ugarit, Ras Ibn Hani, and Other Places*. Edited by M. Dietrich, O. Loretz, and J. Sanmartin. Münster, 1995. (=CTU).
KUB	*Keilschrifturkunden aus Boghazköi*
NAC	New American Commentary
NCB	New Century Bible
NCBC	New Century Bible Commentary
NEB	Neue Echter Bibel
NedTT	*Nederlands Theologisch Tijdschrift*
NIDOTTE	*New International Dictionary of Old Testament Theology and Exegesis*. Edited by Willem A. VanGemeren. 5 vols. Carlisle, UK: Paternoster, 1996.

NSKAT	Neuer Stuttgarter Kommentar Altes Testament
NV	*Nieuwe vertaling*
OBO	*Orbis Biblicus et Orientalis*
OLZ	*Orientalistische Literaturzeitung*
OTL	Old Testament Library
PEQ	*Palestine Exploration Quarterly*
POut	De Prediking van het Oude Testament
QD	Quaestiones disputatae
RB	*Revue Biblique*
Ref	*De Reformatie*
RlA	*Reallexikon der Assyriologie*. Edited by Erich Ebeling et al. Berlin: Gruyter, 1928.
SB	Stuttgarter Bibelstudien
SBLDS	Society of Biblical Literature Dissertation Series
SCSS	Septuagint and Cognate Studies Series
TB	Theologische Bücherei: Neudrucke und Berichte aus dem 20. Jahrhundert.
THAT	*Theologisches Handwörterbuch zum Alten Testament*. Edited by E. Jenni, with assistance from C. Westermann. 2 vols. Stuttgart: Kaiser, 1971–1976.
TRE	*Theologische Realenzyklopädie*. Edited by G. Krause and G. Muller. Berlin: Gruyter, 1977.
ThWAT	*Theologisches Wörterbuch zum Alten Testament*. Edited by G. J. Botterweck and H. Ringgren. Stuttgart: Kaiser, 1970.
TZ	*Theologische Zeitschrift*
UF	*Ugarit-Forschungen*
VT	*Vetus Testamentum*
WBC	World Biblical Commentary
WMANT	Wissenschaftliche Monographien zum Alten und Neuen Testament
ZAW	*Zeitschrift für die alttestamentliche Wissenschft*
ZB	Zürcher Bibelkommentare
ZMR	*Zeitschrift für die Missionskunde und Religionswissenschft*

Introduction

THE IMAGELESS WORSHIP OF Yahweh is regarded as one of the most striking characteristics of the Israelite religion, differing from the idol worship of the surrounding nations. However, the ark of Yahweh functioned as the unique symbol of God's presence. It was located in the most holy place of the temple in the promised land and was the centerpiece of Israelite existence in Old Testament times. A biblical theme deemed of such importance can usually expect to attract much attention from biblical scholars, but only a few studies about the significance of the ark in the Old Testament have been undertaken: the monographs of Dibelius, Sevensma, Brouwer, Maier, and Woudstra.[1] Their scholarly works attempted to investigate the meaning and function of the ark in the Old Testament period. However, the results of their researches hardly reach a consensus, since their presuppositions and methodologies are quite diverse.

Such postulates seem to have been influenced by the philosophies of the day. As a result, these works fail to render satisfactory answers to numerous questions raised about the ark of Yahweh in the Old Testament. Their conclusions will be examined in the following chapters.

Whether or not the methodologies and viewpoints that the authors employed to determine the meaning of the ark are appropriate, the outcome of the research is questionable. However, if such studies are

1. In the twentieth century five major monographs were published: Dibelius, *Die Lade Jahves*; Sevensma, *De ark Gods*; Brouwer, *De ark*; J. Maier, *Altisraelitisch Heiligtum*; and Woudstra, *Ark of the Covenant from Conquest to Kingship*. During the 1970s three further monographs about the ark were issued. However, the writers only cover the ark texts found in 1 and 2 Sam because they regarded these texts as a literary unit, "the ark narrative." These monographs bore the following titles: Schicklberger, *Die Ladeerzahlung des ersten Samuel-Buches*; Campbell, *Ark Narrative (1 Samuel 4:6; 2 Samuel 6)*; and Miller and Roberts, *Hand of the Lord*. In addition, there is Arnold's work, *Ephod and Ark*, a monograph of research about the ark based on the relationship between ephod and the ark in the Massoretic text (MT) and LXX, particularly in the historical books. In addition, there were a huge number of articles that contributed further studies on the ark.

carefully appraised, some may make helpful contributions in assessing the importance of the ark. It is also important to examine the biblical materials, acknowledging the intention of the divine Author as he made use of surrogate authors at various times. This means that in studying biblical writings, the acts of God in history cannot be ignored, since the plain reading of the text roots God's revelation in actual history.

As for its aims and hypothesis, this book seeks to examine the ark of Yahweh in the Old Testament primarily from a redemptive historical standpoint, although a philological-historical-theological method of exegesis is applied (i.e., a three-dimensional approach, in contrast to the historico-literary and traditio-historical [*überlieferungsgeschichtlichen*] approaches that have been employed predominantly when studying the subject of the ark).[2]

Although the contributions of scholars who used the same sort of approach will be acknowledged, this monograph will be a fresh attempt within this field to deal with the ark as described throughout the whole Old Testament.[3] The research will focus on an elucidation of the ark on the basis of the biblical texts while bringing out the richness of their meaning.

The point of departure is the self-evident nature of the scriptures. The Old Testament as well as the New Testament is God-given. The Holy Spirit not only inspired the authors but also moved the people of God to accept the two testaments as the authoritative word of God. The special

---

2. Historical-literary criticism, which has not only been welcomed widely as a comprehensive methodology of Old Testament study since Wellhausen but also was predominantly used in Sevensma's and J. Maier's study of the ark of Yahweh, whereas traditio-historical criticism initiated by Gunkel was applied to Dibelius's research of the ark.

3. Even though Brouwer commences with a critique of both main critical methods, he still aligns himself with this method, to some extent, in that he takes the book of Joshua as "the sheer deuteronomistic" or "the deuteronomistic writing" (*De ark*, 30, 111; see 116). Such a disposition is implied in his explanation of the concept of redemptive history, which he employs as a point of departure for his research. He specifies the term as *exclusief-heilshistorisch*, (exclusive-redemptive historical) that is different from historical facts as such, and from an *inclusief heilshistorische* (inclusive-redemptive historical) which is said to contain actual historical facts (16). However, the biblical documents have to do with bare facts in history as well as historical events that are characterized by God's intention for redemption because the Bible does not allow a distinction between bare facts and meaningful facts. Woudstra's work offers salient theological and exegetical insights on this subject. However, his study is not an all-inclusive research on the ark in the Old Testament.

interest of God resulted in the providential formation of each biblical book and the establishment of the canon.

Primarily, the interpretation of scripture is to be guided by faith, in contrast, for example, to Fohrer, who investigates the Old Testament in terms identical to those of any other literature and who states that understanding the Old Testament does not require faith.[4] In fact, it is preferable that the interpretation of scripture is approached from the confessional standpoint of faith because one can apply all the exegetical instruments available from historical, linguistic, and philological research and never reach the heart of the matter unless one shares the basic experience from which the biblical writers speak, namely faith.[5] Therefore, a priori, Christian faith is essential for an understanding of the scriptures.

Furthermore, the fact that God's revelation consists of two elements (event and word) and also that the scriptures appear in historical form requires the exegete to consider historical and philological approaches in his/her exegesis of the Bible. History is the first context for interpretation. The exegete is to pay due regard to the historical aspect because the nature of scripture, God's eternal word given in human words in history, demands it.[6] The term "philology" is used in many fields including linguistics and literary study. It is necessary to consider literary forms of the biblical texts in a proper way, for scripture has various ways of speaking (Heb 1:1) and the process of interpretation requires a variety of hermeneutical approaches, corresponding to the diversity of texts.

Exegesis also requires theological insight. Without such a perspective the work of exegetical interpretation may become misleading by isolating individual texts. The theological perspective may not only be obtained from the Old Testament itself but from the relationship between the Old Testament and the New Testament and sequential processes through the two testaments. For Christian scholars, the Old Testament should not be regarded as mere Hebrew literature or the Hebrew Bible but should be accepted as an authoritative canon along with the New Testament. The principle behind this interpretation, a tradition already illustrated in Augustine—"The New Testament reveals what is veiled in

---

4. Fohrer, *Theologische Grundstrukturen*, 31.

5. Hasel, *Old Testament Theology*, 200–201; see Körtner, *Der inspirierte Leser*, 60; Cazelles, *Écriture Parole et Esprit*, 89.

6. Fee, "History as Context," 32; see Lion-Cachet, *So het dit begin*, 2.

the Old"[7]—reflects the redemptive historical approach in exegesis at a theological level. Thus, a theological presupposition is required as the starting point of biblical exegesis.

There are different theological themes, motifs, and concepts available for describing the meaning of Old Testament texts: covenant, kingdom of God, promise and fulfillment, redemptive history, the name Yahweh, God himself, etc.[8] Although they all carry some weight in their own right as themes in the Old Testament, redemptive history is preferred and adopted in this study for interpreting the Old Testament. This concept links the two Testaments[9] and acts as the basis of the religious life and faith of Israel.[10] The redemptive history theme is also useful as a comprehensive umbrella concept for a variety of other themes such as covenant, God's reign, promise and fulfillment. In many respects, it deserves to be adopted as a theological point of departure for interpreting the Bible, since redemptive history is not a static topic but has a proper and exegetical perspective as a dynamic theme denoting God's activity in redeeming and perfecting his saving will.[11] The concept of redemptive history is a theological presupposition that is set out by the Bible itself. Needless to say, it is not the only perspective, as Long denotes: "Redemptive history is a necessary condition of the truth of the Christian faith, even if it is not a sufficient condition thereof."[12]

However, because the term "redemptive history" (German: *Heilsgeschichte*) was first introduced in rationalistic circles, it is still flawed like other terms that originated from rationalistic approaches to the Old Testament.[13] However, it should prove useful because the term helps in understanding the historical texts of the Bible, for even the Bible itself is representative of the concept of redemptive history, although it preceded this term and therefore does not directly mention it.

To be sure, the Bible, as the word of God, does more than describe history. The biblical text points to the historical facts but relates the his-

---

7. Augustine, *De Civitate Dei contra Paganos*, 5:18: "reuelante testamento nouo quod in uetere uelatum fuit."

8. See Hasel, *Old Testament Theology*, 139–71.

9. See Fuller, *Unity*; Cullmann, *Christus und Zeit*, 68–69.

10. See Weippert, "Fargen," 419–21.

11. G. Maier, *Biblische Hermeneutik*, 167–73.

12. Long, *Art*, 99.

13. See Trimp, *Heilsgeschiedenis en prediking*, 44.

tory with redemptive significance. Redemptive history, as a process for the historical realization of God's eternal plan of salvation in Christ, plays a key role in God's revelation. Thus, the Bible has a redemptive-historical character. For centuries the Bible has declared that God has saved his people. Within this context the concept of the narrative will not be separated from historicity because narratives that exclude historicity cannot be regarded as portraying God's work.

Redemptive history as an exegetical viewpoint at the theological level has a variety of manifestations. These include *historia revelationis*, history of covenant, salvation history, God-centered, christocentric, and christological approaches. Exegesis based on this is following the historical-philological method of interpretation. This approach, primarily from the perspective of redemptive history, and the basis of my hypothesis, will be applied to the exegesis of the texts in question.

1

The Origin of the Ark

THE TERM "ARK" IN English is rendered from the Hebrew term *'ᵃrōn*.¹ Yet the etymology of *'ᵃrōn* is uncertain. What is known is that it has some cognates from the Semitic language.² In other references outside the texts, this word is used variously for "chest," "cashbox," "coffer," "ossuary," and "sarcophagus," implying some kind of container shaped like a rectangular wooden box. While a secular usage of *'ᵃrōn* occurs in the Bible when it is rendered "coffin" (Gen 50:26) and "chest for money" (2 Kgs 12:10, 11; 2 Chr 24:8, 10, 11), when applied to the cultic object it is always translated as "ark."³ In the Old Testament the vast majority of occurrences specify the ark as a cultic object (195 times) with various qualifications.⁴ Accordingly, research on the ark in the Old Testament requires exegetical and theological work.

A. CRITICAL APPROACHES

Many scholars have offered different suggestions concerning the provenance of the ark, ascribing the biblical references to the ark to P's (Priestly Codex) fabrication, which is allegedly ascribed to the latest document among biblical critics. Specifically Wellhausen, who applied historico-literary criticism to biblical interpretation, doubted the Mosaic origin of the ark in that he thoroughly denied the existence of the tabernacle in Exodus 25 where the instructions for both are found,⁵ while he believed

---

1. It is not understandable why *'ᵃrōn* in Hebrew Bible was vocalized in *nomen regens*.
2. Akkadian *arānu*; Phoenician *'rn*; Empire Aramaic *'rnn* (pl.); Nabatian *'rn'*; Judean Aramaic *'rwnh* (*DISO*, 25; *CAD* A2:231; *AHw* 65).
3. See Zobel, "*'ᵃrōn*," *ThWAT* 1:394.
4. See Seow, "Designation," 185.
5. J. Wellhausen, *Prolegomena*, 6: Georg Reimer, 1927, 40–41: "die hebräische

that the existence of the ark of Yahweh was certainly traceable toward the end of the period of the Judges (1 Sam 4–6).[6] In fact, for him the existence of the ark had nothing to do with the tabernacle because P fabricated it, although the two necessarily belonged together. Moreover his advocacy that the concept of atonement by blood was developed in P in the final stages of the historical evolution of Israelite religion contrasts with the biblical text concerning the origin of the ark, since the atonement place was to be located on the ark from the outset (Exod 25:17–22; 30:6; 35:12; 39:35; 40:20; Lev 16:2, 13–15; Num 7:89). As a proponent of Wellhausen's historico-literary criticism, W. Lotz asserts that the different designations of the ark determine the character of the texts in question as well as the meaning of the ark: JE, the ark of Yahweh or the ark of God: fetish; D, the ark of the covenant; P, the ark of the testimony.[7] This analysis based on Wellhausen's evolutionary view of Israelite religion shows that the pedigree of the ark is not connected with the wilderness period.[8]

As previously mentioned, this approach has dominated in the study of the ark. In particular, the works of Sevensma and J. Maier, wherein documents and dates were classified in accordance with the designations of the ark, demonstrate clearly that they positively applied the method of historical-literary criticism to their research.[9] In the case of Dibelius, despite his *religionsgeschichtliche* (literally, "history of religion"

Überlieferung, . . . für welche doch die mosaische Stiftshütte eigens bestimmt ist, nichts von derselben weiss" (40).

6. Ibid., 43.

7. Lotz, "Die Bundeslade," 154, 157, 172, 183–84.

8. As regards the date of P, Graf's argument on the late dating of P on which Wellhausen's reconstruction rested is substantially based upon Reuss: "Le code sacerdotal date donc d'une époque postérieure à l'exile et c' est code qu'Esdras et Néhémie ont fait accepter par le peuple vers l'an 444 av. J.-C." (*L'histoire sainte*, 241). Reuss had already in 1833 expressed in a lecture this idea that the so-called basic document, i.e., P, was in reality the latest source (see O. Eissfeldt, *Einleitung*, 219). Thereafter, Graf wrote, in a letter of October 7 1862 to Reuss, his teacher that he accepted the notion: "Dass der ganze mittlere Theil des Pentateuch erst nachexilisch ist, davon bin ich vollkommen überzeugt . . ." (cited from Külling, *"Genesis-P-Stücke,"* 7). This conviction seems to go beyond scientific proof and is purely subjective in nature. Wellhausen's confirmation comes not through objective disputation in which he weighs opposing arguments, but through a decision (see Holwerda, *Bijzondere Canoniek*, 26). In the long run, Reuss' "intuition" regarding the dating of the books of the Old Testament became part of Wellhausen's conception of the history of Israel.

9. Sevensma, *De ark Gods*, 90, 99–100; J. Maier, *Heiligtum*, 45–50.

but it is equivalent to comparative religion) disposition, he also basically follows the theory of multiple sources.[10] So for them, in so far as the ark is concerned, the meaning is based on its documentary character: for D it is just a box; for P it is a valuable item for the law. Furthermore, Eissfeldt, who looks upon L as the earliest source, analyzes in detail the materials pertaining to the ark's fabrication according to the historical-literary critical approach. He holds that D, who took over JE^R, must relate the timing of the fabrication of the ark to the story of the restoration of the substituted tablets (Deut 10:1–5), and that P, who depends on JED and retains the framework of the stream of JE^R-narratives by changing and omitting many parts of them, defines the fully qualified priests as Aaron's descendants carrying the ark containing the tablets.[11]

So apart from some negligible differences they have all drawn similar conclusions. If their results and methods were to be accepted, the ark would be merely an imaginative production with theological intent for the Jewish community in the post-exilic period. Such a notion would deprive the ark-related biblical texts of historical reality. Because they tried to explore the meaning of the ark, neglecting the peculiarity of divine revelation and the reliability of the biblical passages, it might be impossible for them to come to proper conclusions. So it is undesirable and unsatisfactory to deal with the ark simply as a retrospective product of the period of the Second Temple. In addition, their conclusions are hardly acceptable if they ignore the biblical evidence for an explanation of the ark.

In the field of traditio-historical criticism, Gressmann, identifying the ark of Yahweh with the chest of Joseph, defends the statement that the ark in the land of Canaan was derived from the Amorite symbol related to Baal worship because it is possible that only in P's thinking does the golden ornamentation of the ark and its connection with *kapporet* and *cherubim* coalesce with the impoverished situation in the wilderness.[12] However the internal and external evidence of the biblical materials does not allow us to imagine that Israel could not afford to manufacture precious things such as the ark and the tabernacle, because of its destitute situation in the wilderness (Exod 12:35–36; 33:5–6).[13] Guthe states

---

10. Dibelius, *Die Lade Jahves*, 47.
11. Eissfeldt, "Die Lade und Gesetzestafeln," 284.
12. Gressmann, *Lade Jahwes und Allerheiligste*, 1–17, 42.
13. See Kitchen, *Reliability*, 279, 495–96. A hands-on excavated tabernacle of

that the ark of Yahweh was derived from the Egyptian processional bark, on which the image of the god stood in a wooden niche with four pillars, in front of which people prayed and worshiped.[14] Possibly the Israelites knew about the Egyptian bark but there is a great difference between it and the ark. While the bark as a house of deity has a divine image behind the curtain, toward which people worship, the ark contains the covenant law without any divine image. Although not an object of worship itself, Israelites were called to worship Yahweh before the ark where God promised to meet with his people. Similarly Hartmann suggests the ark has an Egyptian or Babylonian origin because it is identical to the box of Tammuz or the coffin of Osiris.[15] He thinks the Babylonian Tammuz is identical to the Egyptian Osiris in that both gods were vegetation deities, symbols of a continuously dying and revivifying nature.[16] Yahweh is not a nature deity and nowhere is there any trace of a fertility cult connected with the ark. Likewise Dibelius assumes that the ark was fabricated either inside or outside Palestine as a result of Babylonian influence, completely independent of Yahweh at the outset.[17] Reimpell holds that the ark concept was taken over by the Midianites from the Hittites and consequently borrowed by Moses.[18] Reimpell supposes that Moses made the ark a boxlike shape to imitate the holy stairs and banks found in Midian where Sinai lay and that such a holy stairway played an important role in the cult of the Sinaitic deity. However, all the biblical materials in the early or later stages of Israelite history are silent on the matter. The form of the ark and its function as a container for the tablets of the law bears no resemblance to a holy stone stair. Noth asserts that presumably the ark was originally the movable sanctuary of nomadic clans. For him, although the origin of the ark is unknown, it was regarded as the spatial center of the old Israelite amphictyony whose theory was based on the analogy of Greek and Italian amphictyony.[19] On the other

---

Midianites in Timna now challenges such a notion. "If the Midianites could worship in a multicolored cloth tabernacle in 1130, why not the Hebrews?" (279).

14. Guthe, *Geschichte*, 31.

15. Hartmann, "Zelt und Lade," 209–44.

16. See B. Alster, "Tammuz," *DDD* 828–34.

17. Dibelius, *Die Lade Jahves*, 118. He accepts neither the origin of the ark in Exod 25 nor in Deut 10 because he believes that the texts have no historical value (31, 111).

18. Reimpell, "Der Ursprung," 326–31.

19. Noth, *Geschichte Israels*, 88–91; *System*, 46–48.

hand, von Rad maintains that the ark is a cultic object produced in the land of Canaan to assure Israel of the constant presence of Yahweh, on account of her polytheistic neighbors.[20] For him, the meaning of the ark varies according to the different traditions of P (describing glory of the ark) and D (taking it for a receptacle for the tables).[21] In fact his presupposition is based on the hypothesis that the ark has nothing to do with the tabernacle, which is allegedly fabricated by P, but with a cultic house such as the temple of Shiloh, the house of Obed Edom, or the temple in Jerusalem. Certainly the ark is helpful in assuring Israel of the continual presence of Yahweh in the pagan situation in Canaan, but the function of the ark may not be so confined. The history of God's guidance to the promised land recorded in the book of Joshua by means of the ark would be really of no value if P's theory were accepted.

The attempt to seek the origin of the ark outside of biblical evidence, such as the view of *Religionsgeschichte*, and inside historico-literary criticism, has yet to provide sufficient evidence to substantiate these claims. Even the statements of the scholars who comprehensively applied traditio-historical criticism to the research on the ark can hardly be supported by the biblical texts since the method as such rejects biblical materials as primary sources. Thus this study returns to the reliable testimony of Yahweh testifying to the Mosaic origin of the ark in the wilderness (see Exod 25; 37; Deut 10).

B. BIBLICAL EXPLANATION (EXOD 25:10-15; 37:1-5)

The historical provenance of the ark is considered in this section of Exodus, which describes its size and materials in considerable detail. As far as the form of both passages is concerned, the instruction for building the ark and the narrative of its construction can be juxtaposed in terms of command and execution because the same verbs of both texts for the most part share common objects and sentence constituents.[22]

---

20. Von Rad, "Zelt und Lade," 123, 126–27: "Die Lade ist ein Kultgegenstand, der aus dem Kulturland stammt" (126) which is "gegen die Herkunft der Lade aus Wustenzeit ausgesprochen" (123). Broekhuis also shares this view: "The ark originated in Canaan" ("De ark," 150).

21. This notion is in substantial agreement with J. Maier (*Heiligtum*, 1–3). It may be said that the studies of Lewis ("Ark and Tent") and Campbell (*Ark Narrative*) share this viewpoint.

22. The same verbs were written in the form of perfect *waw*-consecutive and imperfect *waw*-consecutive respectively: make-made, overlay-overlaid, cast-cast, put-put.

With this mutual congruity, the author seems to attempt to exhibit a decisive observance in accordance with the commands.

The first instruction, "they shall make an ark" (*wᵉʿāśū ʾᵃrōn*), demonstrates that the ark is built because Yahweh has initiated its construction rather than because the Israelites decided to do so. The verb (they are to make) is distinctly different from the other wording (you are to make). It appears to intend to establish a link with the same verb in verse 8: "And let the children of Israel make me a sanctuary in the following way: let them make, first of all, an ark, etc."²³ The construction of the ark is about the whole community of Israel rather than just Moses.

The ark was to be made of acacia wood (*ʿēṣê śittīm*) which grew in the vicinity. Identifying the Hebrew word, *śittā* with *Acacia raddiana*, Zohary states that the common acacia (*Acacia raddiana*), which attains a height of about 6 meters and is suitable for building, is compatible with the text.²⁴ The use of this acacia wood, even if expensive,²⁵ appears to imply the wilderness-origin of the ark. After all, this material readily acquired on the spot is qualitatively different from the cedar wood used for the construction of the Solomonic temple (1 Kgs 6:9, 15–18).

From a different angle, Heinemann accepted that *Acacia nilotica*, used commonly as building material in Egypt, was the type of acacia used. Illustrating that the acacia played an important part as a holy tree in religion, he claims that the acacia wood chosen as the material for the ark reflects the influence of Egyptian religion ("Kasten-Kultur").²⁶ However, it is difficult to see how the manufacture of the ark was affected by Egyptian religion with respect to the acacia wood, in spite of the common cultural phenomenon emerging in Israel's religion, for the material was chosen by Yahweh himself. The question that he posed—"to what extent Egyptian religion affected the construction of the ark and the religion of the Israelites and how the 'Egyptian ark' acquired the traditional Old Testament meaning"²⁷—cannot be properly answered unless the distinction between Egyptian animism and Israelite revelation-religion is ignored.

---

23. Cassuto, *Exodus*, 328.
24. Zohary, *Plants*, 116.
25. Ryken et al., *DBI* 42.
26. Heinemann, "Die 'Lade,'" 37–40.
27. Ibid., 40.

The size of the ark is given as two and a half cubits long, a cubit and a half wide, and a cubit and a half high. Cubit (*'ammā*) means literally "forearm": the distance between the elbow and the tip of the middle finger of an average-sized person (see Deut 3:11). It implies that the length of the cubit is flexible. In fact, while Powell distinguishes five different lengths for the cubit in Babylonian history,[28] A. S. Kaufman introduces three kinds of ancient Hebrew cubit depending upon the number of handbreadths into which the cubit was divided: five, six, or seven. According to him, "the cubit of Moses," identified as the "first standard," was the medium cubit, which was equal to the length of six handbreadths or twenty-four fingerbreadths. This division was adopted by other ancient civilizations such as Egypt, Greece, and, Rome.[29] He concludes, "the first standard, known as the cubit of Moses and used in the construction of the Ark of the Covenant and of the Tent of Meeting was 42.8 cm."[30] If his observation were right, this would give external dimensions of 107 centimeters in length and 64.2 centimeters in both width and height. At any rate, the measurements represented the configuration of the object.

Exodus 37:1 states, "Bezalel made the ark," which appears to suggest that Bezalel personally made the ark because of its paramount importance. Yet he must be seen as the director in charge of the construction of the ark and other objects, even though the command was given in the third person plural form (*wᵉ'āśū*). Moses' statement in Deuteronomy 10:3, "I made the ark," is to be understood in the same way as the phrase "the house which King Solomon built" in referring to the temple. Bezalel is the one whom Yahweh filled with the Spirit of God, and with skill, ability, and knowledge in all kinds of crafts. He was the one called to make artistic designs for work in gold, silver, and bronze, to cut and set stones, to work in wood, and to engage in all kinds of artistic craftsmanship (Exod 35:31–33).[31]

---

28. M. Powell, "Masse und Gewicht," *RlA* 7:457–517. The 30 fingers (± 50 cm), two 30-fingers cubits (± 1m), the pace cubit (± 75 cm), the cubit of 24 fingers (± 50 cm), and the Archaemenid royal cubit.

29. Kaufman, "Determining the Length," 120–21.

30. Ibid., 131.

31. The work of the Spirit is different in Old Testament times from that in the New Testament: it is particularly related to the office of service to God with work of art rather than to eternal salvation. See Gootjes, "De Geest," 32–33.

According to the divine instruction—"You shall overlay it with pure gold: both inside and outside, and make a gold molding around it" (Exod 25:11)—the ark was to be overlaid with a double coating of pure gold to enhance its dignity and beauty.[32] Gold was the most precious of metals, because of its scarcity, malleability, and resistance to tarnishing. It is often associated with God and is symbolic of his holiness, majesty, and unchangeable nature.[33] Pure gold is gold of the highest grade, refined till free from all impurities. This was used only for the ark and not the poles, which were covered with ordinary gold. The rings and circlets (*zēr*) too were fabricated of ordinary gold. For the Egyptians, gold has a special meaning: "since gold plays not only an economic but also a religious role, it is considered as the metal of the gods, especially of the sun-god, 'Re,' and its immutability is regarded as an image for the continuation of life after death."[34] However, the Bible does not confer divine meaning to such materials[35] but uses gold as a metaphor for the almighty (Job 22:25–26), the messianic blessing (Isa 60:17), and faith in Christ (1 Pet 1:7). It is likely that in this context the gold molding is associated with the holiness of God.[36]

With respect to overlaying the ark with pure gold, two rabbinic traditions provide concrete descriptions: a nest of three separated chests of slightly varying dimensions was constructed ("Three arks did Bazalel make: the middle one of wood, nine [handbreadths] high; the inner one of gold, eight high, the outer one of gold, a little more than ten high"); the wooden chest was simply overlaid with gold inside and outside.[37] In

---

32. Hebrew term, *ṣippā* is always the verb for overlaying wood with metal (see Exod 13, 24, 28; 26:29, 37; 27:26; 30:3, 5), and this verb had to be repeated in the subsidiary clause, as an adverbial designation might appear in addition to the accusative use of the noun: "*inside and outside.*" The second verb need not be translated repeatedly in English.

33. *DBI*, 557.

34. Heinemann, "Die 'Lade,'" 35. It is in this context that the position of the body of Tutankhamun, a pharaoh in the middle period of the New Kingdom (ca. 1300 BC), discovered reposing within a nest of three coffins can be understood. The innermost coffin had been made of solid gold while the two outer ones were of hammered gold over wooden frames. Settgast, *Tutanchamun*, Abb. 29; Sarna, *Exodus*, 159.

35. See Lurker, *Bilder und Symbol*, 119: "it is true that gold is not divine."

36. See Hague, "'*ᵃrōn*," *NIDOTTE* 1:506. Calvin is cautious about the material itself and stresses the law: "God would have gold over its whole surface, and even shining on its staves, that the dignity of the Law might be enhanced." *Moses*, 2:151.

37. *Yoma* 72b; *Sheqalim* 6:1, 49d.

the light of archaeological finds in Egypt the method of overlaying the ark appears to be by means of attaching hammered plates to the wood with small nails: it would be solid enough to keep the two tablets of stone and the other items.[38] We wonder if a molding of gold is plain or an ornament with the form of a garland.

The ark has four rings and four pedestals: "You shall cast four gold rings for it and place them on its four pedestals, with two rings on one side and two rings on the other side" (Exod 25:12). The rings for the ark serve to hold the poles like crossbars. However, the problem is that the text is almost silent as to the precise placement of the rings on the sides of the ark. The meaning of the pl. f. form of $p^{e'}$ $\bar{a}m\bar{a}$ is far from clear, but it occurs two more times in relation to the feet of an object (Exod 37:3; 1 Kgs 7:30).[39] This word cannot simply be translated as "corners," "sides," as in some ancient versions (LXX, Vg, Pes, Tg), for it was never used in this way. According to Jacob it is something like pedestals: "No object which was flat and even on all sides could possess feet; like beams and pillars it could at most possess pedestals (*a-do-nim*)."[40] Although God does not prescribe it, the presence of the pedestals seems probable. The ark could hardly stand on its bottom plate and its corners and so possibly did not come into direct contact with the ground. The rings would not be fastened on the long side, but along the width and beneath the lower corners, so that the ark was borne aloft, making transportation easier.[41]

"Poles" fabricated of acacia wood and covered with gold were to be long and inserted into the rings on the sides (Exod 25:13–15) so that the bearers might not be in danger of rush against the ark. There is no indication as to the number of poles, but probably two long poles were used.[42] This injunction was observed even after the ark found its per-

---

38. See Cassuto, *Exodus*, 329.

39. Sœbø, "pa'am," 704.

40. Jacob, *Second Book*, 774.

41. Ibid.; Meir, *Rashbam's Exodus*, 308. Rashi has a different view: "It was on the upper corners near to the cover that the rings were placed." *Pentateuch*, 133.

42. It is interesting to note an Egyptian parallel; a chest found in Tutankhamun's tomb is portable, with four poles inserted into each ring inside of the four feet (Settgast, *Tutanchamun*, 29). Of course, it is possible that there were four poles used for the ark if there were eight rings in total by translating *we* at the beginning of the word "and two" (*ūšettē*) as meaning "and" as in *Yoma* 72a. However, the *we* of *ūšettē* should be seen as the so-called *waw explicativum* (GK §154a, n. 1b): "cast four rings . . . *namely* with two rings on one side."

manent resting place in Solomon's temple, as noted in 1 Kings 8:8. This divinely directed arrangement probably originated as a precautionary measure to protect the ark from contact with profane hands.[43] Exodus 25:15 stresses the continuous mobility of the ark both positively and negatively: the poles shall remain in the rings of the ark; they shall not be removed from it.

The order about the Testimony explains the primary function of the ark: "You shall put in the ark (the tablets of) the Testimony, which I will give you" (25:16). This verse is omitted in Exodus 37. Although the tricky point of this verse is the use of the word "testimony," the term in this context is rightly identified with the tablets of the testimony on which the Decalogue was inscribed (34:28–29). It is nowhere stated that God actually gave the testimony to Moses but it is assumed that he received it from God as Exodus 40:20 reports that Moses "took and placed" the testimony into the ark. The fact that the testimony is put into the ark implies that the glory theophany on Sinai is closely linked with the testimony in the ark; this law is given in glorious theophany and is expressly referred to as the testimony indicating a link between the glory and the law.[44] In this context the word "testimony" manifests the covenantal nature of the Ten Commandments, especially with its preface: they testify to the covenant that was made between the Lord and the children of Israel and the testimony is the seal. It reminds the Israelites of the redeeming hands of Yahweh and simultaneously the covenantal obligation that he imposed on them.[45] Yahweh wants to have fellowship with his people, and the ark symbolically signifies his presence (see Ps 132:5–7).

The verses in Exodus 25:17 and 37:6 refer to the divine instruction about the fabrication of an atonement place (*kappōreṯ*). The object is the same width as the ark: two cubits and a half length, and a cubit and a half breadth. It is made of pure gold. That is why the atonement place is an independent object with its own function rather than simply the

---

43. Sarna, *Exodus*, 160.

44. Hague, "'ᵃrōn," *NIDOTTE* 1:507. Schäfer-Lichtenberger merely considers a theological aspect: "Die Lade enthält materialiter in Gestalt der 'edut die Quintessenz der Sinaitheolophanie und deren auf die Gegenwart Israels sich beziehenden Ansprüche JHWHs an Israel. Die 'edut ist das Zeugnis der Sinaioffenbarung, sie vermittelt zwischen einer nur noch im erzählten Mythos existierenden Vergangenheit und einer sakralrituell erfahrbaren Gegenwart." "»Sie wird nicht wieder hergestellt werden«," 237.

45. See Owczarek, *Die Vorstellung*, 171.

cover of the ark. In a broad sense the atonement place is the place of revelation where Yahweh manifests himself (Lev 16:2) and speaks (Exod 25:22; Num 7:89).[46] Yahweh reveals himself above the atonement place, so the presence of Yahweh comes to be associated with a concrete object. It is also the place of atonement. The atonement place as the place of revelation and atonement is an essential cultic object for the maintenance and restoration of the covenantal relationship between Yahweh and his people.

Detailed directions about the cherubim are given next: "And you shall make two cherubim out of hammered gold at the two ends of the atonement place. Make one cherub on the one end, and one cherub on the other end. Of one piece with the atonement place shall you make the cherubim on its two ends. The cherubim shall spread out their wings upward, overshadowing the atonement place with their wings, their faces one to another; toward the atonement place shall the faces of the cherubim be" (Exod 25:18–20). The Old Testament does not depict the exact form of the cherubim apart from describing their two outstretched wings. This may imply that they were well-known figures in ancient society so much that the Israelites needed no further information. According to the biblical account, the cherubim, made of ordinary gold, set at both ends of the atonement place, appear to be two erect figures confronting each other, with the stretched wings. The expression "each shall be turned towards the other, the faces of the cherubim shall be toward the atonement place" is ambiguous. The difficulty lies in that the cherubim should face each other and simultaneously they should face the atonement place.[47] This verse apparently tells that the cherubim possessed faces, which probably are human faces. The phrase "Each shall be turned towards the other" means confronting each other in posture rather than looking at each other. The faces of the cherubim with their heads down slightly should be turned in the direction of the atonement place as if they should guard the ark.[48] The cherubim with their wings

---

46. See Houtman, *Exodus 3*, 371; Janowski, *Sühne als Heilsgeschehen*, 347.

47. Rashbam explains that "facing the covering" means "facing the middle of the covering" (Meir, *Rashbam's Exodus*, 314). Jacob provides a clarification of Rashbam's interpretation: "As their gaze was directed toward each other, they looked over the *kaporet*" (*Second Book*, 777). Yet, this is still not clear to our understanding.

48. The rabbinic tradition regarded the face of the cherub as the face of a little child. See Michaeli, *Le Livre*, 233.

appear symbolic of something heavenly and transcendental because the stretched wing has flying image.

The last part of the divine instruction about the ark is concerned with the location of the atonement place, with the testimony and Yahweh's promise (Exod 25:21-22). "You shall put the atonement place on top of the ark and put in the ark the Testimony, which I will give you" (v. 21). The order of this verse seems illogical but in fact the author wants to make a successive allusion to the atonement place from verse 20. The atonement place is an independent object, but has a close and vital connection with the ark. The ark without the atonement place is unimaginable and vice versa, not because the latter is the cover of the ark, but because they are inseparable in a functional sense (Lev 16:2, 13, Num 7:89). The command to put the atonement place—linked with the cherubim—on top of the ark suggests that they are united in the simple ark. Thus, the instruction commences and ends with the ark. As for the connection between the ark with the testimony and the cherubim, de Vaux draws a remarkable picture: "these are the ark-footstool and the cherubim-seat that together constitute the throne of Yahweh."[49] Yet his mosaic appears to exceed the biblical concept, for he took the meaning of the ark from extra-biblical parallels that show that the instrument of the treaty was placed beneath the feet of the god. He deduced that the concept of the throne pertaining to the ark is a later theological product.[50] There is no steady evidence to support the idea of the ark throne but it is clear that the whole unit, including the ark, represents God's presence and his sovereignty over his covenantal people. The repeated command that the testimony should be put in the ark (Exod 25:16, 21) seems to emphasize the fact that the atonement place and the wings of the cherubim protect the tablets of the law and remind the people that this is where God has promised to meet with them.

There is a promise in the instruction: "There I will meet you and speak to you, from above the atonement place, from between the two cherubim over the ark of the testimony, everything I will command you for the Israelites" (v. 22). The atonement place on the ark is represented as the place of revelation; there Yahweh reveals himself and

---

49. De Vaux, *Bible et Orient*, 234: "Ce sont l'arche-marchepied et les cherubins-sige qui, *ensemble*, constituent le trône de Yahvé."

50. Ibid., 258–60; de Vaux, "Arche et Tente," 67–68: "Il n'y avait pas de chérubins dans le culte du désert, donc pas de «trône» de Yahvé" (67).

speaks. As the Redeemer, Yahweh issues his covenantal commandment to Israel through Moses, who is to be the intermediary of God's will for his people. In this extraordinary promise the proper understanding of Moses' special status before God and for Israel is underscored; he is an authoritative prophet (Num 12:6–8). Thus, from its beginning, Israelite religion was not focused on object worship but on the word of God; the primacy of the divine word was explicit in the worship. In this verse the first designation with qualification is given to the ark—"the ark of the testimony" for the tablets of the law are kept there. The ark of the testimony is meant to encourage Israel's obedience.[51] As a whole, the ark with the cherubim and the atonement place serves to reveal Yahweh himself and parts of his attributes.

---

51. The introduction of the LXX "ark of testimony" (κιβωτὸν μαρτυρίου) in verse 10 seems to underline the unique role of the ark.

2

The "Constituents" of the Ark

A. TESTIMONY

IN EXODUS 25:16–21 YAHWEH commanded that Moses should put the testimony into the ark. Among scholars there is some difficulty over the translation of the word *ʿēdut*, which can have various meanings: "testimony," "covenant regulations," "stipulations" (of a covenant or agreement), "something written," "basic law," "covenant," "pact."[1] Jacob leaves it in the transcribed form of the Hebrew word without any attempt to construe in order to avoid any misleading conclusions.[2] Apart from the texts in which allusion is made to the ark, *ʿēdut* is used as a synonym of *bᵉrît* twice (2 Kgs 17:15; Ps 132:12) and *bᵉrît* in these texts is to be understood as a term of obligation.[3]

The noun *ʿēdut* is mostly regarded as an abstract form of *ʿēd*, which is probably derived from the Akkadian *adê* (pl. tantum of *adû*).[4] It seems incorrect to apply the Akkadian meaning directly to this text since the covenant between Yahweh and Israel is different from a kind of mutual agreement; the commencement of the covenant is completely one-sided in the Old Testament while "the agreement called *adû* was drawn up in

---

1. "Covenant regulations" (Bundesbestimmungen): Volkwein, "Masoretisches ʿēdūt, ʿēdwūt, ʿēdōt," 39–40; "stipulations" (of a covenant or agreement): Kitchen, "Egypt, Ugarit, Qatna and Covenant," 460; "something written" (etwas »Geschriebenes«): Janowski, *Sühne als Heilsgeschehen*, 294; "basic law" (grondwet): Houtman, *Exodus 3*, 357, 370; "covenant": Meir, *Rashbam's Exodus*, 311; "pact": Sarna, *Exodus*, 160.

2. Jacob, *Second Book*, 771.

3. See Owczarek, *Die Vorstellung*, 167; E. Kutsch, "*bᵉrît*," THAT I, 342: "*berît* does not indicate a "relationship," but is the "requirement," "obligation" that the subject of the *bᵉrît* takes over."

4. Ungnad, *Akkadian Grammar*, 46–47; Von Sodon, *Akkadischen Grammatik*, 93.

writing between a partner of higher status (god, king, member of the royal family)" and others.[5]

The basic form of the term *ʿēdut* is used as a legal term in the Old Testament, symbolic of a pact or agreement: a heap of stones between Laban and Jacob (Gen 31:48, *ʿēd*) or giving a sandal to another (Ruth 4:7, *tᵉʿūdā*). The term seems closely tied to "testimony" or "witness" in legal usage (see Gen 31:50; Exod 20:16; Num 35:30; Josh 24:22; Job 16:19; etc.). Basically such a testimony seems to be a concrete symbol of promises made between two parties. Hence, the term is employed to intend something concrete when associated with the ark. So, the word *ʿēdut* refers not so much to the treaty or covenant in the general sense, as specifically to the stone tables, "something written," or to the concrete symbol of the covenant at Sinai (Exod 25:21; 40:20).[6] Although the scroll of the Law was deposited in the ark according to the Talmud (*Baba Bathra* 14b), *ʿēdut* in this verse it is rightly identified with *lū ḥōt hāʿēdut* (the tablets of the testimony) on which the Decalogue is inscribed (Exod 34:28–29). In the context the word *ʿēdut* manifests the covenantal nature of the Ten Commandments and especially of the preface which informs that Yahweh is entitled to claim Israelite observance of the commandments. The testimony is an official mark of the covenant and makes the Israelites realize how to maintain the gracious relationship between Yahweh and them.

Because the tablets of the Decalogue are put into the ark (Exod 25:16), the function of the ark is simply prone to appear as housing them (1 Kgs 8:9). This idea was derived from a prevailed legal tradition in the ancient Near East. Some scholars illustrate a peace pact between Egypt and Hittite: a duplicate of the treaty document between Rameses II and Ḫattusilis III was placed under the feet of the images of Re and Teshub respectively, when the treaty was concluded.[7] However it is questionable whether there is any relationship between this Near Eastern custom and Israel's religion or whether the royal treaty between the emperors actually affected the Israelites, who were liberated from slavery earlier on and were already wandering in the wilderness. Nonetheless, it is said

---

5. *CAD* A1:133.
6. Seow, "Designation," 194.
7. See Seow, "Ark," 389; Sarna, *Exodus*, 160; Vaux, *Bible et Orient*, 258–59; Matthews and Benjamin, *Parallels*, 86–90.

that this ancient custom makes it clear why the testimony to the covenant made between Yahweh and Israel was enshrined in the ark.[8]

The command of Yahweh in verse 12 is supposed to signify other implications for the symbolic meaning of the ark: the footstool of God's throne (1 Chr 28:2), which is an important prerogative of royalty, a token of dignity and power in the Near East: "The instrument of this testimony is deposited in the ark, since this is the pedestal and later, the footstool of Yahweh, this testimony is put under the feet of God in this way."[9] Yet, it is still debatable that an unequivocal elucidation of the meaning of God's revelation rests on a comparison with the religious and political customs of an ancient society, although God did sometimes use the cultural ideas of other societies. It is true that Yahweh is king of Israel and the universe but the concept of footstool has a rather broad application in the Old Testament: the footstool in Psalm 99:5 is Zion[10]; whereas Isaiah 66:1 denotes earth as a footstool. In these cases the expression of footstool obviously appears to have nothing to do with the idea of the kingly protocol that von Rad associates with the testimony in the ark.[11] Thus, suffice it to say that with this command Yahweh unfolds that he is the redeeming savior whom the people should obey in accordance with the covenant; Yahweh wants to have communion with his people on the basis of the covenant made at Sinai.

B. THE ATONEMENT PLACE

Exodus 25:17 and 37:6 refer to the divine instruction concerning the fabrication of an atonement place. An examination of the terms is vital because of disputes over the translation of the Hebrew word *kappōrẹt*. It is a derivation of the verb *kpr*, which has *kaparū* as an Akkadian cognate. While the qal form of the Hebrew verb means "cover," "paint," "smear," its pi'el form means "atone," "appease" (see Gen 6:14).[12] Similarly the Akkadian simple verb *kaparū* has the meaning of "wipe off," "smear

---

8. Cassuto, *Exodus*, 331.

9. De Vaux, *Bible et Orient*, 256: "L'instrument de ce traité est déposé dans l'arche et, puisque celle-ci est le piédestal et, plus tard, le marchepied de Yahvé, ce traité est ainsi mis sous les pieds de Dieu."

10. See Kraus, *Psalmen*, 853; Goldingay, *Psalms 90–150*, 219, 550.

11. Von Rad, "Das judäische Königsritual," 208–9.

12. *HALAT* 470.

on,"[13] and the D stem (intensive form like pi'el in Hebrew) *kuppuru* signifies "wipe off," "clean," "rub," "ritually purify," "pull out by the roots"; [14] the Akkadian noun *kupartu* means "purification."[15] It is observed here that the Akkadian cognate corresponds closely to the Hebrew *kpr*. In both stems, Akk. D and the Hebrew pi'el attract attention to the meaning of *kāppōręt*, since the contemporary debate about the derivation and foundational meaning of the root *kpr* revolves around the pi'el. Thus, *kpr* grammatically does not indicate the meaning "cover" (see Lev 17:11); the basis of such translations, "atonement cover" (NIV), "reconciling cover" (*verzoendeksel*, NV) is weak. The Arabic *kafara*, "cover," "conceal," or "hide," influenced the concept of "cover," since the lexica associated the two terms.[16]

LXX renders *hilastērion epithema* for the Hebrew word *kāppōręt*; the Greek translator inserts the two Greek words *hilastērion* and *epithema* only in this verse (see Exod 25:18; Lev 16:2, 13-15). In the combination, *epithema* has the leading position syntactically, which is an independent noun "lid," "cover," whereas *hilastērion* functions as an attributive adjective "propitiatory," signifying the cultic relevance of that part of the ark.[17] Wevers explains the reason for this translation: "Since this is its first occurrence, Exodus defines it as an *epithema* 'lid, cover.'"[18] Koch points out some problems that the choice of *hilastērion* entails: "The adjective is used in common Greek in connection with gifts or a monument propitiating a deity or a hero"; "With *hilastērion*, an expression was adopted that encompasses a propitiatory effect for this part of the ark of the covenant. The idea could scarcely have arisen from a strict reading of the Hebrew text because there the intention of *kipper* is not to propitiate the deity but rather to cleanse the holy place and the members of the community with the help of God's gracious support."[19] It is reasonable to decline *hilastērion epithema* for the term *hilastērion* points to the only place for propitiating the deity,[20] and the pi'el stem

---

13. *CAD* K:178-79.
14. Ibid., 179-80; *AHw* 442-43.
15. *AHw* 549.
16. Lang, "Kapper," *ThWAT* 4:303-18; *AEL* 7:2620.
17. Koch, "Considerations," 67.
18. Wevers, *Notes*, 398.
19. Koch, "Considerations," 68.
20. Lang, *ThWAT* 4:309: "Nirgends meint *kippœr* ein Beschwichtigen Gottes."

of the Hebrew term *kpr* cannot be translated as *epithema*. Moreover *kāppōręt* is not actually connected with the ark as a lid. "Atonement place" (Sühneort, *verzoeningsplaats*) or "mercy seat" (KJV, RSV, ESV) might be a better rendering of *kāppōręt*.[21]

Most Jewish exegetes tend to regard *kāppōręt* as "cover" or "function of cover" placed above the ark, which was open at the top.[22] This appears to reflect their traditional position, namely, "holy ark" referring to the receptacle for the scrolls of the Torah in the synagogue. However the atonement place does not function as a lid and is not part of the ark. The ark itself indicates a complete object: a chest with cover. The atonement place also is an independent object.[23] There is a difference even between the materials used for the two objects: the ark is fabricated of acacia wood overlaid with pure gold, while the atonement place is made of pure gold without any wood. Although the atonement place is set on the ark, various texts provide an explanation of its independent character in the description of its position: "in front of the atonement place that is on the ark" (Lev 16:2; see Exod 30:6; Lev 16:13).

In a broad sense the atonement place is the place of revelation where Yahweh manifests himself (Lev 16:2) and speaks (25:22; Num 7:89).[24] The presence and appearance of Yahweh comes to be associated with a concrete object.[25] The practical function of the atonement place is found in the regulations concerning the Day of Atonement in Leviticus 16. On the Day of Atonement, in particular, Aaron was to sprinkle the blood of a bull on the front of the atonement place seven times and then he was to slaughter a goat for the sin offering for the people and sprinkle its blood on the atonement place and in front of it (Lev 16:14–15). The blood on the atonement place indicated that Israel's sin of failing to meet Yahweh's requisite standards is put under the atonement place and is expiated by

---

21. See Janowski, *Sühne als Heilsgeschehen*, 273, 346–47. He also translates *kpprth* as "Sühnmal," "Sühneort," recognizing it as "an die Herleitung von *kpr* pi. sühnen, Sühne schaffen."

22. See Rashi, *Pentateuch*, 134; Meir, *Rashbam's Exodus*, 311; Cassuto, *Exodus*, 323; Sarna, *Exodus*, 161; Jacob, *Second Book*, 775.

23. See Houtman, *Exodus* 3, 371; Janowski, *Sühne als Heilsgeschehen*, 275; F. Maass, "*kpr*," *THAT* 1:842–57; de Tarragon, "La kapporet?" 8.

24. Here Cassuto simply states that it connotes the throne of God. *Exodus*, 325.

25. Similarly Janowski elaborately interprets *kāppōręt* as "der in die Form einer »reinen Ebene« gefaßt Ort der Gegenwart Gottes in Israel." *Sühne als Heilsgeschehen*, 347.

a surrogate death. This ritual demonstrates that the atonement place was essential in making atonement for the people.

Moreover, by the atonement place, Moses was able to meet Yahweh without climbing Mt. Sinai. The atonement place is a holy object over which Yahweh manifests himself.[26] The concept of the holiness of the atonement place is strengthened by its location; the placing of the atonement place over the ark appears to emphasize and warrant both its authority and holiness. The atonement place as the place of revelation and atonement in the official rite occupies a central location in the sanctuary; it is indispensable for the covenantal relationship of Israel with Yahweh in the early stage of her history. Its function betrays God's goodness.

C. THE CHERUBIM

The translation of the Hebrew $k^e ru\underline{b}\bar{\imath}m$ is generally substituted by its transliteration. The root *krb* is not otherwise attested in biblical Hebrew, but it has some cognates in the Semitic language.[27] Yet, such homologous words seem insufficient to unravel the significance of the biblical cherubim.

As to the pedigree or background of the cherubim on the ark, Mettinger maintains a Phoenician provenance.[28] However, to what extent such a Canaanite religion affected the revelational religion of Israel is inexplicable.

The Old Testament does not outline the precise form of the cherubim apart from two outstretched wings (Exod 25:18–20; 37:7–9). The general figure of the cherubim is abundantly attested in the Ancient East. It is usually connected with an imaginary creature that mediated between deity and man: it is described as a hybrid creature having a hu-

---

26. Contra de Tarragon, "La kapporet?" 12: "La sainteté de ce socle à chérubins vient alors du rite: ce n'est pas l'objet qui est saint, mais le rite."

27. The Hebrew root is possibly furnished by Akk. *karābu*, 'bless' rather than other roots such as Aramaic, 'plow' or Arabic, *krb* 'nearness' or 'bring near' (see Freedman and O'Connor, "k^{e}rūb," *ThWAT* IV, 326; *AEL* 7, 2603). The Akk. *karābu* has two derivations worth noting: *kāribu* and *kurību*. The form *kāribu* as an active participle describes any person or image in a gesture of blessing and adoration (*CAD* K:216), while the diminutive *kurību* represents a protective genius with specific non-human features which is applied to cultic images (*CAD* K:559).

28. Mettinger, "Israelite Aniconism," 203: "The background of the cherubim throne in Jerusalem is to be sought in the West Semitic ambit, more exactly in Phoenicia, and not in an originally Hurrian-Mitannian tradition."

man face and the body of an ox with wings or in other forms combining elements of the body of a man, ox, lion, or eagle.[29] Such images express the addition of divine nature and power to the creatures. For example, in Egypt, the gods Isis and Nephthys partly play a subordinate role, formed as serpents and guarding the gate of the underworld. The images of winged, anthropomorphic beings protect the mummy in the coffin.[30] In Mesopotamia, hybrids with the body of a winged lion have a lion's head, a dragon's head, a human head—with or without wings—or the head of a goat.[31] In Anatolia and Syria, there are similar images, such as a winged lion with eagle, falcon, or dragon parts.[32] The form of the Egyptian sphinx was prevalent. It had the body of a lion with a human head and was a widespread feature of the art of Mitanni, Syria, and Canaan.[33] The postures of Mesopotamian hybrids were mostly of fighting statues and those of Syrian hybrids are standing or crouching guardians.[34] Such mysterious images appear far from the enigmatic description of the cherubim in Ezekiel 1:6–11 and 10:14–22; they are hardly identical to biblical ones. Besides, the figures of the cherubim over the ark are not found in the extra-biblical materials. There still remains the difficulty to apply adequately such syncretistic parallels to the cherubim, which played a prominent part in Israel's most sacred rites. So, the best way to attempt reconstructing a picture is to return to the text.

Exodus 25:18–19 refers to the material and the rough location of the cherubim: "And you shall make two cherubim out of hammered gold at the two ends of the atonement place." Although the two objects were together interlocked on both verges, there is a physical difference between the cherubim and the atonement place: the one was of ordinary gold, the other was pure gold. It means that the cherubim were not of one piece with the atonement place but independent objects. It appears that the cherubim on it must be erect figures, if their faces should confront each other in posture and be turned toward the atonement place at the same time (v. 20).

---

29. See Freedman and O'Conner, "kerub," *ThWAT* IV, 331–32.
30. Lurker, *Bilder und Symbol*, 103.
31. Collon, *First Impressions*, 32–74.
32. Metzger, *Königsthron und Gottesthron*, 320.22.
33. Keel and Uehlinger, *Göttinnen, Götter und Gottessymbole*, 190–91.
34. Ibid., 320–22.

The instruction about the peculiar shape of the wings mentions outstretched wings. "The cherubim shall spread out their wings upward" (Exod 25:20a). It is widely contended that one function of the cherubim is found here: their outstretched wings would be, so to speak, a throne of God, an empty throne on which God, invisible to the human eye, would sit. It is the empty seat that clearly indicates that God has no likeness whatsoever, for in the very place of his enthronement no representation was to be seen.[35] Furthermore, Haran maintains that the wings, spread horizontally, form the throne in contradistinction to the translation "upward."[36] It is also argued that cherubim thrones are well attested in Egypt and Syria-Palestine. The Pharaohs' thrones discovered in the tombs (the Eighteenth Dynasty, Thutmosis IV, Amenophis, or Amenhotep III) were shaped like the winged sphinx. An engraved ivory plaque (1350–1150 BC), excavated in the LB level of Megiddo, shows a king seated on a throne supported by winged sphinxes in the Phoenician style. On one of the long sides over the sarcophagus of Ahiram king of Byblos (tenth century BC) a procession moves towards the deceased king, who is sitting on a throne supported by the winged sphinx, whose feet are on a stool. He was a deified king.[37] Many scholars contend that these archaeological finds illustrate that the winged cherubim over which Yahweh is sitting functioned as a royal throne; Yahweh reigns over Israel as king sitting on the cherubim.

The repeated references to God enthroned above the cherubim seem to have been stated in order to leave little doubt that the Israelites shared a similar concept (Pss 18:10; 80:1; 99:1; Isa 37:16). Moreover, their meaning is extended by the argument that with the outstretched wings they do not simply represent a fixed throne, but a moveable one reflecting God's omnipresence: the cherub appears to be described as the vehicle of Yahweh, able to carry him through space (Ps 18:11; 2 Sam 22:11; see Ezek 9:3; 10:4). Sarna added theological significance to them: "As bearers of the celestial throne, they evoke belief in divine, transcendent sovereignty. Their permanent place above the ark is God's immanence—his enduring presence in the covenanted community of Israel."[38]

---

35. See Cassuto, *Exodus*, 322.

36. Haran, "Ark and Cherubim," 36.

37. See de Vaux, *Bible et Orient*, 243–47; Haran, "Bas-Reliefs," 14–25; Gressmann, *Lade Jahwes und Allerheiligste*, 190–91; Metzger, "Jahwe," 79–80.

38. Sarna, *Exodus*, 161.

However, in all the texts of the Old Testament there is no hint that the cherubim are a throne. The biblical materials indicate the various functions of the cherubim: first, cherubim as guardians of the way to the tree of life (Gen 3:24); second, cherubim on the ten curtains of the tabernacle (Exod 26:1) and on the veil (Exod 26:31; 36:35); third, cherubim involved in reference to God's movements (2 Sam 22:11; Ps 18:11; Ezek 1, 10); fourth, cherubim in the temple of Solomon (1 Kgs 8); fifth, cherub in God's mountain (Ezek 28:14, 16); sixth, cherubim carved on the walls of the inner sanctuary and on the door of nave in Ezekiel's vision (Ezek 41:18, 25).[39] None of them denotes that the cherubim are God's throne. Such a theological conclusion concerning enthronement requires a more meticulous investigation of the related texts of the Old Testament.

Above all, these statements indicate that the function of the cherubim is not always the same. First, the cherubim as guardians in the east of the garden of Eden appear not to be alien to the garden or unfamiliar to Israelites in that the term has a definite article at first.[40] Even though the figure of the cherubim is not clear, they probably are considered as composite beings connected with the presence of God, just as other texts indicate (Exod 25:18–22; Ezek 1, 10). Their duty is to keep the way to the tree of life from intruders. The keeping duty is likely similar to the cherub in God's mountain, "a guardian cherub" (Ezek 28:14, 16, NIV, ESV). Second, in terms of the cherubim on the curtains of the tabernacle and on the veil, they were to be produced by a skilled craftsman, not by a common embroiderer (see Exod 26:36) or an ordinary weaver (see Exod 39:27). The emphasis on the injunction about the cherubim seems to have an aesthetic concern.[41] Yet their beauty goes beyond great artistic value, to a description of God's splendid glory. The cherubim on the inner surface of the curtain reflect the glory of God from the inside of the inner rooms. This function is associated with the cherubim carved on the walls of the inner sanctuary and on the door of nave in Ezekiel's vision. Third, unlike the above two cases the references to the cherubim concerning God's movements appear to imply a throne. Yet careful consideration of the verses shows us that two passages (2 Sam 22:11; Ps 18:11), which contain the same content, hardly match the cherubim and

---

39. See *HALAT*, 473.
40. Sarna, Genesis, 30.
41. See Janzen, *Exodus*, 343

the throne. The cherub (NIV, cherubim) in the first clause of this verse is paralleled in the second with the wings of the wind, which do not exist.[42] Hence Harman appears to feel that the cherub here may be a poetic term for clouds because of the parallelism in Psalm 18:9–10.[43] In the midst of the storm Yahweh is there, controlling all the forces at his disposal. He comes with majesty to bring deliverance. Likewise the cherub in these verses also is far from the concept of the throne of God, although its interpretation still remains open. Fourth, the wings of the cherubim that stretch from wall to wall in the temple of Solomon are different from the cherubim on the ark. The cherubim covering and protecting the ark reflect the glorious and majestic presence of Yahweh at the ark, positioned in the Most Holy Place of the temple, Yahweh's eternal dwelling place (1 Kgs 8:13). In addition, the cherubim in the vision of Ezekiel draw a vehicle as if they were God's throne-chariot (Ezek 1:9–11). It is difficult to describe this very complex phenomenon but it is important to scrutinize the following verses directly related to the throne: Ezekial 1:26; 9:3; 10:4, 18; 11:22. As to the throne in 1:26, its likeness was above the firmament over the heads of the living creatures considered to be the cherubim. This whole description is quite different from the idea that the cherubim or their parts compose the throne: it is independent from the creatures. So to relate the throne concept directly to the cherubim on the basis of this verse is questionable. The cherubim may be described rather as bearers of the throne. Likewise a close reading of the other passages in Ezekiel demonstrates that the cherubim are hardly related to the concept of the throne, albeit they remind us of the image of the throne. The common expression is *k^ebōd 'ᵉlōhē mē'al hakk^erūb*. Yet the English translation, "glory of God on the cherub," is not clear as to whether the glory is on it or God is on it. Hebrew verbs clarify what the subject is by using the genitive connection between God and glory, which is *nomen regens*. This grammatical structure denotes glory as the subject: God's glory was on the cherub. Then there is the question as to whether the place of God's glory can be equated with God's throne. Indeed God's glory is present in many places such as in a cloud (Exod 16:10), on a mountain (Exod 24:16), in the tabernacle (Exod 40:34; Num 14:10), with the people (Lev 9:23; Num 16:19), in the temple (1 Kgs 8:11), but they are not described

---

42. See Klement, *II Samuel 21–24*, 202.
43. Harman, *Psalms*, 108.

as thrones. So, the cherubim that appear in Ezekiel cannot be directly regarded as a throne.

As mentioned above, the cherubim have a broader meaning: the various self-manifestations of Yahweh. Notwithstanding the functions of the cherubim are mainly focused on only one: divine attributes such as God's glory (see Heb 9:5) or his transcendence. It fits well with the metaphysical notions expressed in physical forms in ancient times. If the cherubim were meant to be the throne, the word *kissē* (throne) would have been used at least once in the Old Testament. Wings are meant for flying, not for sitting on. The general imagery of the outstretched wings of the cherubim seems to convey what is splendid, majestic, omnipresent, and glorious.

Besides, the translation of *yōšēḇ hakkᵉruḇīm* (literally, sitting the cherubim) is too easily juxtaposed with the concept of enthronement. It is frequently assumed that this term invokes an "enthronement theology." The difficulty in the rendering of the expression is caused by the lack of a preposition between the two words. Woudstra gave a detailed explanation of this problem,[44] while most scholars overlooked and paid no attention to it. The puzzling question in translation of the phrase made its variant versions proposed. The KJV and NIV insert the preposition "between," which appears to have been analogized out of the previous verses, Exodus 25:22 and Numbers 7:89,[45] while many commentators with the RSV and ESV add the preposition "on," the idea of "above" between the two terms.[46] In fact, such attempts to translate the words *yōšēḇ hakkᵉruḇīm* are usually based on the presupposition that the cherubim are the throne of Yahweh, apart from KJV. However it still appears to be unfounded.

---

44. Woudstra, *Ark*, 68–73.

45. Strictly speaking, the phrase, "enthroned between the cherubim" implies that the cherubim themselves do not denote the throne because one who is enthroned does not sit between the throne(s) but on the throne, even though it gives us the imagery of the throne. To sit between the cherubim is to sit on the atonement place.

46. Stoebe and Stolz clearly exhibit such a trend, directly rendering *yōšēḇ hākerubīm* as "Kerubenthroner" (Stoebe, *Das erste Buch Samuelis*, 128; Stolz, *Erste und zweite Buch Samuel*, 39). Dietrich also has the same point of view (Dietrich, *Samuel*, 197, 200, 231). Murray seems too easily to link this element with the ark: "He may be summoned to assert his regal authority over his enemies by bringing victory to his people of the divine warrior-king enthroned over the ark in the shrine" (*Prerogative and Pretension*, 119).

However the biblical texts show us different usage of the term. The verb *yāšab* in *yōšēb hakkᵉrubīm* has a variety of connotations, such as sit, sit down, be enthroned, lie down, rest, remain, stay, dwell, inhabit, settle, be inhabited, populated, be set, be established, stand, endure, etc.[47] The term, *yōšēb* is always combined with the preposition *'al* (on, over) (Exod 12:29; Deut 17:18; 1 Kgs 1, 2; 2 Kgs 10:3, 30; 11:19; Pss 47:8; 132:11; Prov 20:8, etc.), when it is juxtaposed with *kissē* (throne). It means that the phrase *yōšēb hakkᵉrubīm* could probably be translated as "one enthroned on the cherubim" without any difficulties if it had the preposition *'al*. Yet it is not always interpreted as throne, even when there is a suitable preposition between the words. For instance the phrases of Psalm 29:10 declare that Yahweh sits (or dwells) on the many waters or the flood: *yahwē lammabbūl yāšab*. On the basis of this expression it may be difficult to maintain that the flood is the throne of Yahweh. In this context the flood may be understood as an object under God's control rather than a throne. Thus the collocation of *yōšēb hakkᵉrubīm* cannot naively be matched with the concept of the throne of Yahweh.

With respect to the translation, it may be acceptable that KJV put the preposition *"between"* in the phrase, which gives a notice of insertion in an italic character, and rendered *yōšēb* as "dwell" instead of "sit": "dwelleth *between* the cherubims,"[48] although we do not know accurately how invisible God is spatially present at the ark. It implies at the least that the cherubim are not related to the idea of a throne. Otherwise, as a last resort, it would be tolerable rendering it literally "inhabiting the cherubim," without a preposition, if possible (see YLT).[49] If the cherubim convey the thought of majesty and glory, the phrase *yōšēb hakkᵉrubīm* can be paraphrased as "one who is dwelling in glory and majesty."[50] Accordingly, the expression need not be intimately affiliated to the ark so as to grant room for the concept of enthronement. Above all it is necessary to remember that in ancient times metaphysical concepts, such as

---

47. See *DCH* 4:317–18.

48. Calvin also has the same translation: *Dieu habite entre les Cherubins*. *Predigten*, 136.

49. LXX's translation literally follows MT (καθημένου χερουβιμ, sitting cherubim), although the verb, κάθημαι (sit) requires preposition επι, when it is used as the meaning of "sitting" (see Lk 22:30): e.g. καθηστο επι θρονου, "He was seated upon a chair." Josephus, *Antiquities*, 5:192.

50. See Woudstra, *Ark*, 70–73. In relation to the preposition, he suggests that "Yahweh dwells, or tarries, *at* or *with* the cherubim" (73).

divine omnipotence and omniscience, were often expressed in physical forms like the cherubim.[51] Therefore the spread wings of the cherubim seem to be associated with the idea of the power and the majesty of Yahweh rather than a throne concept derived from heathen situations outside Israel. We need to be cautious of directly applying extra-biblical materials to biblical texts in order to get their meanings because of the uniqueness of the Israelite religion.

The instruction of Exodus 25:20b shows the direction of the statues and their faces: "Overshadowing the atonement place with them, and each shall be turned towards the other, the faces of the cherubim are to be toward the atonement place." In this verse another function of the cherubim is introduced. The Hebrew word *sōkēk*, the participle form of *skk*, means literally "overshadowing," "screening," but is translated as "guardian." In Genesis 3:24, the task of the cherubim is to "guard" or "keep" (*lišmōr*) the garden of Eden, and it is also applied to God's appointment for a cherub to drive the king of Tyre from power for abuse of trade and violence (Ezek 28:14, 16), although the cherubim in this text is not related to the ark.[52] Thus, it appears that the cherubim have a function to protect and guard the atonement place and the ark beneath it; their wings form a kind of canopy. The cherubim, as hybrids that have excellent qualities from various creatures such as power, rapidity, and intelligence, are suitable for guardians and protectors.[53] Josephus's description about the wings of the cherubim covering the ark "as under a tent or dome" renders the verb for the cherubim's overshadowing of the ark as "cover."[54] This appears to imply a protective function, even though his understanding is lacking.

In conclusion, the cherubim as symbolic and celestial beings are primarily regarded as expressions of Yahweh's attributes such as transcendent sovereignty, omnipresence, glory, and majesty.

---

51. See Borowski, "Cherubim?" 36–41.

52. For classical exegesis, see Monique Alexandere, "L'Épée de flamme (Gen 3:24)," 403–41.

53. Houtman, *Exodus* 3, 374.

54. Josephus, *Antiquities*, 7:103–4.

3

The Appellations for the Ark

IN CONFORMITY WITH THE results of literary-critical and traditio-historical investigations, J. Maier classified in chronological order more than twenty different designations of the ark in order to trace the development of the ark in its function and meaning throughout various periods of its history.[1] Although it appears nearly impossible to discern any consistent pattern in usage with such numerous references to the ark, Seow helpfully simplified and reclassified a total of 195 instances that clearly refer to the ark: eight epithets in four categories, namely, ark, the ark of God, the ark of Yahweh, the ark of the covenant, the ark of the testimony, the ark of holiness, the ark of your power.[2] This section will consider some designations of the ark, roughly following this arrangement.

A. ARK

The term $'^a r\bar{o}n$ (ark) occurs by itself, with or without the definite article, a total of fifty-eight times. This simple name as a seemingly neutral designation appears in most texts of the Pentateuch and the historical books.[3] For Maier this appellation is the oldest.[4] This is true because it was used in neutral form for a box in every period, even before the ark of the covenant was manufactured. The term $'^a r\bar{o}n$, which is rendered as "ark" or "chest," at first seems neutral, with no special theological significance, when it is mentioned in Yahweh's injunction and its implementa-

---

1. J. Maier, *Heiligtum*, 82–85.

2. Seow, "Designation," 185. The last two phrases seem simply to reflect divine attributes with the ark rather than the epithets of the ark.

3. Ibid., 186.

4. J. Maier, *Heiligtum*, 82.

tion (Exod 25:10; 37:1; Deut 10:1–5). However the simple designation is often associated with other terms of some significance (Exod 25:22; 26:33–34). As regards its definition, it is hard to define the theological meaning of the simple expression "ark." The fact that it is often used in a simplified or abridged form alongside another epithet shows that the word appears to convey the same meaning as the name suggested in the context, since the hearers are able to understand it perfectly in the texts (see Josh 3:15; 4:10; 6:4, 9; 1 Sam 6:13). For instance, the abridged expression "ark" used in Joshua 3:15 and 4:10 could easily be understood as similar to the "ark of the covenant," mentioned in the previous verses. Thus, it is plausible that the specific meaning of the simple word "ark" should be derived from the context, even if the term as such, in the sense of cultic object, basically carries the significance of the divine presence.

B. THE ARK OF YAHWEH/GOD

The most frequent occurrences among the variants of the ark are those used in conjunction with two divine names (eighty-two times): the name *'ĕlōhîm* (God) and the name Yahweh. Most of these designations occur in the historical books in accord with Christian classification. In consideration of the relationship between the ark and God, Seow may well argue that "there can be no doubt that the ark came to be associated with divine names from the earliest periods of its history because of its function as a symbol of divine presence."[5] However it is questionable if the divine names related to the ark can be employed as criteria to classify documents and their dates. On the basis of documentary hypothesis, von Rad suggests that the ark of God is the original name of the ark.[6] In the same vein, Houtman conceives that the ark of God and the ark of Yahweh can be distinguished from each other from a historical perspective: "The ark of God would be the oldest appellation and indicate one of the original Canaanite cultic objects that could be named as the ark of Yahweh after acceptance in the cult of Israel."[7] Still, it seems arbitrary

---

5. Seow, "Designation," 187.

6. Von Rad, "Zelt und Lade," 121: "daß die Lade eines Elohim sich da draußen aufhielt, war der Anlaß all dieser Komplikationen, sondern die Landfremdheit! . . . Die ganz Jugendgeschichte Samuels kennt den Namen *'ărōn yahweh* nicht. Man kann also getrost behaupten, die Bezeichenung für die Lade war ursprünglich *'ărōn hā' ĕlōhîm*."

7. Houtman, *Exodus* 3, 359.

to divide historical periods according to the divine name.[8] The problem that the epithet "the ark of Yahweh" often occurs in the books belonging to periods earlier than Samuel still remains unsettled and subjective. So, there is no biblical proof that the name $hā'$ $^e lōhīm$ (the God) was earlier associated with the Israelite cultus (see Gen 4:26).

As Seow notes, it is extremely difficult to claim that the two sets of names represent two different strata in the texts pertaining to the ark.[9] Indeed, the occasional juxtaposition of the two, and sometimes the translation of the names in the versions (e.g., LXX 1 Sam 4:3, 22; 5:2) and their mutual exchange in the parallel between 2 Samuel 6:17 and 1 Chronicles 16:1, demonstrate that the designations "the ark of God" and "the ark of Yahweh" are probably to be treated, for the most part, as interchangeable. The variations between the two are usually stylistic rather than ideological, even if the divine name $'^e lōhīm$ is frequently connected with God's omnipotence as creator, while the epithet Yahweh is related to God's faithfulness to his covenant. With the appellations of the ark,

---

8. The variety of designations of God has for a long time been obstinately accepted and applied as an explanational criterion for biblical texts. However some Near Eastern literature provides us with proofs that different divine names had nothing to do with the origin of the literature. Many deities bore multiple names. In the Sumerian myth, *The Deluge*, Nintu is known under the names of Ninhursag and Ninmah (*ANET* 43). In the Babylonian *Enuma elish* (*ANET* 61–72), Ea is also Nudimmud (Tablets I, II), Tiamat is also Mother Khubur (Tablets I, III), and Marduk is also Bel (Tablet IV). In the Ugaritic texts such as *Poems of Baal and Anath and Aqhat* (*ANET* 129–42; 149–55), Kothar-wa-Khasis is also Hayyin (Aqht A, v), and Baal is also Hadd (IV AB ii, iii). In the Sabaean Inscription (*ANET* 665) of Old South Arabia, 'Almaqah or 'Ilumquh has epithets Thahwân, and Thwr-Ba`lm. In the Hittite *Song of Ullikummi* (*ANET* 121–25), Ullikummi is referred to as Kunkunuzzi-Stone (the diorite man) (III-d, KUB XXXIII, 106:iv). It is striking that the different names of one deity were freely put down in one tablet or the text and not in separated documents. In consideration of these phenomena, there is no real warrant for attributing any significance to YHWH and Elohim as literary markers.

In terms of the literary approach, Schmidt (*Einführung*, 50) acknowledged the impossibility of the classification of sources according to the variation in the divine name: "In den meisten Fällen bleibt der Wechsel (of God's names: my note) aber sachlich unerklärbar." On a different level Soggin (*Introduction*, 87–88) rejected God's names as a criterion by observing that in the Samaritan Pentateuch an ancient translation such as LXX lacked consistency in rendering and setting God's names, viz. Elohim and Yahweh. Thus it is the opinion of this paper that these two names might be used in turn, according to the preference of certain religious groups and the progress of time in the history of Israel.

9. See Seow, "Ark," 387.

the ark of God and the ark of Yahweh, the ark generally symbolizes the awesome presence of God in the midst of his people.

In addition, there are the designations of the ark with special modifiers. In particular, Joshua 3:13 introduces the term "the ark of Yahweh, the Lord of all the earth," which gives a cosmic dimension to all the events surrounding Israel's entrance into the promised land, already hinted at in Rahab's confession (Josh 2:11). Yahweh, the God of the whole earth (Gen 19:25; Exod 19:5; Ps 24:1), chose a people for himself "out of all the peoples that are on the face of the earth" (Deut 7:6). This is suggested by the words of Joshua 4:24: "that all the people of the earth might know that the hand of Yahweh is mighty." Yet, the modifier "the Lord of all the earth" is about Yahweh, rather than the ark; it is not an epithet of the ark but of Yahweh. This also applies to the name associated with the divine name "Yahweh Zebaoth who dwells between the cherubim" (1 Sam 4:4; see 2 Sam 6:2; 1 Chr 13:6). It is held that this is usually regarded as the fullest and most ancient liturgical name of the ark. However, the term "Zebaoth" is intimately associated with Yahweh rather than the ark. Yahweh Zebaoth in those texts seems to be an epithet that stresses his omnipotence rather than one directly concerned with the ark. This is seconded by Isaiah 37:16, in which the phrase has nothing to do with the ark.

C. THE ARK OF THE COVENANT/ TESTIMONY

The appellations "the ark of the covenant" and "the ark of testimony" appear forty times (thirty times with various forms of the divine name) and twelve times, respectively, throughout the Old Testament. Critical circles posit that while the association of the ark with the covenant is typical of the Deuteronomists (it is their special designation of the ark), P uses the ark of testimony as a substitute name for the ark.[10] Yet it is still doubtful to argue that the various names of the ark originate from various sources. Indeed, it is inexplicable that the so-called P, for whom the notion of God's eternal covenant plays a central part (Gen 17), would not have characterized the ark as the ark of the covenant.[11]

10. Ibid.

11. In his dissertation, Külling maintained that it is absurd that in 1869 the "P" portions were assigned to the exilic/post-exilic era with one fell swoop based on literary-analytical grounds without proof, and that not until later were arguments brought out to undergird the thesis. "*Genesis-P-Stücke*," 43–57.

In practice, the Hebrew words for the covenant (*bᵉrît*) and the testimony (*'ēdut*) are interchangeable with respect to the ark (see Deut 31:9, 25, 26; Josh 3:3, 6, 8; Exod 25:22; 26:33, 34; 30:6, 26; 39:35; 40:3, 5, 21; Num 4:5; 7:89; Josh 4:16), as above mentioned. Regardless of the ark, *'ēdut* is used as a synonym of *bᵉrît* twice (2 Kgs 17:15; Ps 132:12). Strictly speaking, however, *'ēdut*, which is rendered "testimony," basically refers to something concrete, such as the tablets of the covenant or "stipulations" of the covenant at Sinai, rather than to the covenant itself. In particular, the meaning of *'ēdut* was intimately linked with the Ten Commandments, even though the covenant had been established previously. The Decalogue as testimony basically is God's requirement for his covenantal relationship with the Israelites, who had already experienced God's redemption from Egypt. It should be underlined that Yahweh wanted the covenant relation with his people liberated through the exodus. This relationship is the foundation for the people to be "a kingdom of priests and a holy nation" (Exod 19:6). On the one hand the Decalogue was provided as a means of fulfilling the holy destiny God intended for them. It was, on the other hand, given as a means for the people to dedicate themselves with thankfulness to the God of redemption. Highlighting this aspect of the covenant character, the word *'ēdut* itself indicates the ark (Exod 16:34; 26:33, 34; 30:6, 26). Nevertheless, both the ark of the covenant and the ark of testimony symbolized the commands of the covenant that formed the people of Israel as a faithful community. These appellations of the ark represent the principal character and function of the ark as a marvelous emblem of God's presence; God's presence implied in the ark is not automatically realized in the midst of his people but there has to be communion with God based on the covenant law, the Decalogue inscribed on the tablets as a fundamental law of Israel's legal corpus.[12]

---

12. See the section "Testimony" in the previous chapter for a detailed explanation of the testimony.

4

The Suggested Functions of the Ark

A. FETISH-CHEST

LOTZ CONTENDED THAT THE designation "the ark of God/Yahweh" belonged to the primitive stage of Israelite religion and that the ark was used as a fetish-chest in the early phase of Israelite history.[1] For him the ark itself was an object of worship that could bring good fortune. He believed that the covenantal character of the Israelite religion evolved from a primitive religion. This idea reflects an attempt to reconstruct Israel's religion and history on the basis of Hegel's historical philosophy.[2] In terms of Hegelian speculation, all religions can be classified as higher or lower religion according to their various phenomena. For Hegel the truth is a process of emerging truth since everything is movement. However, such a superstitious notion that the ark of God/Yahweh was simply a fetish-chest loses its biblical base because Israelite religion was substantially characterized by revelation and covenant from its beginning, even though its institution became more sophisticated later on.

This idea reminds us of religious practices in China, where ancient Chinese people brought stones from T'ai shan (literally, huge mountain)

---

1. Lotz, "Die Bundeslade," 154.

2. If religion is understood in the framework of Hegel's dialectical structure, which was applied to his historical philosophy, religion is the relationship between the limited and unlimited spirit that progresses through history, namely, the unlimited spirit continuing to advance to a higher stage of self-consciousness. Clinging to the scheme of thesis-antithesis-synthesis (he used these terms, Sein-Nichts-Werden), it proceeds from the position where it last achieved its highest stage: nature religion-practical religion-absolute religion. See Hegel, *Hegels Religionsphilosophie*; 189–237, 248–318, 320–31; *Phänomenologie des Geistes*, 443–506.

for good fortune.³ They believed that they could earn the benefit of god's protection when they went on pilgrimages to the mountain. But as they could not stay there long, they would take a stone from the mountain back to their homes to ensure that the protective presence of god's mountain remained with them.

However, the ark was not a magic object, even though the Israelites sometimes attempted to use it in that way (1 Sam 4). There are two contrasting outcomes from association with the ark in 2 Samuel 6: the death of Uzza and the blessing of Obed-Edom. Uzza died beside the ark, punished by God, because Uzza had violated the law of God by touching the ark (Num 4:15). In fact, the infringement resulted from a lack of respect for the prescription God himself gave. However, Obed-Edom experienced the blessing of Yahweh in all that he had (1 Chr 13:12) while the ark was sheltered on his property for three months. Yahweh blessed him for the sake of the ark. These events demonstrate that blessing and curse do not arise from the ark itself but from the free will of God, who is faithful to his promise.

B. BEARER OF GOD'S IMAGE

Guthe considers the ark of Yahweh to be a bearer of God's image just as the Egyptian bark bears the image of a god standing in the wooden niche with four pillars.⁴ In addition, Gressmann, who buttressed Gunkel's traditio-historical critique, believes that the image of deity resides in the ark. In regard of the contents of the ark, he argues that the ark originally contained a golden calf as Yahweh's image,⁵ and later on, the tablets of the Mosaic law. Moreover, he connects the idea of a golden calf with the image of Yahweh as a god of war and then relates it to "the Mighty One of Jacob" in Psalm 132:2, 5, which is identical to ephod.⁶ Gressmann also supposes that there were probably two images, including an image of a female deity. The image of Yahweh's wife was added to Yahweh's image, by noting the number "two" of cherubim, as if Yahweh were Baal.⁷

---

3. Eichhorn, *Die Religionen Chinas*, 47.

4. Guthe, *Geschichte*, 31.

5. Gressmann, *Mose und sein Zeit*, 231: "Die Lade ist der von Jahve selbst gewollte Ersatz für das willkürlich geschaffene goldene Kalb."

6. Gressmann, *Jahwes und Allerheiligste*, 25, 28–30.

7. Ibid., 44, 64–65, 68.

In these statements the biggest problem is that Guthe and Gressmann attempted to establish the meaning of the ark not so much from biblical literature as from the practices of the pagan religions surrounding Israel. Israelite religion does not allow any images of deity. In particular, the worship of the golden calf was definitely prohibited throughout its history: the characteristic of the religion was imageless. Thus the mythological view that the ark was a bearer of God's image hardly matches the biblical idea: in the Old Testament nowhere is there found any clue about its function as the container of a golden calf. Moreover Gressmann connects the ark with the name "the Mighty One of Jacob" in Psalm 132:2, 5 but this divine epithet, which occurs also in Genesis 49:24 and Isaiah 49:26, seems to reflect the intimacy between Israel and God. In fact it is unnecessary to interpret this as an epithet of the ark.

C. A MINIATURE TEMPLE

This concept is derived from an archaeological parallel. On the basis of archaeological findings in Megiddo, May presented the thesis that the ark should be understood as a "miniature temple" where the deity resided or sat.[8] These are findings from an excavated temple of Megiddo. The discovery is significant as the miniature temples date from the days between Solomon, who built Megiddo, and the exile, coinciding with the time when the ark stood in the temple of Jerusalem. They are obvious figures of the Megiddo temple: "The row of holes above the windows of this model shrine represent the openings for the dovecote of the sacred doves of the mother-goddess who was worshiped at Megiddo sanctuary."[9] These features are far from those of the biblical ark, but May thinks that their function is analogous to that of the ark. "Model shrines, however, as a part of temple furnishings may have served several different functions, although, in each case, they would have had a special sanctity by virtue of the fact that they represented the temple in which the Deity dwelt."[10] He supposes that this conception of the ark as the dwelling of the deity lends support to the hypothesis that the ark was a miniature temple. In the same vein, May believes that there were mani-

---

8. May, "The Ark," 215–17.
9. Ibid., 218.
10. Ibid., 224.

fold arks in different places, which were formed according to the model of the temple in Jerusalem, and that they functioned as a processional instrument, as a divination or oracle box, as a military mascot, as a depository for the tablets of the law, and as an altar.

The finding from Megiddo can be a miniature temple where the deity was believed to dwell, as May proposed. However, it is still difficult to connect the two objects in the same function. Even if the worshippers might perhaps go to the shrine to expect that the deity was present at the miniature temple, their ritual was no more than a superstitious practice because it was not the legitimated process of the worship in Israel. It seems difficult to explain the function of the ark with a miniature temple. In addition, the notion that the ark is a part of the tabernacle or the late temple in Jerusalem hardly matches the biblical view, because the ark was used by itself and had existed before the temple was built, even if the ark amplified God's glory in the temple. The ark is an independent object. In particular, May's explanation about the relationship between the cherubim over the ark and the cherubim in the temple is not sufficient. We cannot say that the ark that is associated with cherubim is a part of the temple because cherubim are a part of the temple ornamentation. There is a unique difference between the small pottery shrines of Megiddo (30 20 20 centimeters) and the ark that is overlaid with gold that reflects God's holiness. As for function, they seem to be different from the historical ark that represents the glorious and special presence of God. From this standpoint, it seems relatively easy to undermine the uniqueness of Israelite religion by concluding that "the ark was thus most probably an institution of the popular cult, both pagan and Yahwistic, and traces of it, or of a similar institution, should be found not only at the Palestinian sanctuaries but in other places in the Near East where a similar cult predominated."[11] Although Israel's religion reflected Canaanite-Israelite syncretism in its practice, this does not imply that the ark itself was not unique in biblical perspective.

D. THRONE

Gunkel considers the ark to be a throne-seat, particularly in relation to cherubim on the grounds of the (extra-) biblical passages such as Jeremiah 3:16; Numbers 10:35.36; 1 Samuel 3:3; Exodus 25:22, 30:6;

---

11. Ibid., 219.

Numbers 7:89; Ezekial 1; Revelation 4; and Near East parallels.[12] The gist of Gunkel's article is almost identical to the statement of Meinhold, who writes that Moses manufactured the ark after the Egyptian model and the Israelites gave the concept of the empty throne to the ark in Sinai.[13] In a similar vein, referring to the writings of Herodotus, Xenophon, and Curtius, Dibelius clarified the meaning of the ark by analogy with the empty throne-wagon of Ahura Mazdâ, the Persian god, which was drawn by eight white horses.[14] Undoubtedly, his idea of a throne that emanated from the *religionsgeschichtliche* view, which basically has its fundamental positive relationship with phenomenological and religious parallels, requires much discussion.

Some biblical passages that appear to support the "throne theory" need to be closely examined, such as Numbers 10:35–36 and Jeremiah 3:16–17. In the text of Numbers 10:35–36, it is broadly stated that "rise up" obviously matches the image of the ark as the throne-chariot of Yahweh. With respect to the throne theory, Reimpell appears to compromise Dibelius's theory of the evolutional development of the religion.[15] The moving of the ark signifies that Yahweh is about to stand, "return" again suggests the image of the ark as the throne-chariot. They tend to equate the two imperative verbs, *qūmā* (arise) and *šūḇā* (return), with "stand up" and "sit down," like the action of standing and sitting on a chair.[16] Kristensen contends that this verse undergirds the theory of throne-box by analogizing Yahweh of Israel with Horus of Egypt.[17] Care should be exercised in making such an analogy because the attempt is again rooted in a failure to note the unique character of the revelatory nature of Israel's religion.

---

12. Gunkel, "Lade Jahves," 35–42; *Märchen*, 97: "der alte Orient stellt solche Thronträger nicht selten dar; in dieser Obliegenheit sind sie an der Lade jahves abgebracht."

13. Meinhold, *Die "Lade Jahwes,"* 17–18, 25–27, 43–45.

14. Dibelius, *Die Lade Jahves*, 60–63. To be sure, he suggests prooftexts on the notion as if it were a syllogism: "Nach Ez. 1 ist die Lade ein Abbild des Himmels,... Denn auch der Himmel ist ein Thron Gottes" (55). But this seems debatable, since the picture of Ezek 1 has nothing to do with the ark.

15. Reimpell, "Der Ursprung," 331: "Als Jahwe im Laufe der Zeiten geistiger verehrt wurde, und man gelernt hatte, in religiösen Dingen weniger konkret zu denken, wurde die Lade als Thron umgedeutet."

16. *qūmā* and *šūḇā* have forms of intensive imperative.

17. Kristensen, "De ark van Jahwe," 180.

In fact, Moses' prayer contains a feature different from what might generally be expected; a deity, presumably seated on a throne, is not invited to rise when that throne moves forward. At the resting of the ark Yahweh is not invited to be seated but rather to return, not to the ark, but to the Israelites, according to the content of the prayer.[18] Thus, contrary to the statements of the scholars mentioned above, this text certainly has nothing to do with the concept of a portable throne or a throne-chariot of Yahweh.

In the case of Jeremiah 3:16–17, verse 17 appears to reinforce the thesis that the ark was understood to be a throne for Yahweh, as many scholars suppose.[19] However, it is hard to contend that Jerusalem, as a futuristic throne of Yahweh, can be substituted for the ark; at that time, the people of God were fickle and unfaithful (2:27; 7). Most likely there was maltreatment and misunderstanding of the ark among the people, as Jones states.[20] One example of this misuse is that they mobilized the ark as a war-palladium in battle (1 Sam 4). In consideration of Jeremiah's preaching to the people, there is a possibility that they did not treat the ark properly during his time. They may have believed that the ark was an image or a material symbol of Yahweh, as special reverence of the Torah follows from the divine nature attributed to it in the Jewish community.[21] They probably confused essence and symbol, and so the ark became much the same as a fetish. The people may have called it Yahweh's throne because of a misunderstanding, but Yahweh's revelation through Jeremiah's prophecy may have had the intention of correcting this wrong idea: "At that time, they will call Jerusalem Yahweh's throne" (Jer 3:17a). Thus, it is perhaps difficult to conclude that verse 17a is firm evidence that the ark was considered Yahweh's throne.

In fact, it is stretching the imagination to extract biblical significance from the cultural phenomena of the countries surrounding Israel. The Old Testament succinctly testifies that Yahweh dwells upon a throne in heaven (Exod 17:16; 1 Kgs 22:19; Isa 6:1; 66:1), whereas the ark with its box-like shape is never directly associated with the throne concept.

---

18. See Woudstra, *Ark*, 93.

19. See Holladay, *Jeremiah*, 121; Carroll, *Jeremiah*, 150; Craigie et al., *Jeremiah 1–25*, 61; Schreiner, *Jeremia*, 29; Soggin, "Ark of the Covenant," 221, etc.

20. Jones, *Jeremiah*, 103.

21. Van der Toorn, "Analogies," 242.

Instead, Jerusalem or the sanctuary is described as Yahweh's throne on earth.

E. FOOTSTOOL

It has been broadly accepted that the ark is Yahweh's footstool on the basis of a comparison with an ancient and widespread Near East legal tradition, but a copy of the legal record is always put "under the feet" of the god of the contracting king respectively, whereas the testimony is placed in the ark (see chapter 2A). It is interesting to explain the ark in the light of the practice of pact-making but there are still doubts about applying ancient diplomatic customs to explicate biblical documents.

In Psalm 132:7 is found the clearest expression about the footstool in relation to the ark: "Let us enter his dwellings, let us worship at his footstool." This phrase has been frequently used to support the theory that the cherubim are regarded as the actual throne and the ark as a footstool to that throne. However, the expression is somewhat ambiguous, for it can be a metaphorical and figurative description set in a poetic context rather than a theological definition. Here his footstool may have to be considered his dwellings: "After taking up the expression 'dwelling' from v. 5, the people gloss that as Yhwh's footstool."[22] The people might enter the court of tabernacle but not worship at the ark because they could not have access to the ark in the holy of holies. The sequence of the verbs "enter" and "worship" shows an advancement of their action.

Likewise the same phrase "at his footstool" in Psalm 99:5 does not necessarily mean the ark because the phrase "at his footstool" is interchangeable with "at his holy mountain" (v. 9), which functions as a refrain in the parallel structure.[23] In this psalm the footstool seems also to be identical to "my resting place" (Ps 132:14) because it is synonymous with footstool (see Isa 66:1).[24] The biblical concept of the footstool is not ascribed to the ark but is, in fact, fairly broad. For instance, the term in Isaiah 66:1 refers to the earth. The idea of the footstool in Lamentations 2:1 is broadly applied in view of a lament over the destruction of Jerusalem, Zion, and the temple.[25] The expression of 1 Chronicles

---

22. Goldingay, *Psalms 90–150*, 550.
23. See Tate, *Psalms 51–100*, 527.
24. See H. J. Fabry, "hdm," *ThWAT* 2:347–57.
25. See Goldingay, *Psalms 90–150*, 219, 550.

28:2, where "footstool" and "ark" are in apposition to one another,[26] also appears not to point to the ark, the chest, exclusively, but to the "whole unit" of the ark containing the cherubim above the ark.[27] Therefore the biblical idea of the footstool does not give room to suppose that the cherubim are regarded as the actual throne and the ark as a footstool to that throne, as de Vaux and others attempt to explain them on the basis of a Hittite parallel.[28]

F. A SIMPLE RECEPTACLE

Critical theory generally contends that the ark in Deuteronomy is completely void of any sacred character and is described as a simple receptacle in which the tablets of the Ten Commandments were kept. According to this theory, this was in line with typical deuteronomistic expression.[29] For an exposition of the primitive feature of the ark, von Rad maintains that the ark described in Deuteronomy 10 should be understood as a container to store the tablets of the Ten Commandments (1 Kgs 8:9) and this idea is to be differentiated from the older view which regarded it as the throne-seat of Yahweh (Num 10:35–36; 1 Sam 4:4; Jer 3:16–17).[30] Here we find his presupposition that there are divergent traditions about the ark. His view of the tradition is improper and simultaneously his exposition about the traditions is skeptical. Von Rad's more explicit description of the ark in Deuteronomy is that the deuteronomistic view, which considers it as a simple storage receptacle for the tablets of the law, evidently concerns "demythologization" and rationalization of the old idea that endowed it with some sacred significance.[31] So according to

---

26. R. W. Klein and T. Krüger, 1 *Chronicles,* 520.

27. Kraus, *Psalmen,* 853: "Lade und Kerubenthron sind nicht voneinander zu trennen." See Woudstra, *Ark,* 89.

28. De Vaux, *Bible et Orient,* 256–60; 243–47.

29. Brouwer, *De ark,* 82; Eissfeldt, "Die Lade und Gesetzestafeln," 283; von Rad, "Zelt und Lade," 112; Fretheim, "Ark," 4; *Kings,* 52; Labuschagne, *Deuteronomium,* 220; Clements, *Deuteronomy,* 54; Seow, *ABD* 1:391; see Tigay, *Deuteronomy,* 105.

30. Von Rad, *Das fünfte Buch Mose,* 56: "Die Lade ist in unserem Text recht nüchtern als ein Behälter zur Aufbewahrung der Tafeln verstanden (1 Kön. 8:9). Diese Auffassung unterscheidet sich erheblich von der älteren, die in ihr den Thronsitz Jahwes sah (4. Mose 10:35f.; 1. Sam. 4:4; Jer. 3:16f. u.ö.)."

31. Von Rad, *Deuteronomium=Studien,* 27: "es handelt sich bei der dt. Auffassung als eines Aufbewahrungsbehälters für die Gesetzestafeln offenbar um ein 'Entmythologisierung' und Rationalisierung der alten Anschauung!"

him, the ark in deuteronomistic writings has no theological meaning for the Israelite faith. Although Deuteronomy appears to put special stress on the law rather than the ark as such, it seems unreasonable to maintain that in Deuteronomy the ark is described as a simple box used for the tablets of the law. The relation of the ark to the tablets presents another significant function of the ark that is concerned with strengthening the importance of Yahweh's law.

For a precise evaluation, it is vital to understand the character of the ark passage in Deuteronomy 10. The narrative of the ark in this text (Deut 10:1–5) is severely truncated because it is unnecessary to restate all the details of the original injunction in Deuteronomy itself and the goal of this book is different from that of Exodus. While the ark passage in Exodus is focused on God's glorious presence on the way to the land of Canaan, the text of Deuteronomy emphasizes God's mercy to renew the covenant with his rebellious people.[32] So, it is not desirable to say that this brief account of the ark ignores some of the characteristics of the ark.

Contrary to von Rad's view, there are some references to a sacred meaning of the ark in deuteronomic language, behavior in treatment of the ark (Deut 10:8), and its relationship with the law (Deut 31:26). Above all, Ian Wilson meticulously examined the phrase "in his presence" or "before Yahweh" in Deuteronomy and "deuteronomistic books" by using a linguistic method to oppose von Rad's concept on the ark of the covenant. According to Deuteronomy 10:8, the Levites should stand "in the presence of Yahweh" to minister to him. The phrase "in the presence of Yahweh" denotes the ark as a symbol of the divine presence of Yahweh.[33] This phrase shows us that Deuteronomy still uses language that attaches sanctity to the ark. Furthermore, the connotation of the phrase suggests a holy object even in Deuteronomy. In addition, the same verse (Deut 10:8) informs us that the ark bears not only a significant role as the repository of the law tables but is circumspectly conveyed by the Levites and set apart in accordance with holy writ. Great reverence for the ark is exhibited in the treatment of it. In particular, according to Deuteronomy 31:26, the law Moses wrote should be placed beside the ark. This verse suggests that the law was also to be conceived as constitutive of the com-

---

32. Thompson, *Deuteronomy*, 161.
33. Wilson, "Merely a Container?" 212–49.

munity and authoritative for it.[34] Here the law is firmly tied up with one aspect of the significance the ark bestows: it has divine authority. It plays an important role as a sacred object affiliated with Yahweh's presence and authority. The "deuteronomic" texts related to the ark still describe its sacred character and does not suggest that it is a simple chest. Thus there is no fundamental difference on the matter of the characteristic of the ark between Exodus and Deuteronomy.[35]

G. WAR-PALLADIUM

The notion that considers the ark to be a war-palladium, as many scholars suppose,[36] differs from the biblical description of the ark, even if the Israelites sometimes thought of it in this way. The result of the Israelite battle against the Philistines truly reflects the absurdity of such a superstitious use of the ark (1 Sam 4).

Besides the account of the war in 1 Samuel 4, two other verses appear to show that the ark is associated with war. The Massoretic text of 1 Samuel 14:18 reads: "Saul ordered Ahijah, 'bring the ark of God,' for in that day the ark of God was with the Israelites." This passage seems problematic since Saul's order is not in harmony with the situation of the same chapter, according to which "Ahijah carried the Ephod" (v. 3). The rest of the books of Samuel comply by showing that Saul had no particular interest in the ark (see 1 Chr 13:3), and moreover the ark was stationed in Kiriath-Jearim until the initial reign of David (2 Sam 6). To overcome this incongruity, Arnold maintains that the ark Saul ordered to bring is another ark.[37] Yet biblical materials do not support his hypothesis of multiple arks when we consider that the other ephod that Gideon made is negatively evaluated: "Gideon made the gold into an ephod, and he put it in Ophrah, his town. All Israel prostituted themselves after it there, and it became a snare to Gideon and his family" (Judg 8:27). Instead, the Hebrew text can be emended to read ephod, not ark, according to LXX[BL], which read ephod for "ark of God." The LXX's

---

34. See Fretheim, "Ark," 5.

35. See McConville, *Deuteronomy*, 188.

36. Gunkel, "Lade Jahves," 34-35; Dibelius, *Die Lade Jahves*, 110; Wellhausen, *Prolegomena*, 47; Stoebe, *Das erste Buch Samuelis*, 95; Kraus, *Psalmen*, 632; De Robert, "Arche et Guerre Sainte," 52; Dietrich, *Samuel*, 228-29; etc.

37. Arnold, *Ephod and Ark*, 26-27.

rendering, which most exegetes accept, appears to be more plausible.[38] Thus, this passage demonstrates that the ark is not associated with war.

Another verse regarded as proof that the ark was in the battlefield is 2 Samuel 11:11. In this verse we read about Uriah's rejection of David's suggestion. The expression "the ark and Israel and Judah are staying in tents" is ambiguous. The term "tents" (*sukkōṯ*) is not normally used of tents for the Israelites (Lev 23:42, 43; Neh 8:14, 17), whereas the word that mentions the ordinary tent is *'ōhęl* (Gen 4:20; 12:8, 2 Sam 6:17; 16:22; etc.). Woudstra carefully considers the term as a reference to the festival of Sukkoth described in Exodus 34:22 and 23:16–35.[39] However, Uriah's statement seems to stress the seriousness of the battle as a whole. Moreover, there seems to be no reason for him to reject the comforts of his house in such unusual circumstances, while people were celebrating the Feast of Tabernacles staying in booths (see Judg 21:19–21). Yadin's proposal that the term *sukkōṯ* should be understood as the place "Succoth" located forty-five kilometers from Rabbath-Ammon is plausible.[40] Then the militia (Israel and Judah) remained at the secure base of Succoth, serving as strategical reserves both against unexpected eventualities of fresh Aramean interventions and as reinforcements for Joab's army. At any rate, it appears that the militia with the ark was kept in reserve. In this case, the Israelites seem to have used the ark as an object of divination (see Judg 20:23–28), quite differently from the war against the Philistines in 1 Samuel 4. This may have been a rare occasion and another example of Israel's abuse of the ark. Therefore this verse may not be used as evidence that the ark frequently functioned as a war-palladium in the Old Testament.

H. SPATIAL CENTER OF AMPHICTYONY

It would not be fallacious to say that the ark was the central point for the twelve tribes of Israel in the land of Canaan. Israel did have one central sanctuary but it was not fixed to one place: it moved to several central places such as Shechem (Josh 24), Bethel (Judg 20:18), and Shiloh, which appears as the most important center of worship (1 Sam 1–4). Unlike the sanctuary, the portable ark was believed to be the symbol of God's pres-

---

38. See Kio, "What did Saul ask for: ark or ephod?," 240–46.
39. Woudstra, *Ark*, 119–21.
40. Yadin, "Strategy," 341–51.

ence wherever it was carried. In this sense, the ark was the central focus for all the tribes.

However the hypothesis of amphictyony that Noth spread is based on skepticism about biblical history. His concern was to reconstruct a factual history of Israel from biblical history, which means that he considered Israelite history in the Old Testament as an unreal or traditional history purely related to what Israel professed. In his study of the Israelite tribes, he argued that Israel as a twelve tribe organization had only come into existence after it had settled in Canaan.[41] This stance was prompted by his discovery of an analogy with Israel's tribal structure in Greek and Italian amphictyonies—the union of independent communities united through common worship at a central shrine.[42] As a result the ark functioned as a centripetal point for amphictyonic formation. In terms of religion, the ark, which was probably originally the movable sanctuary of nomadic clans, is regarded as the spatial center of the amphictyony in ancient Israel.[43] Then the reason the twelve tribes joined in the league was to take charge of offerings at the shrine each month for a year in turn.[44] For him, the amphictyony is a cradle of Israelite tribes as well as a religious organization. Consequently he rejected the Old Testament report of the historical narratives in which Israelite tribes consisted chiefly of the children of Jacob, concurrent with the conquest of the promised land by the Israelite tribes.[45] This hypothesis is another by-product brought forth by the traditio-historical method.[46] It is seem-

---

41. Noth, *System*, 61.

42. Ibid., 46–55; *Geschichte Israels*, 88–104.

43. Noth, *System*, 95: "Ich wage daher die Behauptung, daß 'Jahwe, der Gott Israels' mit der Lade zusammengehört und daß auch im Kult der Zwölfstämmeamphiktyonie die Lade das eigentliche Zentralheiligtum war."

44. Ibid., 85–86.

45. However the historical study based on the findings of modern archaeology is sufficient to drive a wedge into his hypothesis, that Jericho's destruction (where the ark played a key role) was a direct result of the conquest itself while Ai and the surrounding territories were destroyed by subsequent military attacks. See A. Mazar, *Archaeology*, 331; Wood, "Conquer Jericho?" 44–58.

46. A characteristic of tradition-historical criticism is to regard historical events in biblical documents as etiological sagas that mold fictional occurrences of the past in endeavoring a reply to the questions of curious humans on the determinative phenomena of general-human, ethnological, or local nature. See Gunkel, *Genesis*, viii–ix; Noth, *Das Buch Josua*, 31–33; see Noort, *Das Buch Josua*, 148; Mowinckel, *Tetrateuch-Pentateuch-Hexateuch*, 33–35; Langlamet, *Gilgal et les recits*, 128.

ingly true that the ark was the main focus of tribal organization in Israel. Yet it would be unwise to attempt reconstructing the origin of Israel with the theory of amphictyony at the cost of historicity of Scripture.[47] Thus, it is insufficient to explicate the ark by employing Noth's ideological framework within which to understand phenomenologically the biblical history about early Israel and its organization.

---

47. His theory was challenged by many scholars: G. E. Wright, *Old Testament and Theology*, 128–29; G. Anderson, "Israel," 148; Herrmann, *Geschichte Israels*, 146; Gottwald, *Tribes of Yahweh*, 356–57; Bock, *Kleine Geschichte Israels*, 40–42.

5

The Ark in the Pentateuch

A. "THE SONG OF THE ARK" (NUM 10:33–36)

WITH REGARD TO THE circumstances of the text, the whole chapter of Numbers 10 reports another preparation, regulations, and departure of the march of the Israelites from the wilderness of Sinai, where they stayed for some one year (Ex 19:1; Num 10:11). The latter half of this chapter (Num 10:11–36) deals with the departure of the tribal organization of Israel and God's guidance. It is impressive that Moses solicited Hobab's accompaniment and assistance for the Israelite march in treacherous wilderness (Num 10:29, 31).[1] As a Kenite who was familiar with the topography of the wilderness, Hobab's experience was to help the people: he knew how to encamp in the wilderness.[2] He might be able to give some effective advice to them, when the people of Israel would have to camp in a new evironment, the place where the cloud guided. Besides, Moses' request seems not simply for his human leadership but also for him to join a kind of faith in Yahweh: he said to Hobab, "We are journeying into the place about which Yahweh said, 'I will give it to you.'" It might have been difficult for Hobab to understand what Moses said because the land of Canaan was in the reign of Egypt at that time. At any event, it must be good for both Hobab and Israel that he accepts Moses' request (Num 10:32). However the dialogue between the two keeps silent about Hobab's response, although the texts of Judges provide evidence that he accompanied Moses (Judg 1:16; 4:11). Thus this

---

1. Hobab is probably Moses' brother-in-law; see Cole, *Numbers*, 175–76.
2. NIV and ESV rendered *yāḏaʿtā ḥanōtēnū* as "you know where we should camp." The versions appear, in a certain aspect, to stress a human leadership but the Israelites should camp by the movement of the cloud under the divine guidance.

context seems to be subject to the text that illustrates divine guidance by the ark of Yahweh.

Eventually, the camp of the twelve tribes of Israel, with God's presence in its midst, begins its climactic march from the wilderness of Sinai toward the promised land: "And they departed from the mount of Yahweh and went three days' journey" (10:33a). The first stage of the march is a three-day journey to Taberah (Num 11:3) in the wilderness of Paran (Num 10:12). "The mount of Yahweh" generally designates Mount Zion after the temple was built (Ps 24:3; Isa 2:3; 30:29; Mic 4:2), but here it denotes Mount Sinai where Yahweh revealed himself.[3] A day's journey does not usually imply specific length measurements.[4] Although "three days' journey" sounds like quite a long distance (see Jonah 3:3), the march of Israel for three days would not be so far, in view of the number of people of all ages as well as all their equipment. In this march the ark plays a leading role: "The ark of the covenant of Yahweh went before them (three days' journey) to scout a resting place for them" (Num 10:33b). "The ark of the covenant of Yahweh" is a new name for the ark. This description connotes the ark in which the "tablets of the covenant" were deposited (Deut 9:9, 11, 15). In this text the ark signifies the covenantal relationship between Yahweh and Israel: his protection and her obedience in the wilderness. The phrase "the ark went before them" seems difficult to understand on the basis of Numbers 10:21 and 2:17; it should be placed between the camp positions of Reuben and Ephraim. While it is acceptable that the ark marched at the head of the Israelite camps and that the other holy objects the Kohathites took care of were carried between Reuben and Ephraim, it is inconceivable that there are two arks: one in front and one in their midst as some rabbis suggested.[5] From passages such as Numbers 14:44 and Joshua 7:6 and 8:3 it appears that the ark was in the midst of the camp when the camp was at rest, but it traveled in front during the march. The literal rendering "a distance of three days" for the phrase "three days' journey" in the second part of Numbers 10:33 cannot be sustained, for the ark had to be visible in

---

3. Targum provides, instead of its translation, an explanation of this phrase: "from the mountain upon which the glory of the Lord was revealed." It reflects the periphrastic tendency of Targum. It is also supported by Gen 22:14, if the vocalization of MT is accepted (*bᵉhar yhwh yērāʾě*).

4. See Powell, "Weights and Measures," 901.

5. Milgrom, *Numbers*, 80.

order to serve as a guide.[6] The sentence makes sense without the phrase, for the same phrase is syntactically connected with the second part of the sentence. Here the task of the ark is to scout a resting place, which means a place to encamp.[7] The context of the word relates to the seemingly military function of the ark on the march. Indeed the phrase "the ark scouted it," which is written in an almost personifying fashion, is a symbolic expression for the guidance of Yahweh, who is closely associated with it. The fact that the ark leads the Israelites to the resting place reminds Christians of the true rest that can be found in Christ.

Numbers 10:34 shows us a phase of God's presence: "The cloud of Yahweh was over them by day when they set out from the camp."[8] The cloud was over the marching Israelites as a sign of the presence and protection of Yahweh (see Num 12:4, 5; 14:14b; Ps 105:39) while the ark served symbolically as a guide; both are signs that Yahweh is at work in their midst.

This couplet of Numbers 10:35 and 36 is generally called "the song of the ark," which is enclosed by the inverted nuns:[9] "When the ark set out, Moses said, 'Rise up, O Yahweh! May your enemies be scattered and

6. Ibid., The second phrase, *dęrękh šelōšęth yāmīm* looks like dittography.

7. The verb *tūr* (circumambulate, scout, survey) is frequently employed in Numbers 13 and 14, especially to scout the land of Canaan. "The Hebrew noun, *menūḥā* usually connotes a permanent, secure habitation (Deut 12:9; Jer 45:3; Ruth 1:9), but this is not its sense here" (Levine, *Numbers 1-20*, 317).

8. In LXX this whole verse is located after the contents of v. 36, thereby connecting the song of the ark with the statement about the ark. This arrangement appears as the result of reflecting the order of occurrence.

9. In fact, there is no satisfactory answer to inverted *nuns* (*nun menuzzeret*). The general concept on the inverted nun is that the concerned verses stand in an improper place (GK §5 n.). According to the rabbinic tradition (*Sif. Num.* 84) this is not their proper place nor do the enclosed two verses form a separate book. The latter is supported by the Mishnah (*Midrash Yadayim* 3:5): "A biblical scroll that contains eighty-five letters, as in the section that begins: 'when the Ark was to set out,' defiles the hands" and is confirmed by similar signs (something like *diplē, antisigma*) in Greek papyri and grammatical literature (Lieberman, *Hellenism*, 38-43). It is unknown if this couplet was taken from "an apocryphal book of Eldad and Medad" (see 11:26) in a medieval tradition from Cairo (see Leiman, "Inverted nuns," 353). Levine states that the status of Num 10:35-36 is given the syntax of medieval Hebrew ("Inverted nuns," 123), but the verses' orthography shows antiquity: "On notera Asia dans ces vv., un abondant usage de la «*scriptio defectiva*», ce qui semble nnouvel indice d'antiquité du texte" (De Vaulx, *Les Nombres*, 146). Milgrom states that this couplet may be a fragment of a larger saga on the life of Moses (Milgrom, *Numbers*, 81) but it is uncertain. Nevertheless, it is possible to say that a certain scribe or Massoretic scholar appears to have understood this part as an independent unit at least if he inserted the inverted *nuns*.

your haters flee from your face.' When it came to rest, he said, 'Return, O Yahweh, to ten thousand thousands of Israel.'" It is difficult however to determine whether it was used as a song, for the first word in each stanza is grammatically structured as an imperative. The idea that Moses could command Yahweh as to whether and when he was to set out is in direct contradiction to Israel's knowledge concerning man's position relative to God. It would be more proper to see this part as a prayer rather than a formula such as a song or incantation.[10] Moses' prayer in the first verse of the couplet is nearly same as the prayer of Psalm 68:2: "May God arise, may his enemies be scattered; may those who hate him flee before him." This poetical expression appears to have been considered as an independent part but roughly harmonized with the historical context of the march in the wilderness.

The verb *qūm* in *qūmā*[11] is often used to express "rising" in order to attack enimies (see Judg 5:12) but has the meaning of "advancing" in the text. The words "your enemies" and "your haters" connote that the enemies and haters of Yahweh are those of Israel as well: the problems of Israel are also those of Yahweh. Moses wished Yahweh to arise and to attack his enemies and haters, meaning that Israel wanted to enter the land of Canaan safely behind Yahweh. Here the setting forward of the ark, in sacramental manner, signifies the symbolic rising of Yahweh.[12] Corresponding to this sacramental connection between Yahweh and his ark is Moses' urgent plea that Yahweh should arise. We might also say this is Moses' active cooperation with the sacramental realization of the sign as embodied in the ark's motion.[13] It is not a magical incantation.

Since it lacks the preposition, it is contestable whether the phrase *rib^{e}bōt 'alpē yiśrāēl* (ten thousand thousands of Israel) is linked with

---

10. Ohmann, *Tellingen*, 67.

11. *qūmā* does not simply serve "zur Vermeidung eines Hiatus gewöhnlich" (GK §72:3), but here as an emphatic usage (Joüon, §33), for this term might be used as a exclamation.

12. This is contrary to Eichrodt's view, according to which the ark is identified with Yahweh himself, even if the same term is applied to Yahweh himself in the passage such as Deut 1:30 (*Theologie*, 43). Calvin used the phrase, "in sacramental manner" in his explanation of atonement and reconciliation in the Old Testament as well as in the lesson of sacrament (Calvin, *Moses*, 2:321–24).

13. Woudstra, *Ark*, 93.

Israel[14] or with Yahweh.[15] The former provides the direction of Yahweh's return, while the latter offers a divine epithet. Primarily, it seems natural that the phrase is connected with the direction of Yahweh's return (KJV, NIV, NASB, ESV, etc.) rather than an epithet of Yahweh. This expression differs from Yahweh of hosts ($ṣ^eḇāōṯ$) which refers to celestial hosts or armies (Josh 5:14–15), including the sun, moon, and stars (e.g., Deut 4:19).[16] Here the phrase "ten thousand thousands of Israel" appears to be associated with the huge number of Israelites (Deut 1:10). It is plausible to pray that God who fought their enemies may return to his people.

As a whole, Moses' prayer reveals that the main purpose of the ark was to stimulate the Israelites' faith in Yahweh, who is symbolically associated with the ark, and obedience of God's demands in terms of the covenant. Hence, Moses spoke to Yahweh rather than to the ark. After all, without God on their side, victory was not possible for Israel.

In Numbers 10:36 Moses asks Yahweh, the militant God, to return to his people and his habitual place in the camp when the battle is over. It is completely unknown if Moses expressed this phrase whenever the ark set out and came to rest, but it appears to exhibit that, to a degree, the march of the Israelites in the wilderness had a kind of liturgical character. At any case, this ark passage that describes Yahweh's guidance and protection for the Israelites in the wilderness shows us another divine attribute: goodness.

B. THE ARK AND THE LAW (DEUT 10:1-5, 8 AND 31:26)

The ark passage of Deuteronomy gives us the second information about the fabrication of the ark. Thus, the pericope Deuteronomy 10:1–5 did not have to be written in such detail as the text containing the pedigree of the ark in Exodus 25. It was written in a general way to supply information about God's gracious devices to his people in giving the Decalogue and the ark.

The time when Yahweh commended Moses is expressed by "at that time." It denotes the time of Moses' intercessory prayer for atonement of the people and the time when he acted more than just as a mediator of the covenant (Deut 9:25–29). The interpretation of the verses immediately following is significant. That is to say, this ark passage consists

---

14. Gispen, *Numeri*, 1:164; Wenham, *Numbers*, 119; Budd, *Numbers*, 112.
15. De Vaulx, *Les Nombres*, 146; Milgrom, *Numbers*, 81; Seebaas, *Numeri*, 4.
16. Milgrom, *Numbers*, 81.

of Yahweh's response to Moses' intercession over Israelite sin. Yahweh's command, "Hew for yourself two stone tablets like the first ones and come up to me on the mountain" (Deut 10:1a) shows how the broken covenant can be restored; "This is an invitation to covenant renewal."[17] The injunction for the construction of the ark also should be understood within this context: the ark as such is not accentuated in the text referring to it.

According to the substantial tradition of the Jews, the ark in Deuteronomy 10:1, 3, was not the same as the ark of Exodus 25:10–22: "it was a provisional ark into which the tablets were placed immediately after Moses' descent; they remained in it till the final ark could be prepared, for the new tablets were not to be broken" (Exod 34:1).[18] It seems possible to conceive of a temporary container for the two stone tablets at this time. However, this view creates a problem that revolves around the expression *wayyihyū šām* (and they are there); this phrase can be translated as "and they are there till now" in content, which denotes the time of the composition of Deuteronomy.[19] It tells that the ark is the same one as in Exodus 25. Moreover, the ark also was made of the same material, "acacia wood," even though its traits in this text are not described in more detail than that of Exodus 25. Even the information about the construction of the ark, "I made the ark out of acacia wood," need not be seen as conflicting with the report of Bezalel's construction of it (Exod 37:1–9); Moses would commission him to fabricate it. Thus, instead of "an ark of wood," the NIV translation of "a wooden chest" can wrongly lead us to think it was a different ark.

The expression, "Yahweh wrote on these tablets as the first writing, the Ten Words" (Deut 10:4) underlines the agreement of the new document with the first, emphatically marked as "Ten Words" and, simultaneously, Yahweh's activity to announce it directly to his people.[20] Yahweh wanted to reestablish the covenant between himself and his people by rewriting the Ten Commandments; Moses' intercessory prayer was granted.

The sentence "Then I . . . put the tablets in the ark I had made, as Yahweh commanded me, and they are there now" (Deut 10:5) supports

---

17. See Merrill, *Deuteronomy*, 198.
18. Jacob, *Second Book*, 772; see Tigay, *Deuteronomy*, 105.
19. See Merrill, *Deuteronomy*, 198.
20. See Rose, 5: *Mose 1–11/26–34*, 513.

the important function of the ark as a repository of the tablets of the Ten Commandments. Here Amsler's comparison of the Decalogue with the suzerain pact looks awkward because Yahweh's restoration of the covenant is one-sided in this case.[21] The text, as a whole, exposes Yahweh's gracious response to Moses' intercession. The emphasis rests on the tablets of the covenant in this whole chapter rather than on the ark; on how the covenant is restored and remains with them. This context is concerned with the obligations to the covenant faith, in accord with the contents and character of the book of Deuteronomy. It still upholds the ark as the visible symbol of Yahweh's presence, for the people's communion with him is based on his commandments.

Deuteronomy 31:26 shows the importance of the ark in reference to the Book of the Law: "Take[22] this book of the law and put it beside the ark of the covenant of Yahweh your God. There it will remain as a witness against you." This Book of the Law appears to indicate all of the law and the book of Deuteronomy that Moses wrote. The law Moses wrote should be placed beside the ark; it is here, at least, called "the ark of the covenant." This verse suggests that the law was also to be conceived as authoritative for the community. Here placing the law beside the ark signifies that the ark adds divine authority to the law. Before his death, Moses exhorted the people of Israel to stick to the covenantal law. This law is not directly linked to the tablets of the Decalogue but to the ark containing them. The significance of the law is underscored in that it is placed in a specially designed, sacred place, namely, in the presence of Yahweh, even if the context is not directly to accentuate the divine presence as such, but rather the permanent location of the tokens of the covenant.[23] The ark plays an important role as a sacred object affiliated with Yahweh's presence and authority.

The ark passages in Deuteronomy demonstrate the covenantal restoration of Yahweh's plan of redemptive history on the basis of his promise to the patriarchs. Through amazing grace, disobedient people are given another chance to obey the commandment of Yahweh and to sustain the covenanal relationship by keeping the law whose authority was highlighted beside the ark.

---

21. Amsler, "Loi orale et loi écrite," 54.
22. Gk §113 bb. The infinitive absolute of *lāqaḥ* functions as an emphatic imperative.
23. See McConville, *Deuteronomy*, 443.

6

The Ark in the Book of Joshua

A. THE ARK IN JORDAN (JOSH 3:1—4:24)

THIS SECTION DEALS LARGELY with how the people of Israel crossed the Jordan under the guidance of Joshua. It shows how the ark of Yahweh plays a decisive role in this event.

After camping by the Jordan River, the Israelites were given instructions for passing over it: "When you see the ark of the covenant of Yahweh your God, and the Levitical priests bearing it, then you are to depart from your place and follow it" (Josh 3:3).[1] The name given to the ark that is the sacred chest containing the tablets of the law (Exod 25:21; Deut 10:1) is used here to express the idea that Israel's privilege as God's people was linked to the sacred obligation to keep the covenant that God in his grace had made with them. Because of its sanctity, the ark was to be carried by designated persons: the Levites, especially the sons of Kohath (Num 4:4, 15). The office with its double emphasis, "the priests the Levites," in this text is to stress that it is to be strictly regulated.[2] The primary task of the priests is to take care of the sanctuary (Num 1:53; 3:28, 32). This office is characterized by its protective function (i.e., to

---

1. Pitkänen, *Joshua*, 126. The object of preposition, *'ah"rāw*, should be singular, "him" (*w*), rather than plural, "them." Pitkänen translated it as if the Israelites are to follow the priests but they are to follow the ark of the covenant.

2. It is confined to the tribe of Levi. In fact, the phrase "the priests the Levites" occurs frequently in Deuteronomy (17:9, 18; 18:1; 24:8; 27:9; see Josh 8:33). Although all Levites are not priests, on the basis of the reference to the offices in Joshua 8:33 and Deuteronomy 27:9–14, it is likely that the author of this book equates "the Levites" with "the priests the Levites" for the latter term is used for those who actually participated in the ceremony at Gerizim and Ebal. See McConville, *Law and Theology*, 137.

protect God's holiness in the holy area). In the same way, the priests were called to serve by carrying the ark.

Emphasis on the holiness of the ark is given in the next verse: "there will be a distance of about two thousand cubits between you and the ark; do not go near it" (Josh 3:4). "About two thousand cubits" is rendered around nine hundred meters. Such a distance is not found elsewhere[3] but it was probably a special protective measure that God ordered for this once-for-all-time event in the redemptive history of Israel, namely, crossing the Jordan River. The Israelites were not to approach the symbolic object of Yahweh's presence with them by keeping an optimum distance. The divine presence brought enormous responsibility; Yahweh's presence was certainly a blessing but, coincidentally, it was also a threat. Geographically, the distance of two thousand cubits is approximately from the outer bank of the Jordan (el Ghôr) to the inner bed (ez Zôr) that is located on a lower level.[4] Then the people from the higher position could see when the priests touched the water of the river.

In relation to the holy nature of the miracle that Yaweh is about to work with the ark, the people are commanded to be sanctified (Josh 3:5). The outward ordinances for sanctity that are applied to other important events (Exod 19:10, 14–15; Num 11:18; Josh 7:13) and appear in the purification of clothes and sexual abstinence (Exod 19:10–15; Gen 35:2)[5] are meant to induce spiritual reflection and a humble attitude. Both of these are necessary in order to experience Yahweh's presence. On the condition of preserving sanctity, Yahweh will do wonders among the Israelites.[6] In particular, this marvelous act of Yahweh in enabling them to cross over the Jordan, a natural barrier, will be a significant moment

---

3. Brouwer claims that this section is inserted by a later scribe on the ground that such distance between the ark and the people is not to be found again in the future ark narratives. *De ark*, 109.

4. Woudstra, *Joshua*, 81. According to Jewish tradition Midrash *Tanḥuma*, two thousand cubits was the extent of the permitted Sabbath day's journey: "In the future you will stand there and observe the Sabbath. Do not go more than two thousand cubits from the ark on any side, so that you can go and pray before it on the Sabbath." Cohen, *Joshua, Judges*, 13.

5. See Hess, *Joshua*, 110.

6. The wonders, *niflāʾōṯ* (ni. ptc. f. pl. of *pālā*) generally are such impressive acts as miracles that astonish people. However, the substantive *niflāʾōṯ* (13x) with *peleʾ* (10x) is frequently associated with Yahweh's acts of salvation: the Exodus event (Exod 3:20; Mic 7:15; Ps 98:1), the wilderness journey (Ps 78:12–20), the crossing of the Jordan (Josh 3:5) and the conquest of the land of Canaan (Exod 34:10).

for the Israelites as they experience a new phase of the redemptive history of Yahweh.

Before they cross over the river, Joshua's position is to be exalted: "Today I will begin to exalt you in the eyes of all Israel, so they may know that I will be with you as I was with Moses" (Josh 3:7). God is now about to fulfill publicly what he promised to Joshua (1:1–9). Joshua's exaltation is an official confirmation of his leadership before all the people of Israel. Yahweh knows that it is vital for both the people and Joshua to have confidence in his leadership for the upcoming wars in Canaan. Yet, his leadership is of a more spiritual than military or strategic nature (1:10; 3:2–4, 5–6, 9–13, etc.). Yahweh's exaltation of Joshua as a spiritual leader does not stress his position as such but that the Israelites might know that Yahweh is with Joshua.[7] This accentuation can also be found in this subordinate clause with *nun paragogicum*.[8] Naturally, Yahweh is with all his people but he is with Joshua in a special way. He encourages him by stating that as he was with Moses so he will be with him. The people who had experienced Moses' leadership in the wilderness are able to apprehend this. With Yahweh's proclamation, Joshua is to be recognized as Moses' successor.[9]

Joshua had to command the priests who carry the ark of the covenant: "when you reach[10] the edge of the Jordan's waters, you shall stand in Jordan" (3:8). The purpose of this command is to give an opportunity

---

7. See Howard, *Joshua*, 124.

8. As for the grammatical construction, *ʾăšer yēdeûn, nun paragoicum* in the clause, Hoftijzer explains, "is concerned with an aim which will certainly be attended (provided the action in the principal clause takes place)" (*Function and Use*, 44). According to this grammatical structure, the principal clause is Yahweh's exaltation of Joshua and the subordinate clause points to a conviction of the people's acknowledgement that Yahweh is with Joshua.

9. Coats asserts that Joshua's initiative with the ark is comparable to Moses' initiative with the rod, used in the separation of the waters of the Red Sea. However, such a comparison between the ark and the rod appears a bit clumsy. The latter may symbolize Moses' authoritative position but the former has nothing to do with Joshua's status. In fact, the function of Joshua differs from that of Moses in the performance of the miracles, even though Yahweh exalted both of them as prominent leaders of the Israelites. Joshua's role with respect to the impending miracle of the parting of Jordan's waters is less direct than that of Moses at the Red Sea. Moses was himself instrumental in the miracle (Exod 14:6, 21), but Joshua merely gave orders. It may be that the promise of Yahweh's presence with the ark also plays a role in this difference. Coats, "Ark," 140.

10. In the conjunctive sentence with the preposition, *kᵉ* of *kᵉbōʾăkem* (literally, "as you enter") serves as leading a time clause. Brockelmann, *Hebräische Syntax*, §163c.

for all the people to affirm realistically that Yahweh is with Joshua, as he was with Moses. In addition to the order to the priests, Joshua calls for the attention of the Israelites in order to instruct them: "Come here and listen to the words of Yahweh your God" (3:9).[11] In fact, the words of Yahweh that the people should listen to are to indicate "the wonders" that were previewed in verse 5 and $b^ez\bar{o}t$ (by this) in verse 10, namely, the blocking of the Jordan's flow as depicted in verse 13. Joshua's command is to require the people to believe that Yahweh is with him and simultaneously with them: "by this you will know that the living God is in your midst" (3:10a).[12] It is understandable for the term to be regarded as the wonders described in verse 13. Here, Joshua introduced Yahweh as "the living God." This term is employed as a polemic against the pagan gods whom the Canaanites worshiped (see Jer 10:10-11).[13] Since Yahweh is the living God, totally different from dead idols, Joshua said, "he will certainly drive out before you the Canaanites, Hittites, Hivites, Perizzites, Girgashites, Amorites and Jebusites" (Josh 3:10b) according to his promise (Gen 15:18; Exod 23:28; 33:2; 34:11; etc.).[14]

Among the various lists of Canaanite peoples in both number and order, these seven nations appear to form a standard list (see Gen 15:19-21; Exod 3:8, 17; 13:5; 23:23, 28; 33:2; 34:11; Num 13:29; Deut 7:1; 20:17; Josh 3:10; 9:1; 11:3; 12:8; 24:11; Judg 3:5; etc.). The biblical texts offer information on the territories that these seven peoples were occupying at that time.[15] If the number has a symbolic meaning, the seven symbolizes

11. Grammatically, a curious form (GK §66c) of *gōšū* (qal, imp. 2. m. pl. of *nāgaš*) is exceptional. Bergsträsser, *Hebräische Grammatik*, §25c.

12. The NIV rendering of $b^ez\bar{o}t$, "this is how," is not clear.

13. See Howard, *Joshua*, 125.

14. The assurance of Yahweh's ejection of the peoples is expressed in the paronomastic use of the inf. abs. form of the verb, *yāraš*.

15. The Canaanites probably are the people living near the sea and near the Jordan River (Josh 5:1; Num 13:29), even though the term "Canaanites" is frequently an all-inclusive word referring to any people living in Canaan. The Hittites are found in the hill country of Judah (Gen 23:1-3, 26:34; Judg 1:22-26; Ezek 16:3, 45). The Hivites lived in the mountainous region to the north (Josh 11:3; Judg 3:3). The Perizzites seem to have lived in the region of central Palestine (Gen 13:7; Josh 17:15). The Girgashites appear only in the lists of peoples of the Bible. According to Hostetter, they lived toward the north of Palestine, because the region is the only area left in Palestine (*Nations*, 63). In this case, the Amorites probably refer to the people east of the Jordan River (Num 21:26; Deut 4:46; Josh 13:10, 21), although the name of the people seems often to be synonymous with the Canaanites (Gen 15:16, 36:2-3; Josh 24:15; Judg 1:34.35; Ezek 16:3). The Jebusites inhabited Jerusalem (Josh 15:8, 18:28). In fact, there were more

the entire number of the oppressive and corrupt authorities ruling the land.[16] By God's miraculous action, the people of Israel will be assured that Yahweh will expel all these Canaanite nations from the land.

As a sign of God's expulsion of the pagan nations from Canaan, the ark is called "the ark of the covenant, the Lord of all the earth" (Josh 3:11). Yahweh is the owner of all the earth including Palestine. As its possessor, he has right to claim ownership of the land of Canaan. In consideration of the construction of this phrase, the author seems to intend to show the ark as identical to Yahweh in this situation because the relation between "the ark of the covenant" and "the Lord of all the earth" is not a genitive connection but appositive. Thus, the ark preceding the people signifies God's guidance through the Jordan River. Their attention to such divine leadership is drawn by the first word of this verse, "behold," which indicated the focus is on the ark of Yahweh.

The sequential arrangement of the next verse appears rather clumsy: "Now then take you twelve men out of the tribes of Israel, out of every tribe a man" (3:12). As for grammatical peculiarity of distribution, in this case, the numbered object too is repeated (Num 13:2; 34:18).[17] The content of the verse has nothing to do with the preparation or the event of passing over the Jordan River. The choice of twelve men is linked with what was to happen after the people had crossed over it (Josh 4:2).

"And when the soles of the feet of the priests bearing the ark of Yahweh, the Lord of all the earth, set in the waters of Jordan, the waters of Jordan shall be cut off. The waters coming down from above will stand in one heap" (3:13). This verse discloses the identity of "the wonders" stated in verse 5: the disruption of the waters flowing downstream. It will produce a dramatic scene since the miracle will occur at the moment when the priests bearing the ark set foot in the Jordan. Joshua's explanation for God's miracle contains an element that challenges the people's faith: God's guidance is not one way. Yahweh wants to work through the covenantal obedience of the people: "when they set" ($k^e n\bar{o}^a\d{h}$).[18] Here, the ark of Yahweh is modified once more by the phrase "the Lord of all

---

nations living in Palestine than these seven peoples (see Gen 15:19–21) but these are deemed as representatives of the nations occupying the entire land of Canaan at that time (see Num 34:2–12).

16. Hamlin, *Joshua*, 28.

17. GK §134q.

18. In $k^e n\bar{o}^a\d{h}$, $\bar{o}$ in inf. cons. of $n\bar{u}a\d{h}$, replaced $\bar{u}$. Bergsträsser, *Hebräische Grammatik*, §28d.

the earth," showing that he is sovereign over the whole earth. Thus, the magnificent qualification of the ark appears to have a suitable function in this military context, for Yahweh will exhibit his power by expelling the Canaanites and proving himself the victor and Lord over the gods of the defeated nations of Canaan.

Now the procession towards this miraculous event commences with Joshua's command, "take up the ark of the covenant and pass over in front of the people" (3:6).[19] And Joshua's command is executed: "when the people moved from their tents to cross the Jordan, with the priests bearing the ark of the covenant ahead of the people" (3:14). This march is a sort of parade of faith because they would not dare to risk marching towards the Jordan River without faith. In this verse, the emphasis centers on the ark.

"When those who bore the ark reached the Jordan, and the feet of priests bearing the ark touched the water's edge" (3:15a), "the waters of the Jordan from above stopped" (3:16a).[20] The climax is an impressive description of how the waters of the Jordan were stopped. The main features are described by the two verbs, "rise" and "cut off." But the expression "the water piled up in a heap very far from the town Adam in the vicinity of Zarethan" is not clear. It may have to be paraphrased as the piling up of the water extended very far from the town Adam to the Zarethan, if Qerē, *mēʾādām* is accepted.[21] Geographically, Adam is located twenty-seven kilometers north of Jericho, controlling the Jordan fords just below the confluence of the Jabbok, and its vicinity was famous for the occasional landslides that could dam the floods of Jordan.[22] The wall of water stretched out very far into the region. They could watch the stoppage of the water and its consequences. The water was suddenly cut

---

19. Joshua 3:6 does not seem to be in chronological order since the content of this verse is directly linked with v. 14. Such a phenomenon sometimes happens in the process of describing an occurrence (see Jonah 4:5). Thus, it may be natural that Joshua 3:6 is placed next to vv. 7–13 because it is overlapped chronologically with what is described in v. 14.

20. With respect to the structure of this sentence, the writer wanted a dramatic unfolding of the narrative in vv. 14–16, for he delays the climax the reader longs for by using subordinate clauses in vv. 14–15: he leaves us in suspense as to what actually happens until v. 16, which contains the principal sentence (see Kroeze, *Het Boek Jozua*, 57; Howard, *Joshua*, 130). In this kind of syntax, the author causes the readers' attention clearly to converge on the miracle, not the crossing.

21. See Glueck, *River Jordan*, 157.

22. Bimson, *Illustrated Encyclopedia*, 18; Aharoni, *Land*, 34.

off all the way downstream to the Sea of the Arabah. Finally, they could affirm that Yahweh, the living God, was with Joshua, as they saw this marvelous miraculous fulfillment of Joshua's prediction (v. 13).

The second part of this verse underscores the supernatural nature of this occurrence: "The Jordan overflows all its banks all the time of harvest" (3:15b). This parenthesis has respect to the time of crossing, which is dated as the tenth day of the first month, Abib, April (4:19). At this time, the river is at its fullest, swollen first by the long winter rains and later by the melting snows in the Anti-Lebanon Range.[23] This information about natural conditions reveals that it is impossible for the Israelites to pass over the natural barrier for themselves under such unfavorable circumstances: it is a miracle performed by Yahweh. While the Jordan was cut off, "the people passed over opposite Jericho" (3:16). The location, "opposite Jericho" describes a place between the Jordan and Jericho.[24]

"The priests that bore the ark of the covenant of Yahweh stood firm on dry ground in the midst of Jordan, while all the Israelites passed over on dry ground, until the whole nation had completed the crossing on dry ground" (3:17). Yahweh's marvelous activity is highlighted even more in this situation. The people passed over the Jordan on dry ground, while the ark remained in the middle of the river on dry ground with the priests who were bearing it standing firm. In the description of this event, the writer employs the term "completely" twice (vv. 16–17) to paint a vivid image of the successful crossing of the Jordan River. The term is not found in Joshua's explication of the same event (4:7, 22). The ark, the supreme symbol of God's indwelling, is viewed as silently directing the whole proceedings as the priests stood firm on dry ground.[25]

The successful entrance into the promised land is brought about because of Yahweh's guidance by means of the awesome miracle and the

---

23. Boling, *Joshua*, 168.

24. Actually, the phrase, *neḡer yerīḥō* (opposite Jericho) is vague. Vulgata (3:17) found an alternative term "contra Iordanem" to avoid the difficulty. However, such an attempt is not a desirable solution. Although the basic meaning of the preposition, *neḡer*, is "against" and frequently used in the sense of "before" (Exod 19:2; Neh 13:21; 1 Kgs 8:22), here it is rendered as "opposite," which describes a place between the Jordan and Jericho. The most satisfactory point would be the ford that Arabs call al-Maghtas, about seven miles southeast from T. es-Sultan and eight miles due west from T. el-Hammam. Boling, *Joshua*, 170.

25. Woudstra, *Joshua*, 88.

people's fidelity to the covenant. The event did not occur as a result of a simple ritual ceremony as Coats suggests, even though such a possible cultic element cannot be ruled out entirely from this section.[26] In the whole historical event the central role of the ark of Yahweh is underlined although the ark itself is not the cause of the miracle, as Soggin assumes, because the ark as such was not to be used in a magical or superstitious way.[27]

However, the narrative of the miracle to which the ark is central is not finished in Joshua 3: the Israelites have one more task to complete. For the sake of progeny, significant events are marked in history through the erecting of monuments. This was no different for Israel: they had to set up a sign to inform future generations of the *Magnalia Dei*. The sign is marked with twelve stones out of the midst of Jordan, out of the place where the priests' feet stood firm, according to the number of the tribes of the Israelites. Joshua set up the twelve stones as a historical monument in Gilgal (4:20). Each stone would not be large but the set of the twelve stones bears tremendous significance: "the waters of the Jordan were cut off before the ark of the covenant of Yahweh; when it crossed the Jordan the waters of the Jordan were cut off" (4:7) and "Israel crossed over this Jordan on dry land" (4:22).

The interpretation of the setting of the memorial stones (vv. 5, 9) has yielded different conclusions. Generally, those who contend that there was just one set of twelve stones in the narrative believe that verse 9—"Joshua set up twelve stones in the midst of Jordan"—shows another independent tradition.[28] Yet there is no foundation for the assumption that the biblical text consists of a collection of different traditions. In particular, on the ground that verse 9 is a parenthetical aside, Howard declines the traditional idea that there was one set of twelve stones set up on the bank (vv. 3, 5, 8) and another set of twelve stones set in the riverbed by Joshua (v. 9): "only one set of stones existed" . . . "Joshua had initially set up twelve stones in the riverbed itself, where the priests had stood." He connects the term, "there" of verse 9 with the last word, "there" of verse 8: "'there' refers to the stones on the riverbank (not in the

---

26. Coats, "Ark," 140–41.

27. Soggin, *Josué*, 51: "Pour le liturge ancien, la présence de l'Arche dans le lit du fleuve était la cause efficiente du miracle."

28. See Gray, *Joshua, Judges and Ruth*, 65; Butler, *Joshua*, 49.

riverbed)."²⁹ Primarily, his clarification looks attractive enough to solve the tricky issue, since the setting of the memorial stones demanded a slightly complicated process (3:12; 4:2–5, 8), while Joshua's action seems prompt. Furthermore, putting the stones under the water seems meaningless (4:9). However, if his notion is accepted, there are grammatical difficulties with such an interpretation and in addition verse 9 would be superfluous.³⁰ Besides the grammatical problem, if the "there" in the phrase "they are there to this day" (v. 9) signifies "there" in verse 8, "laid them down there," this additional formula should have been placed after verse 20 in which Joshua set up the stones in Gilgal. Thus, it is more likely that Joshua set up an additional twelve stones at the spot where priests carrying the ark of the covenant stood, as ancient biblical translators (LXX and Vg) understood.

Joshua's initial action seems natural to mark the precise place where the priests had stood with the ark of the covenant. The stones Joshua set up in the riverbed can proclaim at low water level that the ark then stood in that spot: "Yahweh your God dried up the waters of Jordan, . . . as Yahweh your God did to the Red sea" (4:23).³¹ Thus, the message of the memorial stones would sink deep in their minds. The children of the Israelites must not forget Yahweh's gracious guidance with the ark and the fulfillment of the promise to their fathers. It was a gift from Yahweh; they could enter the promised land without fighting. The success or failure of the entrance completely rests on the people's faith and not on their ability. God's promise is fulfilled as a result of their faith and obedience to his commandments. They could undergo another phase of redemptive history of Yahweh through this marvelous event.

With respect to the different titles such as "the ark of the covenant" (Josh 3:3, 6, 8, 11, 14, 17; 4:7, 9), "the ark of Yahweh" (3:13; 4:11) or

29. Howard, *Joshua*, 136.

30. When Joshua's setting up the stones is regarded as his initial action, the tense of the verb *hēqîm* should be understood as pluperfect and then the object *bānîm* necessitates an attribute, such as the definite article. Moreover, it seems unnatural that the "there" of v. 9 resumes the narrative of v. 8 to link two "theres" together because the demonstrative adverb "there" usually refers to location, which is mentioned in the close sentence, and the subject of *wayyahyû* should be *bānîm* in verse 9, for the imperfect consecutive *wayyahyû* serves apparently to represent a progress in the narrative. GK §111d.

31. "The interpretation of both occurrences becomes clearly from Ps 114 that mets both occurrences each other. Both events are both sites of God's saving hand." Ballhorn, *Israel am Jordan*, 173.

"the ark of the testimony" (4:16), their designations of the ark remind the people of its varied significance. "The ark of Yahweh," carried as the people journeyed, symbolized their belief that Yahweh went with them, guiding them to places of rest (Num 10:33). "The ark of the covenant" or "the ark of the testimony" symbolized the commands of the covenant that formed the people of Israel. This whole covenant relationship and way of life went with them as they crossed over the Jordan.[32] The ark was thus a symbol of the awesome presence of the God of the covenant in their midst as they crossed over into the new land.

In conclusion, the purpose of the crossing of the Jordan River is to affirm that the living God is with Joshua and among the people (Josh 3:7, 10), so that they might always fear Yahweh their God (4:24). This remarkable guidance requires them to fear God and fulfill the goal of life (Eccl 12:13). Although the word "fear" is used in various ways (see Jonah 1:5, 9, 10, 16),[33] in this context, the word is employed with "serve," reminding the people of God's marvelous guidance (Deut 6:13; Josh 24:14; 1 Sam 12:14, 24; 2 Kgs 17:33, 36) and their willing and loyal response in the Lord's service. The Israelites who crossed over the Jordan on dry land are to serve Yahweh with loyalty and commitment: it is holy fear based on respect and trust. This is the ultimate purpose of the miraculous event wherein the ark of the covenant played a crucial part.

B. THE ARK IN JERICHO (JOSH 6:1–21)

The pericope recounting the downfall of the walls of Jericho can be outlined as follows: Yahweh's promise and instruction for victory over Jericho (Josh 6:2–5), Joshua's command (vv. 6–7, 10, 16–19), and the people's implementation of God's instructions (vv. 8–9, 11–15, 20–21). The conquest of the land of Canaan commences with the assault against Jericho—the gateway to the land. The text denotes that this should be read as a sequel to the crossing of the Jordan because the conjunction "and" joins the verses together. Jericho is usually identified with Tell es-*Sulṭān*, on the western outskirts of the modern city of Jericho, but ques-

---

32. Hamlin, *Joshua*, 24.

33. According to Akkadian literature, the fear, *palāḫu* (verb), *puluḫtu* (substantive), is defined as man's essential attitude before gods and king, which is not only for right conduct but for respecting the order established by the power and right cultic service (Derousseaux, *La crainte de Dieu*, 58). This appears to be used as its general definition, implying an idea of distance and feeling of terror.

tions about the identification of these ancient sites continue to concern scholars.[34] The site is strategically located, giving access to the heartland of Canaan. The name Jericho probably indicates that this city was "a city of the moon."[35] This pagan city is destined to be destroyed by the people of Yahweh. The parenthetical statement of the first verse—"Jericho was tightly shut on account of the Israelites[36] and there was none who went out or came in"[37]—outlines the situation when the Israelites arrived at Jericho, which was apparently hopeless, as they did by Jordan River. The shut gate is a barrier to Israel's divinely ordained destiny to take possession of the land.[38] The king of Jericho chose to face down this desert people who had no experience in storming a fortress, although he had heard of the exodus, of the crossing of the Red Sea and of the Jordan, and of their military victories. However, Yahweh had promised Joshua that he would overcome any hindrance: "See, I have given into your hand her king and the mighty warriors" (Josh 6:2). The signal term "see" strengthens this initiative. The expression "I have given into your hand" means, quite literally, that the victory has already been won (see 2:8–11; 5:1).[39] The phrase as an idiom was prevalent among the ancient peoples

---

34. See Noort, *Das Buch Josua*, 164–66. Noort contends explicitly that the Jericho recounted in Josh 6 has nothing to do with Joshua's conquest: "in the related period, there was no Jericho that could be conquered, and in a historical sense Joshua 6 has nothing to do with the 'Landnahme'... The city itself is not important for the theological tendency of Joshua 6. The story might theoretically be able to be told about another city also. That was topographically impossible. The falldown of the large city, Jericho was not military, nor historical, but necessarily *topographically*. Man could not literally march around Jericho." "Jericho," 278–79.

35. *yᵉrī ḥō* appears to be derived from the term *yārēᵃḥ*, "the moon" (*HALAT* 418), Akk. *warhu*, the moon (*AHw* 1466).

36. According to A. Besters, the phrase *bᵉnē yiśrāʾēl* (literally, sons of Israel) mostly is used by the priestly tradition, Deuteronomist and post-priestly and post-deuteronomistic redactors (*Israël et Fils*, 5–23). Yet, this is not persuasive because the phrase *bᵉnē yiśrāʾēl* appears approximately 630 times throughout the Old Testament at random (Kühlewein, "bēn," *THAT* 1:316–25).

37. The double use of the participles (*sōḡeret*, act.; *mᵉsuggeret*, pass.) of *sāḡar*, "shut up" in v. 1 in combination with v. 1b, "come in," "go out" is indicative of the absolute inaccessibility of the city; the active participle appears to have to do with "go out" and the passive one with "come in."

38. Hess, *Joshua*, 141.

39. *nātattī* is declarative perfect that expresses future actions, when the speaker intends by an express assurance to represent them as finished, or as equivalent to accomplished facts (GK §106m; Lettinga, §72b3).

in the Middle East.⁴⁰ The statement "I have given into your hand" testifies, from the first, that this conquest belongs to Yahweh, not to Israel; it is Yahweh's war. What Israel has to do is to maintain the covenantal relationship by obedience to the divine orders. According to Yahweh's instructions, they had to march around the city in procession for seven days. Therefore, the detailed directions focus upon a daily progression around Jericho, culminating on the seventh day. The signal horns are to be blown and the people are to raise a shout. This scene indicates Yahweh's leadership of a military expedition.⁴¹

The priests carried the signal horns and armed men preceded the ark. A rear guard followed the ark, perhaps to protect it. Recognizing the pivotal role of the ark in this event, Coats interprets this victorious occurrence from a cultic viewpoint: "Just as the ark marks the entry into the land as a symbol of God's presence with Joshua as the people cross the Jordan in cultic procession, so the ark marks the first major victory of God over the Canaanites in the land, an event effected by cultic procession."⁴² It is true that the description of the event defined by the divine instructions is not a description of normal military strategy, a plan that will permit Joshua to assault the city, to gain entry by breaching the walls with the machinery of war. However, it is difficult to say that the ritual, properly executed, effected the collapse of the walls of Jericho. A purely ritual ceremony would not require armed men in the cultic procession and the blast of the signal horns, used when people went to war (see Num 10:9) or to inform of a coming calamity (see Amos 3:6), nor the shout that encourages military morale (see 1 Sam 4:5-6). Obviously, the ritual as such is hardly effective for razing the walls of Jericho. Rather, it should be regarded as an act of faith in Yahweh, who promised the destruction of Jericho (Heb 11:30). "The biblical worldview stands opposed to that of magic, although the popular mind of the Israelite may at times have shown traces of magical thinking."⁴³

---

40. The victory formula, "I have given into your hand," has "the corresponding Akkadian expression, *ina qāti nadānu*, "give into the hand," which is used with reference to a god granting victory over enemies, as early as the Old Akkadian period." Moran, "End," 337.

41. Brouwer, *De ark*, 110.

42. It is not acceptable to maintain that "the ark is no longer the holy symbol of God's leadership" (Coats, "Ark" 147) on account of its position in the procession.

43. Woudstra, *Joshua*, 109-10. The procession of the Israelites disassociates the ritual procession such as that recorded in the Babylonian New Year's festival, the *akitu*,

As Joshua's command, the people march around the city once a day,[44] in regular sequence (Josh 6:7-9). In the minds of Jericho's inhabitants, this procession might possibly be seen as eccentric behavior, a strange strategy to attack the city. However, Israel displays the ark, the symbolic presence of Yahweh, to the people of Jericho; Yahweh, the God of Israel who had stopped the flow of the Jordan before the Israelites until they had crossed over, will fight for them.

The new beginning in verse 12 and the description in verse 13 are made clear by verse 14 as the practice from the second to the sixth day: they marched around the city once each day for six days. The launch with the phrase *wayhī* (and it happened, v. 15) as a historical formula underscores the new phase of divine action. At this point, the Israelites perhaps have to get up at daybreak in order to accomplish the seven circuits of the march around the city on the seventh day.[45]

---

accompanied by incantations of the king (*ANET* 331-34) and the royal procession of the Hittite king followed by the heavily armed bodyguards: UGULA LIM (overseer of the Clanmen), ERIN.MES (provincial contingents), NIMGIR.ERIN.MES (herald of the troops), and heavy and golden spear men, which presents a purely political and military character (Beal, *Organization*, 528).

44. LXX translated that v. 11 revolves around the ark as a whole; the ark is rendered as the subject of three different verbs: "and the ark went around . . . entered . . . lodged," even though *wayyasseḇ* should be read in the hif'il form: "he made the ark of Yahweh go round . . ." and the two verbs, *wayyāḇō'û, wayyālīnû*, form qal, imperfect-consecutive, third person, masc., pl. Schwienhorst correctly observed that "'Lade' als Objekt zu *sbb* im Hif'il wird aber sonst immer mit Partikel *'aet* angeschlossen (1 Sam 5:8b, 9-10; 1 Chr 13:3)" (Schwienhorst, *Jerichos*, 25). However he fails to seriously consider that this verb bears the double accusative; it looks unnecessary for each of two accusatives to receive nota accusativi, *ēṯ*: Joüon classifies this sentence as one of various kinds of accusatives (Joüon, §125r N). Thus, the versions of LXX and Vg. (*circuivit ergo arca Domini*) tend to accentuate the ark's semi-independence of movement.

45. Regarding the expression "at daybreak" in Ps 46:6-7: Janowski explicates that the motive of Yahweh's help *am Morgen* reminds that "Jahwe die gegen die Gottesstadt anstürmenden Feindvölker in einer dem kosmischen Chaoskampf analogen, anfänglichen Tag überwunden und in dieser Bewahrung der kosmischen Ordnung seine universale Schöpfermacht erwiesen." He connects the motive with "die transzendente Herkunft des Kommens und Eingreifens Jahwes" in cultic and individual invocation (*Rettungsgewißheit und Epiphanie*, 184-91). However, the Israelite petition for assistance to extricate themselves from adverse circumstances and God's help are not restricted to some designated times such as "at daybreak" (Judg 7:9-25; Ps 22:3; 42:9; 77:3, 7; 78:14). The prayer at daybreak may be associated with the pattern of the daily life of the people; the Israelites start their daily work early in the morning. Although Yahweh's help *am Morgen* may signify his particular act in the poetic supplication, it is unknown whether the term "at daybreak" in v. 15 has especially to do with Yahweh's marvelous intervention in the same way.

The number "seven" of the seven days it took to defeat Jericho is symbolic of completeness, fulfillment, totality, and perfection. It has fundamental significance in the time scheme of the created world (Gen 1:1—2:3).[46] The fact that Yahweh's direction is linked with the number "seven" appears to imply the triumph of completion over Jericho. It issues from Yahweh's initiative rather than from priestly tradition that regards God's creation as the key to Israel's religion. It becomes an integrating and unifying theme between creation, history, and worship, as a result of the development to an extraordinary degree of the progression of revelational history.[47] At the end of the seventh encirclement around the city the blast of the signal horns occurs and the people raise a shout of triumph founded on the divine promise: "for Yahweh has given you the city" (Josh 6:16). At the sound of the signal horns, the people broke into shouting (v. 20a): "And the wall collapsed; so the people stormed the city right from where they were and took it" (v. 20b). The core of the event is to be found in verse 20: "the wall fell down flat." At the cry of the people the walls collapsed downward: it happened not by attack from outside. This is the moment when the divine promise about Jericho was fulfilled (v. 5): "By faith the walls of Jericho fell, after the people had marched around them for seven days" (Heb 11:30).[48] The function of the ark of Yahweh in this remarkable event primarily is to illustrate his omnipotence, even if the fall of Jericho's wall shows his goodness to Israel and his righteousness to the Canaanites (see Gen 15:16–21).

C. THE ARK NEAR SHECHEM (JOSH 8:33)

This verse recounts how Joshua implemented Moses' command to bless the people, after he built an altar to Yahweh on Mount Ebal, and he sacrificed burnt offerings and peace offerings on it according to the instruction of Moses preserved in the Book of the Law of Moses and after he, in the presence of the Israelites, inscribed a copy of the Law of Moses on stones.[49] The text shows the ark played a significant part in the cer-

---

46. The motive "seven" in such Mesopotamian literature as the Epic of Gilgamesh (*ANET* 77, 94–95), in which seven is a key organizing principle, probably originated from an event that coincided with the biblical report on the six-day creation and rest on the seventh day.

47. Jenson, "šęba'," *NIDOTTE* 4:35.

48. Coats mentions "the power of the ritual" and "the gift of the ritual" as the cause of the successful conquest over Jericho. "Ark," 149.

49. The article in 'al-hā*ᵃ*bānīm (v. 32) need not mean a peculiar thing like the altar

emony, presided over by the Levites, in accordance with the command of Moses (Josh 8:33). Carried by the priests, the ark of the covenant of Yahweh was located between Ebal and Gerizim. Perhaps the ark was in the narrow valley between the two mountains.[50] It means that the ark was at the center of the ceremony. With its position settled, Joshua read all the words of the law, the blessings and the curses, in the midst of the whole assembly of Israel, including the women and children, and the aliens who lived among them (v. 34–35). It is remarkable that while the movement of the ark comes at Joshua's command, it is observed according to the Law of Moses. This does not imply that Moses still had some personal influence over Israel but that Yahweh's law was to be kept from generation to generation (Deut 6:2).

Although all the Israelites were gathered around the ark, the representatives of the people—such as their elders, officials, and judges—seem to be particularly emphasized in the ceremony. The ark was surrounded by two groups of Yahweh's own people, both aliens and native-born.[51] No class of the Israelites was exempted from the worship service. They were divided so as to stand on both sides of the ark of the covenant of Yahweh. Facing the priestly Levites, half of them stood in front of Mount Gerizim while the other half stood in front of Mount Ebal in seemingly slightly altered positions from what Moses had commanded: 'el-mul (opposite) instead of 'al (on) or b^e (in) (Deut 27:12–13). It may be that they were indeed on top of the two mountains and that those on Mount Gerizim were considered those to be in front of Mount Ebal and vice versa.[52] The ark appears to be positioned not in Shechem but in its vicinity because ancient Shechem, as "the navel of the land," was located between two

---

because in Hebrew the employment of the article denotes a single person or thing as being present to the mind under given circumstances (GK §126q). So, the stones on which a copy of the law was written were probably not the stones of the altar, the large white-washed stela prescribed in Deuteronomy 27:1–7. Thus, presumably we would have to assume that he set up a second set of stones. See Woudstra, *Joshua*, 147.

50. Pitkänen, *Joshua*, 191.

51. The presence of aliens in the ceremony was assumed and commanded (Deut 16:11, 14), based on Yahweh's love for them; the law of Deuteronomy viewed such aliens as economically underprivileged and provided special means of support for them (14:29; 16:11, 14; 24:17, 19–21; 26:12–13; 27:19). Special protection (1:16; 5:14; 24:17; 27:19) and even privilege (14:21; see 17:15) were granted to them. See Howard, *Joshua*, 216.

52. Ibid., 217.

high mountains Ebal and Gerizim.⁵³ This can be assumed, even though the actual name Shechem is not mentioned in the text.

According to the command of Moses (Deut 27:9, 14), the Levites (or the Levitical priests) had to proclaim both blessing and curse in front of the assembly of Israel. Yet the context necessitates that Joshua be seen as the subject of the sentence (Josh 8:34), even if the reading of the law leaves the subject of the verb (*qārā*) ambiguous.⁵⁴ Here Joshua functions as a Levite and a worthy successor to Moses. The passage does not specify the range of all the words of the law—the blessing and cursing Joshua inscribed and read. Yet this law probably refers to the content of Deuteronomy 27:15–26 on account of a close correlation between the altar commandment in Deuteronomy 27 and the description of the building of the altar in Joshua 8.⁵⁵ Most of the curse-formular (Deut 27:15–26), consisting of twelve parts, corresponds to the Decalogue in some way.⁵⁶ Even though the law contains only curses, the law also contains positive ideas of blessings, by highlighting the degree of obedience; this is not a list of curses in the strict sense but a list of statutes whose violation brings a curse.⁵⁷ Hence presumably all the words of the law—the blessing and cursing Joshua read in front of the people—appear to be associated with the fundamental law centered on the Decalogue rather than the whole legal corpus. This ceremony of the reading of the law for the entire assembly of Israel freshly underscores the significance of covenantal loyalty to Yahweh, who had faithfully led them to the promised land. That is to say, the covenant renewal takes place when Israel has entered the middle area of the land (see Deut 27:2). The covenant unilaterally commences from God's side on the basis of his redemptive grace but thereafter the covenantal relationship is maintained in a

---

53. See G. R. H. Wright, *Ancient Building*, 43.

54. Joshua is inserted as the subject in LXX: *anegnō 'Iēsous*.

55. It goes beyond our concern to verify whether or not the ceremony in Josh 8:33–35 is the original one as Naʿaman contends at the standpoint of source criticism ("Law," 154). In any event it may have to be comprehended in the light of deuteronomic passages because it is natural that the injunction precedes the performance in historical progress.

56. The prohibition of images, 1st, 2nd commandments; despising parents, 5th; moving neighbor's boundary stone, 8th; withholding justice, 9th; improper sexuality, 7th; murdering neighbor, 6th.

57. See Merrill, *Deuteronomy*, 346.

mutual commitment.⁵⁸ On the side of the people, steadfast love is the quality typifying the covenantal relationship. The balance between God's initiative and Israel's required response is illustrated by its varied use of the term, $b^e rīt$, sometimes in parallel with the idea of an oath (Deut 4:31), and sometimes with that of a command or law.⁵⁹ The oath is a form of conditional self-cursing; the breach of the covenant is directly connected with the curse. Thus, blessing and cursing are the two poles around which the history of the covenant revolves (Deut 11:26; 30:1).⁶⁰

The blessing⁶¹ basically signifies power; it is associated with the ability to meet all the desires of the human condition, including the enjoyment and improvement of life, harvest, achievement, and the prosperity of descendants.⁶² For instance, the promise of God's blessing to the patriarchs consists of property and wealth (Gen 24:35; 26:12), descendants (Gen 28:3), and land (Gen 35:12), and the deuteronomic blessing mentions prosperity, abundance, fertility, health, and victory (Deut 7:12–16). The blessing is something good, something fundamentally required for happiness. Eventually all kinds of visible and material blessings in the Old Testament reflect the spiritual blessings in Christ. In this context, the blessing is connected with life on the land received as a gift from Yahweh, while the curse calls the Israelites' attention to the danger of abrogating the covenantal relationship. With the epithet "the ark of the covenant of Yahweh" the ark stood between the blessing and the curse (Josh 8:33). At the moment, Yahweh with the ark displays his faithfulness to his promises, and unfolds a new epoch of redemptive history in the promised land.

---

58. See Straus, "Schilder," 25–27.
59. See McConville, "$b^e rīt$," *NIDOTTE* 1:746–55.
60. See Woudstra, *Joshua*, 150.
61. The Hebrew term *bārak* appears usually in the pi'el form in the Old Testament (233 times), while the qal form of the verb is used in the passive form only seventy-one times. This presents a blessed status; it has a factitive form to get an objective. See Jenni, *Pi'el*, 216–17.
62. See Mowinckel, *Religion und Kultus*, 64–65.

7

The Ark in the Book of 1 Samuel

A. CONTEXT

THE BOOK OF SAMUEL begins with an introduction to a pious family who make their annual pilgrimage to Shiloh during the period of the Judges (1 Sam 1:3). Here Hannah's barrenness was used as a point of contact through which Yahweh opened a new era in Israel's history. Yahweh would provide a new future for his people in the period of trial through a faithful woman. Her prayer soliciting a male child would result in the birth of a Nazirite who would reform the perverted state of Israel (see 1:11; 2:1–10).

However, the attitude of the religious leaders in Israel was in conflict with Yahweh's design for the future of Israel. The priests, Hophni and Phinehas, committed sin before Yahweh and the people. The author disclosed the seriousness of their sin (2:12): they were called *sons of Belial*, "wicked men" (Judg 19:22; Ps 18:5; 2 Cor 6:15). Although they were priests, they did not know Yahweh and lacked respect, love, and loyalty to him.[1] their depravity is characterized by contempt for Yahweh's offering and by the practice of Canaanite religion in Shiloh (1 Sam 1:13–17; 2:22).[2] As corrupt priests, they prevented the people from restoring their impaired relationship with God. Their serious transgressions spiritually contaminated the sanctuary at Shiloh and the people of Israel.

---

1. See Fretheim, "*yāḏaʿ*," *NIDOTTE* 2:413.

2. In the phrase "they slept with the women," the tense of the verb, *yiškeḇûn* (sleep), is imperfect, which is usually employed to signify a repeated and habitual behavior. It is clear that their sexual misdeeds cannot be considered as a simple moral mistake. They behaved in the same way as the Canaanites who dedicated themselves to their gods through sexual intercourse.

In the religious situation of Israel the disregard of such an important office—appointed to usher the people towards salvation and to assist them in maintaining their relationship with God—hindered their redemption. So, Yahweh was forced to dispose of such corrupt leaders (2:27–36; 3:11–14) in order to protect his people. He could not grant Israel a king who would rule the people in accord with Yahweh's law without first reforming the priestly office. A king is susceptible to the temptation of dominating people with his own political power like the pagan kings surrounding Israel. That is to say, for an effective reign a king needed capable leaders such as priests and prophets, since the king was commanded to govern Israel as the people of the covenant, in conformity with all Yahweh's laws and decrees (Deut 17:14–20).

Yahweh's will to innovate their religion emerges in the judgment of Eli's house and in Samuel's calling. The calling of Samuel provides a light to Israel in the spiritual darkness because Yahweh was planning to appoint a prophet who would deliver his word to his people (Acts 3:24; see 1 Sam 3:1). Just before the era of Israel's kingship, Yahweh called Samuel as a prophet. In a befouled sanctuary, he called Samuel four times, which reflects his sustaining attachment to a people who numerously abandoned him. It also shows his indomitable will to build a new kingdom for Israel. The section of 1 Samuel 4:1—7:1 concerning the ark is to be conceived in the context of Samuel's inauguration as a prophet who, like Moses (see Deut 18:15–19),[3] functions as Yahweh's impeccable and revered spokesman. At the same time, Eli's house must be punished so that God can innovate the corrupted priests of Israel and make straight the way of a king. This background to the texts provides the direct source of the catastrophe that Israel experienced as delineated in the "ark narrative."

A. THE ARK CAPTURED (1 SAM 4:1B–22)

This section commences with Israelite involvement in a fight against the Philistines, which seems to reflect Yahweh's retribution on the house of Eli (see 1 Sam 2:25).[4] They had become a serious threat to the Israelites

---

3. See Garsiel, *Samuel*, 45.

4. The Philistines are thought to have migrated in large numbers from the Aegean area, esp. Crete or Cyprus, to the coastal regions of southwest Israel during the first half of the twelfth century BC, where they assimilated with the various foreign and local Canaanite influences. See Dothan, *Philistines and Culture*, 21; A. Mazar, *Archaeology*, 307–8.

during the period of the Judges, most likely because they saw in Israel an intimidation to their security or to the security of their trade routes leading inland from the coast. Thus, they moved to gain control of the whole of western Palestine.[5] The Philistines were not a particularly numerous people but were formidable fighters with a strong military tradition due to their mastery of a superior technology in iron. This provided them with a military edge in controlling the surrounding areas both militarily and economically (see 13:19–22). The Philistine army encamped along the banks of the Yarkon River at Aphek (modern *Tell Rās el-'Ain*) where they could easily maneuver military equipment, such as their iron chariots, while the Israelites pitched a base camp 3.2 kilometers to the east at Ebenezer (modern *'Izbet ṣarṭah*), which offers a wide view over Sharon plain.[6] In this battle, the Philistines deployed their forces to meet Israel, and Israel was defeated with the loss of about four thousand men (1 Sam 4:2). Perhaps, this battle should not be regarded as a mere skirmish or preliminary small-scale battle but as a full-scale war that would exert a decisive influence upon the national destiny of Israel. Moreover, the combat had a particular significance for the Israelites; at stake was whether or not they could defend the everlasting possession that Yahweh gave them as a guarantee of a blessed life on the basis of the promise to the patriarchs (see Gen 17:8). The Israelites did not understand the cause of the unprecedented defeat nor realize the need for repentance. It is interesting to note that the elders of Israel superintended the war council to plan their counterattack in the absence of Eli, the "high" priest and the judge who was in charge of the deliverance of the people from calamity.[7] The responsible elders attributed the defeat to Yahweh: "Why did Yahweh bring defeat upon us" (1 Sam 4:3a). They finally decided to use the last instrument that might save them from their enemies: the ark of Yahweh's covenant (4:3b).[8] The ark, based on the vital concept

---

5. See Bright, *History*, 185.
6. See Bergen, *Samuel*, 90; Dietrich, *Samuel*, 223–25.
7. Originally, the institution of elders (*zᵉqunīm*) was perhaps an organ of nomadic government. After the group had settled in one place the old system of government, often for a long time, continued to function with little change: they came to have the extensive power of the city (Ruth 4:1–12) and of the larger areas (Judg 11:5–11). See Mulder, *I Kings*, 378.
8. It appears impossible to settle whether the subject of two verbs, *wᵉyāḇō* (and come) and *wᵉyōši'ēnū* (and save us), is "he" (Yahweh, RSV) or "it" (the ark, KJV, ASV, NIV, ESV), but the latter is deemed appropriate because their attitude was presumably changed after the meeting.

of Yahweh's presence with it, was now expected to give victory. Thus, for the Israelites, the utilizing of the ark signifies something more than improving the morale of the troops, because they were confusing the symbol with its essence. In any event, according to the decision of the elders, probably with the consent of the whole camp (see 3:5), the ark as the visible sign of Yahweh's presence was about to function as a battle-palladium in the war against the enemies of Israel.[9] They did not seriously consider whether it was permissible to mobilize the ark in battle or not. In fact, it is rare to find any biblical evidence that the ark went onto the battlefield at any point in the history of Israel. With the expectation of a similar victory, perhaps they were hoping to revive the strategy of Jericho instead of looking for the reason for their defeat and trying to rectify their broken and tarnished relationship with Yahweh.

The specific designation "the ark of the covenant of Yahweh Zebaoth dwelling between the cherubim" is introduced in 1 Samuel 4:4. In this text, the ark is at first associated with "Yahweh Zebaoth," a phrase whose original meaning is obscure.[10] The divine epithet appears to be associated with a kind of "might" concept referring to a multitude. The Hebrew word $ṣ^eḇāōṯ$ (fem. pl. of $ṣāḇā$), has a variety of connotations in diverse biblical documents.[11] In spite of the different conceptions about the word, the consensus is that the designation calls attention to God's might and victory.[12] That is why LXX versions appear to read *yahweh*

---

9. McCarter, 1 Samuel, 109; Caquot and de Robert, Livres de Samuel, 77.

10. The Akkadian $ṣābu$ or $ṣābûm$, equivalent word to Hebrew $ṣ^eḇāōṯ$, provides variant meanings (group of people, contingent of workers, troop of soldiers, army, people, population), but mostly is used in the collective sense. CAD 16, 46; AHw 1072.

11. E.g., the multitudes of Israelites (e.g., 1 Sam 6:26; 7:4; 12:17, 41, 51; Num 1:3, etc.). The appellation reminds us of Yahweh as the God of the Israelite army (1 Sam 17:45), powerful in war (Ps 24:8–10), and the God of war (Ps 46:7–11; Isa 13:4). However, this name in the Old Testament implies a broader meaning (e.g., 1 Sam 1:3, 11; 2 Sam 7:8, 26; Pss 69:7; 84:2, 4, 9; Isa 6:3). On the basis of the verses mentioned above, the name $ṣ^eḇāōṯ$ does not always indicate an earthly army.

12. Ross separated the concept of a "multitude army" from the designation for three reasons: 1) $ṣāḇā$ is used in this sense only in the deuteronomic and later strands of the Old Testament. 2) With this meaning it is always singular. 3) A prophet such as Jeremiah, who strongly opposed the worship of the host of heaven, could speak freely and without embarrassment of "Yahweh Zebaoth" ("Jahweh $ṣ^eḇāōṯ$," 77). According to Ross, all the verses of Samuel and Psalms in which Yahweh Zebaoth stands do not point out the military character of Yahweh except 1 Sam 17:45 and Ps 24. He is of the opinion that "this (1 Sam 17:45) may be due to the hand of glossator" (ibid., 82) and that "the battle (in Ps 24:8) is the primeval conflict of creation between God and

ṣᵉḇāōṯ as *kurios* "the Lord of the mighty" (2 Sam 6:2) or "the almighty Lord" (7:8). On this ground, it is held that the name "Yahweh Zebaoth," which refers to the ark, reminds us of the holy object that played a principal role in the holy war of Israel and that the name "Yahweh Zebaoth" invokes Yahweh as the divine warrior who defeated the enemies of Israel, particularly the Philistines.

In relation to the connection of the ark with Zebaoth, the theory that regards the ark as a war-palladium inevitably associates the ark with the epithet in a martial sense. According to this view, Yahweh was originally a god of war and his symbol, the ark, was necessarily an emblem of war.[13] But the Old Testament texts seem not to suggest that the two words are closely linked because only two verses (1 Sam 4:4; 2 Sam 6:2) employ the connected form of the two words among the 285 cases in which Zebaoth occurs.[14] The phrase "Yahweh Zebaoth" in the present text seems to stress his omnipotence rather than to be directly concerned with the ark. This conception is particularly supported by Isaiah 37:16, in which the phrase has nothing to do with the ark.

The other problem concerning the translation of the phrase was treated in the section on the cherubim, which represent God's glory, revealing his omnipotence and omniscience (see chapter 11A).

Hophi and Phinehas, the sons of Eli, were there when the ark, the prominent emblem of the glorious and majestic presence of Yahweh,

---

Chaos" (ibid., 88). However, his argument does not seem cogent because there is no reason for the meaning of the plural form of the word being altered. Besides, a fight between God and Chaos cannot be found in the Bible. H. J. Zobel has the propensity to easily grasp the sense of the word in view of the cult allegedly formed later: "Zwar hat der Titel seinen Siegeszug im Raum des Tempelkults begonnen, doch er wäre nicht zu dieser hohen Wertschätzung ohne die Mithilfe der Prophetie gekommen" ("ṣᵉḇā'ōṯ," *ThWAT* 6:876–92). Yet, his conjecture is to be dismissed when considering the possible dating of the formation of the book of Samuel. Schicklberger comprehends it as a relative idea by approving of Maag's explanation ("die depotenzierten mythischen Naturmächte Kanaans") as the most appropriate: "Jahwe sei demnach Herr auch über die kanaanäischen Mächte und Gewalten" (*Ladeerzählung*, 27–28). Eissfeldt explains the term as "kosmische Macht" and Yahweh Zebaoth as "Machtfülle Jahwe" ("Jahweh Zebaoth," 103–23).

13. Stoebe's contention pictures this supposition vividly: "Das Zebaoth ist ursprünglich von der sakral-kriegerischen Funktion der Lade zu verstehen und hat erst später eine Ausweitung ins allgemein Kosmische erfahern." His assumption appears to be rooted in the evolutionary theory applied to the religious history of Israel. Stoebe, *Das erste Buch Samuelis*, 95.

14. Jer 82 times; "Proto-Isa" 56; Zec 53; Mal 24; 1 Sam 5; 2 Sam, and "Dt.Isa." 6, etc.; see Zobel, "ṣᵉḇā'ōṯ," *ThWAT* 6:878.

was carried to the battlefield. The arrival of the ark raised the morale of the Israelites and it was welcomed with their great shouts so that the ground resounded (1 Sam 4:5). The phrase "all Israel" appears to reflect the scale of the battle. Despite the first triumph of the Philistines, they seem to believe that they are in a defensive position just before the second engagement: "when they realized that the ark of Yahweh had come into the camp; 'God has come into the camp,' they said. 'We are in trouble! Nothing like this has happened before . . . Woe to us! Who will deliver us from the hand of these mighty gods? They are the gods who smote the Egyptians with all the plagues in the wilderness'"[15] (1 Sam 4:7–8). The Philistines disclose themselves as typical pagans by referring to the ark as the Israelite gods and they confound the plagues in Egypt, which happened before the exodus, with the sojourn of Israel in the wilderness. Nevertheless, they understood an aspect of the redemptive history of Israel in their simplistic thinking.[16] Their vague knowledge that Israel had experienced a supernatural deliverance from Egypt energized the Philistines to fight with determination: "Be strong, Philistines! Be men, or you will serve the Hebrews, as they have served you. Be men, and fight!" (v. 9). In fact, they did not have to encourage their army to overcome fear and to take the field against Israel because Yahweh was about to punish the corrupt priests through the downfall of Israel (see 1 Sam 2:25, 34). The battle drove Israel into catastrophe; she lost three thousand infantry, the ark was captured, and the two priests, Hophni and Phinehas, were slain (1 Sam 4:10–11). The Israelites mobilized the ark, a tangible representation of God's presence, and used it as if it was a sort of war-palladium. Yet even the ark could not deliver them. This defeat demonstrates that the ark of Yahweh was not intended to be used as a war-palladium, as was the case with many of the nations surrounding Israel. Besides, it is apparent that they failed to realize that

---

15. The expression "in the wilderness" is contrary to biblical history (Exod 7:20—12:30), so that many scholars prefer to amend it as *ūbadāber* or *ūb^emō-deber* "and with pestilence." Wellhausen, *Text*, 55; Driver, *Introduction*, 47; de Boer, "Research," 83; Dahood, "Lexicography," 401–2; McCarter, 1 *Samuel*, 104; Klein, 1 *Samuel*, 38. However, there is no reason to believe that the Philistines had precise information on Israel, because the plagues were in Egypt but not in the wilderness; see Smelik, "Hidden Messages," 46.

16. See Timm, "Die Ladeerzählung," 521: "Mit jener Kriegspredigt unmittelbar vor Eröffnung der entscheidenden Schlacht haben die Philister auf ihre Art das heilsgeschichtliche Urbekenntnis Israels an sich gerissen."

the presence of Yahweh is made secure in a saving manner only through faith. Brueggemann notes that the defeat of Israel is not so much due to Yahweh's absence, but rather the will of Yahweh, for Yahweh is present with the ark.[17] This disaster fulfills the prophecy by the anonymous man of God against Eli and his house (1 Sam 2:27–36). Yahweh could no longer take care of the Israelites in the battle because they declined his protection by refusing to obey his holy law. Yahweh's retribution, sustained for centuries, was executed and is re-echoed in Psalm 78:59–61. Shiloh, generally identified with Khirbet Seilun, where the ark was once housed, was overrun and became a forgotten place in the religious history of Israel.[18] Yet, it is reasonable to believe that the tabernacle was protected (1 Chr 16:39; 2 Chr 1:3).

At any event, the occupation by the Philistines obstructed the development of Israel until the reign of David. Their garrisons were placed at strategic points (1 Sam 10:5; 13:3–4, 23) and they deprived Israel of the metal industry. In doing this, they protected their own monopoly in iron and prevented Israel from manufacturing weapons (13:19–22).[19] Above all, the occupation exhibits that Israel, due to her unbelief, failed to maintain the possessions given her by Yahweh.

The last part of this chapter (vv. 12–22) outlines two further occurrences: the death of Eli and the death of his daughter-in-law after she gave birth to Ichabod. The tragic news reaches a climax in 1 Sam 4:17 when the messenger recounts the death of Eli's two sons, Hophni and Phinehas, and the capture of the ark of God. Eli might be anticipating the loss of his sons since he had already heard of Yahweh's decree from a man of God (2:27–36) and Samuel (3:13). Eli, who had led Israel for forty years, died not from the shock of news of his sons but from the report of the ark's capture: "When he mentioned the ark of God, Eli fell off his chair backward by the side of the gate. His neck was broken and he died" (1 Sam 4:18). His death appears to be a disaster for the office of high priest, when in fact it is, in a sense, an act of God's faithfulness to an office he had instituted.[20] Through the death of Eli and his family, the

---

17. Brueggemann, *Samuel*, 32.

18. The archaeological evidence of the city is dated as eleventh century BC; see Delcor, "Jahweh et Dagon," 143; Bishop, "Shiloh," 62–64.

19. See Bright, *History*, 186.

20. See De Wolff and de Boer, *Godsopenbaring*, 49.

holy office of "the priest" is protected and honored. As a result, Yahweh prevented his people from going the way of corruption.

The following scene (vv. 20–22) recounts the death of Phinehas's wife, who was giving birth to a baby. With the news of the collapse of the Elide house and the captivity of the ark, fatal complications in the birthing process caused the woman to die shortly after giving birth to a son. A hopeful birth turns into a sorrowful, tragic fatality. Instead of rejoicing in the most honorable achievement a woman in the Near East could attain, she was listless and distracted despite words of comfort because of her anxiety over the ark. With her dying gasps, she gave a significant name to the child, *Ichabod*, "the glory has departed" (literally, Where is glory?),[21] the explication of which she mentioned twice (vv. 21–22). She recognizes that the fact that the ark is gone symbolizes that Yahweh is absent and Israel bereft. The service of the priest without the ark will be of no use in Israel even though the priesthood is hereditary.[22] The ministration of the office, a mechanism of salvation, disappeared with the ark and this fact necessitated the impeccable work of the eternal office of Jesus Christ.

C. THE ARK IN PHILISTIA (1 SAM 5:1—6:1)

The captured ark was brought first from Ebenezer to Ashdod, located in the northern end of the Philistine pentapolis. The first Philistine settlement was a well-planned and densely built city of some twenty acres in area. At the end of the eleventh century BC, Ashdod had expanded to a size of about one hundred acres, thus, becoming one of the largest cities in the country.[23] The ark was placed beside the idol of the Philistine god Dagon, inside his house. Dagon was the patron deity of the middle Euphrates region from the third millennium BC and was responsible for blessing the spheres of military expansion, fertility, living and deceased human rulers, and divine advice.[24] Just like the Israelites, the Philistine

---

21. See *HALAT*, 38. Tsumura understands 'î in 'î-*kābôd* as "where" on the basis of Ugarit. *Samuel*, 201.

22. Campbell rightly observed that the loss of the ark and the interpretation of that event are the primary concerns of chap. 4 and the fate of the Elides is not the central issue ("Yahweh and the Ark," 37). Nevertheless, it is natural to consider the deaths of the Elides as the fulfillment of the prophecy in chapter 2.

23. A. Mazar, *Archaeology*, 308.

24. See Handy, "Dagon," *ABD* 2:1–3; Healey, "Dagon," *DDD* 216–18.

people committed the mistake of taking the symbol for reality. They performed a ritual to Dagon,[25] the deity who was thought to have given the Philistines victory over both Samson (see Judg 16:23) and Israel's God, by dedicating the ark as a war trophy to Dagon. They seem to ascribe the triumph to their god; they saw the combat as not simply between Israel and the Philistines, but between Israel's deity and Dagon (see Exod 12:12). In so doing, they thought that they could degrade the God of the Israelites and declare Dagon's superiority over him. However, they could not help but be frightened at what they had done by placing the ark beside the idol. This fear was reflected in their curiosity: "the people of Ashdod rose early the next day" (1 Sam 5:3a). Dagon was found in a posture of reverence and submission before the ark of Yahweh: "there was Dagon, fallen on his face on the ground" (v. 3b). The text implies the futility of the Philistines' idolatrous practices (see Pss 115:4-7; 135:15-17; Isa 44:9-20). Yet, it was actually hard for them to accept the unprecedented event as reality. The closing phrase of 1 Sam 5:3, "they took Dagon and put him back in his place," shows how they did not understand Yahweh's power and freedom. But in fact the capture of the ark signified no real restriction of Yahweh's actual potency. Dagon's act of humiliation was repeated the next morning and was even more shocking than on the previous day; his head and hands had been cut off in a manner reminiscent of a grisly military execution (see 1 Sam 17:51; 31:9; 2 Sam. 4:12).[26] Yahweh, by desecrating Dagon, substantiated his superiority over the Philistine god once again. As a result, this accident caused the non-Semitic Philistines to enact a new regulation in their pagan cult: "Thus, to this day neither the priests of Dagon nor anyone entering Dagon's house at Ashdod step on the threshold" (1 Sam 5:5).[27]

---

25. The Hebrew etymological definition of his name (*dāg-ān*, grain) appears hardly to be separated from a god of grain even if such a notion finds no solid evidence in *ANET*.

26. At this point, Bergen rightly denotes that Zwickel misses the parallels noted in the other scriptures that suggest that Yahweh was "executing" Dagon using a technique of military execution. Zwickel does this when he compares the broken statue with archaeological data and concludes the story has been modified during the postexilic period to conform to later iconoclastic customs. Bergen, *Samuel*, 97; Zwickel, "Dagons abgeschlagener Kopf," 239-49.

27. "This custom is said to have survived, 'at least in Gaza, into the first centuries A.D.'" Tsumura, *Samuel*, 206.

Yahweh's supremacy is further demonstrated over the Philistines, including the people of Ashdod, in the resulting plagues. "Yahweh's hand" is typically a metaphoric and anthropomorphic expression that covers a wide range of power.[28] The Philistines had to experience the scourge in order to understand that this was the same Yahweh who had brought plagues against Egypt (see 4:8). The specific plague cannot be pinpointed in modern medical terms but it was probably some kind of epidemic.[29] In consideration of Yahweh's judgment against Dagon, a deity of fertility, it may well have been related to venereal disease.[30] LXX has these sentences: "It brought up against them mice who swarmed in their ships and came up into the midst of their land. There was a great panic in the city—a deadly one." If it reflects the Hebrew *Vorlage*, where this part appears to be missed, the disaster would be more severe.[31] Yahweh's judgment was brought against not only their religion but also against the physical and economical well-being of the inhabitants of Ashdod (see Exod 12:12). Perhaps as a result of experiencing a severe catastrophe, the Ashdodites decided "the ark of the gods of Israel must not remain with them" (1 Sam 5:7). According to the Aegean model,[32] all govenors of five Philistine cities gathered as a council and determined to have the ark moved to Gath (5:8), closer to the district of Judah.

The attestation of Yahweh's supremacy was made anew in Gath with the multiplication of his punishment against all the residents in Gath: "Yahweh's hand was against that city, throwing it into a very great panic. He afflicted the people of the city, both young and old, with an outbreak of tumors" (v. 9a). Due to the magnitude of Yahweh's chastisement of the people of Gath, the ark was sent to Ekron, where its arrival

---

28. Dreytza, "yād," *NIDOTTE* 2:405.

29. Harrison, a former physician explicates it cogently: "This description, remarkably objective as it is, furnishes abundant evidence symptomatically for a diagnosis of bubonic plague, the dreaded scourge of antiquity, which is conveyed to man by the rat flea (*pulex cheopis*), and spread by droplet infection with a short incubation period." *Introduction*, 714.

30. De Wolff and de Boer, *Godsopenbaring*, 52.

31. Van Zyle's statement appears to reflect LXX: "According to ugaritic texts, we can make a connection between this religion and the fertile cult. That also suggests the association of Dagon with Astarte (see 31:8–10; 1 Chr 10:10). The threat of the grain harvest through the mouse plague (6:4) indicates the same direction, even as the possible connection between the name Dagon and the Hebrew word for 'grain' (dagan)." 1 Samuël, 75–76.

32. See Freeman, *Egypt, Greece and Rome*, 117–20.

created even more distress than it had in Gath: "Yahweh's hand was exceedingly heavy upon" the city (v. 11). The tumors or buboes afflicted the citizens of Ekron and many of them died. The town too was thrown into the horrible situation and cried desperately: its cry reached the heavens (1 Sam 5:12). The ark had been in Philistine territory for seven months (6:1). The number indicates "wholeness" or "completeness" and in the Old Testament often refers to complete periods of chastisement and purification (see Lev 26:21, 24, 28; Dan 9:1–2). Perhaps the seven months the ark was in Philistia was a period of complete chastisement for the Philistines. During these seven months, they paid in full for all their iniquities.[33] All these events demonstrate that even the enormously powerful Philistines are powerless before the God of Israel. Through his sovereign power, Yahweh himself opened the way for the ark to be returned to his people. The return of the ark by the freedom and initiative of Yahweh signifies that salvational history is resumed.[34]

D. THE ARK SENT BACK TO ISRAEL (1 SAM 6:2—7:1)

This chapter shows how the Philistines recognized their defeat and surrendered to the God of Israel.[35] On account of their disaster, the priests and diviners (oracle priests)[36] were summoned to decide what to do with the ark and how to send it back to its place. The Philistines assumed that the plagues were caused by the anger of the God of Israel and advised their people to return the ark with a guilt offering and pay honor to Israel's God to lessen the severity of the disaster from themselves, their gods and the land (1 Sam 6:3, 5). The intention of their plan to return the ark in that way was to heal the disease and to know the cause of the scourge. A guilt offering is generally defined as a cultic ceremony the purpose of which is to make atonement for desecration of sancta, that is, the mishandling of sacred things by treating them as if they were common rather than holy (see Lev 10:10).[37] Then their sin is misappropriation of Yahweh's ark. The recommended objects for guilt offering

---

33. Robinson, *Samuel*, 37.
34. See Klein, *1 Samuel*, 39.
35. The psalmist sings that Yahweh woke up from sleep: "And the Lord awoke as one out of sleep, as a mighty man wakes from the stupor of wine. He smote his enemies; he put them to everlasting shame." Ps 78:65–66.
36. *HALAT*, 1041.
37. See Averbeck, "*ʾāšām*," *NIDOTTE* 1: 559.

were precious but detestable things: golden models of rats and tumors, according to the number of the governors of the Philistines.[38] Their disease was not caused by the rats but related to the ark of Yahweh. In this case the rats appear to be associated with the work of their fertile deity because they ravage the land to hinder the fruition, Dagon's blessing. In addition, the Philistine priests and diviners asked the Philistines not to harden their hearts as the Egyptians and Pharaoh by applying the plagues experienced in Egypt to their situation. This historical event gives them instruction that it was wise to prevent extra calamities.

Whatever the case, according to the direction of the priests and the diviners, the Philistines attempted to use a very unusual method to transport the ark on a cart pulled by two milkcows that had never been put to yoke, leaving their calves behind them (1 Sam 6:7). Despite clear evidence that they were afflicted by the hand of Yahweh, they wanted to see once and for all whether the disaster really came from the might of Israel's God or not: "Watch, if it goes up to its territory, Beth-Shemesh, then he has brought this great disaster on us. But if it does not, then we will know that it was not his hand which smote us, but that it happened to us by chance" (6:9). The transporting of the ark was carefully organized as a test on the advice of the priests and the diviners, who were supposed to be able to understand this accident. The Philistines used natural maternal instinct for the test, by letting two cows pull a new cart. These two cows that had calved and had never been yoked had been forcefully separated from their unweaned calves to pull the cart (v. 7). Nevertheless, "Then the cows went on the straight road toward Beth-

---

38. On the ground of Milgrom's finding a Hittite parallel, Geyer contends that the mice should be understood as a mouse used to remove disease in the Hittite ritual of Ambazzi thus rejecting LXX's explanation of a plague of mice bringing bubonic plague ("Mice and Rites," 300–301). His statement looks plausible in consideration of the cultural influence of the Hittites on the Philistines. Yet this parallel is still difficult to understand. While the Hittite patients believed that the mouse carried disease on a long journey from the bowstring to the high mountain, the devastation of the Philistine cities appears to have been more than simply the outbreak of a disease (see 1 Sam 5:6). Moreover, the parallel seems to fail to settle the question of the golden images of the tumors that were sent with the mice. Nevertheless, there is a slight connection to the cultic ritual in their magical performance that requires the images of tumors and mice as apotropia: "Die Anfertigung der Figuren der Mäuse (und Beulen) wurde durch den Auftrag der philistäischen Priester und Wahrsager motiviert, so daß sie nicht (wie innerhalb der Bilderpolemik üblich) der Willkür, sondern der Auskunft des kultischen und göttlisch autorisierten Personals (und damit letztlich göttlichem Willen) entsprang." Berlejung, Theologie, 309.

Shemesh, along the highway and lowing all the way; they did not turn to the right or to the left" (v. 12). The might of Yahweh transcends natural law to confirm that the plague was caused by himself, which demonstrates clearly that only Yahweh is the universal king before whom all should kneel (Ps 95:6; 1 Cor 15:25–28; Eph 1:22). The most powerful maternal instinct of the animals was not able to frustrate Yahweh's sovereign will for the establishment of his design for redemption. The fact that the ark was sent back to Beth-Shemesh forced the Philistines to recognize Yahweh's omnipotence and simultaneously to accept these disasters as the result of his wrath.

When the ark entered the city, the people of Beth-Shemesh were out harvesting wheat in the valley (1 Sam 6:13). The arrival of the ark during the harvest season of May/June appears to explain why there were so many people present to greet it. The people of Beth-Shemesh, in the valley of Sorek, rejoiced over the return of the ark that they believed to have lost. They dare not meet God without ritual protection, and prepared a great sacrifice to Yahweh with joy and awe.[39] Here, the great rock in Joshua's field served as an impromptu altar for the burnt offering.[40] By the way, it remains unsettled why there is no conflict over the sacrifice of the milkcows. The law, after all, mandated that sacrificial animals were to be unblemished males (Lev 1:3; 22:9).[41] Their careless behavior may be understood as an early indication of impending divine judgment against the Beth-Shemeshites.[42] After the Philistine governors saw that their test was satisfied, they returned to Ekron that day, leaving behind the five gold tumors and five gold rats as well as the ark (1 Sam 6:17–18).

The people of Beth-Shemesh rejoiced at the arrival of the ark but did not pay homage to Yahweh, who symbolically abides with it: "they had looked into the ark with curiosity" (v. 19). Yahweh instantly reacted on such inadvertent behavior that infringed the ark's sanctity: "He smote

---

39. Dietrich, *Samuel*, 288–89.

40. Geoghegan viewed the phrase *šām ʾeḇen geḏōlā* as a stone standing "until this day," a redaction formular indicating one of the places where the sanctity of the ark is compromised. Geoghegan, "'Until This Day,'" 220.

41. Klein, *1 Samuel*, 59.

42. See Bergen, *Samuel*, 102.

of the people (fifty thousand and) seventy men."[43] "When Israel ignores Yahweh's holiness, the ark's presence is a matter of grave danger."[44]

The questions of the men of Beth-Shemesh sound like a useless lamentation: "Who can stand before Yahweh, this holy God? To whom will the ark go up from here?" (6:20). They would not have asked that, if they had understood that it was caused by a violation of the law. The question of the Beth-Shemites is answered when the inhabitants of Kiriath-Jearim accept their request: "The Philistines have brought again the ark of Yahweh; come down, and take it up to you" (6:21). Eventually, the ark came to be housed under the protection of Eleazar in Kiriath-Jearim (7:1),[45] a Canaanite city, one of the four cities that formed the Gibeonite league (Josh 9:17). This was also known as Baalah (Josh 15:9) or Baale-Judah (2 Sam 6:2) whose name may be attributable to the city's prominence as a traditional religious center.[46] The fact that the ark was taken to Kiriath-Jearim and not back to Shiloh may be an indirect proof that the Shiloh worship center had been destroyed previously by the Philistines.[47]

It is possible that Eleazar belonged to the Levitical tribe,[48] but most importantly they sanctified Eleazar his son to keep the ark of Yahweh, which was so different from the Beth-Shemites' behavior (1 Sam 6:19). The picture of 7:1 shows at least that the ark is treated on the basis of the

43. According to MT and LXX, the number is "fifty thousand and seventy." However the much smaller number seems more likely to be correct because the population of Beth-Shemesh could not have been so numerous, as it was a small town of, at most, a few thousand inhabitants (Gordon, *Samuel*, 103). It is still not clear why the inhabitants as a whole should have been afflicted; it reads better as "seventy men" and most modern versions and Josephus have made this alteration (*Antiquities*, 6:16).

44. Firth, *Samuel*, 101.

45. The modern site of Kiriath-Jearim is Tel el-'Azhar, eight miles northwest of Jerusalem and it means "City of Forests." Tsumura, *Samuel*, 228.

46. It is interesting to note that extra biblical evidence of the ark's returning to Kiriath-Jearim was found in the form of an ostracon at the site of 'Isbet Sartah (Ebenezer) during the 1976 season of excavations. This ostracon did much to support the biblical account of the ark coming back to reside at the Judahite site of Kiriath-Jearim (Shea, "Travels," 73–79). The text on the ostracon appears to challenge Ahlström's position that "the ark narrative" is a literary fiction with a tendentious, religio-political thread (Ahlström, "Travels," 142).

47. See Bergen, *Samuel*, 104.

48. Miller and Roberts argue that Eleazar was Eli's successor because it is apparent that he was consecrated to have charge of the ark (*Hand*, 20, 25–26), while Willis contends that Samuel was Eli's successor as leader of Israel ("Samuel Versus Eli," 209–11).

law: The ark's installation and protection at Kiriath-Jearim also prove how important it was that correct procedures in accord with the law were implemented.

The ark remained concealed and Israel would have to wait a long time until the ideal worship of Yahweh, which included the presence of the ark, was restored. The return of the ark signified the importance of the physical symbols of God's ongoing redemption of the people; without the ark, a symbol of the covenant, Israel was not complete. In the long run, the ark sent back to Israel shows that the ark was indispensable for unfolding a new era of kingdom in the redemptive history of God. Here the ark was employed as a tool to disclose Yahweh's sovereignty and goodness.

8

The Ark in the Book of 2 Samuel

A. THE RELATIONSHIP BETWEEN 1 SAMUEL 4–6 AND 2 SAMUEL 6

WITH REGARD TO THE relationship between 1 Samuel 4–6 and this chapter, there are two major arguments: a closure of the ark narrative, and a separate unit. After Rost identified the "ark narrative" (1 Sam 4:1b—7:1; 2 Sam 6:1–20) as a separate narrative, a majority followed his theory.[1] Just a handful of opponents suggested a variety of reasons for dissension: linguistic problems, content, genre, etc. The likes of Miller and Roberts disagree about the connection between the two parts by holding that only four expressions are shared and that 2 Samuel 6 tends to be a historical chronicle reporting the return of a lost cultic image.[2] Van Seters maintains that the ark narrative is just part of the wider theme of the ark as the symbol of the divine presence in exilic deuteronomistic history and says it is never an independent document.[3] In the same vein Smelik insists that there are no compelling reasons to assume the preexistence of an ark narrative before the composition of the book of Samuel, by suggesting problems of historical improbabilities, its thorough-going theological nature *Sitz im Leben*, disagreement among scholars, an earlier source, and oral transmission.[4] However, Eynikel recently refuted the arguments against the existence of an independent ark narrative, by concluding that the ark narrative (1 Sam 1–6;

---

1. Rost, *Überlieferung*, 4–47; see Eynikel, "Eli Narrative," 88–89.
2. Miller and Roberts, *Hand*, 23–24.
3. Van Seters, *Search*, 346–53.
4. Smelik, "Hidden Messages," 35–58.

2 Sam 6:1–19) contains the Eli narrative (1 Sam 1–4). In particular, he attempts elaborately to analyze the arguments of the opponents separately and to settle the subjects of discussion.[5] In this article, his introduction to five arguments for the connection between the two narratives is of assistance to understand the relation.[6] Yet it is hard to accept 2 Samuel 6:1–19 as the conclusion of the ark narrative because the suggestions appear not to be persuasive enough and still open to some objections.[7] Whether or not the ark passage of 2 Samuel 6 is the closure of the ark narrative, it is important in this study to recognize that the two narratives show the progression of redemp-

---

5. Eynikel, "Eli Narrative," 88–106.

6. Ibid., 96. 1) A quotation of van Seters's statement: "the connections between the two parts of the ark narrative greatly outweigh their differences." 2) "Second Samuel 6:2–19 provides an excellent closure for the ark narrative." 3) "The enormous power that the ark radiates is the same in both parts." 4) "Abinadab's house is mentioned in both parts." 5) "The shared vocabulary of 1 Samuel 4 6 and 2 Samuel 6 is admittedly limited but important."

7. The problems of the above quoted suggestions can be respectively indicated. 1) Van Seters's intention seems not to argue that the two narratives are originally composed of one literary unit but probably to denote that there is a historical continuation between 1 Samuel 7:1 and 2 Samuel 6. 2) Since generally a great literary work does not finish with incomplete contents such as in 1 Samuel 7:1, it seems plausible on these grounds that the ark narrative is recognized as independent literature, but this conjecture would be altered if the emphasis resides in what happened chronologically rather than from the literary point of view. 3) The phrase "power that the ark radiates" gives the impression that the ark is a fetish. It differs from the description of the text that tells us "the anger of Yahweh was kindled against Uzzah and God smote him" (2 Sam 6:7). This power is not of the ark itself but of God; it occurred as a token of his wrath. Such a demonstration of God's power in association with the ark is not confined to "ark narrative" but is also found in the crossing of the Jordan River (Josh 4) and the destruction of Jericho (Josh 6), even though the results of God's mighty actions were different. 4) It seems natural if the two texts are reliable in showing their historical continuity as a kind of chain, prior to considering any literary unity. 5) He gives two examples: "the new cart" and the queries of the Philistines (1 Sam 6:20) and David (2 Sam 6:9). If it is right that the new cart is a shared vocabulary, then it would be a significant proof for a literary connection between the two materials if they are fictional writings. Yet such terms would have to be used if the texts report historical events. The following example is the shared vocabulary that Eynikel quoted from van der Toorn and Houtman: "What shall we do with the ark of the God of Israel?" (1 Sam 5:8) and "How can the ark of Yahweh come to me?" (2 Sam 6:9). Their contents are fairly different and there is only one shared word between two sentences: the ark. Thereby these two phrases hardly match well. In fact it may be sufficient to say that the phrases he suggested would better be regarded as a common response to such a disaster rather than as a clue to the literature. Moreover he did not explain the reason why the shared vocabulary is more important than the rest.

tive history in Israel. Under this condition there is no reason to oppose that the ark narrative existed as an independent unit in an oral tradition between the historical events related to the ark and the composition of the book of Samuel. The problem is that those who consider that the ark narrative originally contained two parts believe that the ahistorical tradition was properly arranged in a historical setting. So, it may not be necessary to stress their literary unity as a mere story by undermining the historicity of the narrative. Thus, this study is interested in how the historical event concerning the ark in the present text unfolds a new epoch of redemptive history.

B. CONTEXT

After the death of Abner and Ish-bosheth (2 Sam 3:31–39; 4:9–12), all the tribes anointed David king over all Israel (5:1).[8] David had to fight the Philistines as soon as they saw his anointing as the proclamation of Israel's independence.[9] David repulsed the attacks of the Philistines with the help of God (5:17–25). David's first undertaking was to conquer Jerusalem, the last Canaanitic enclave, which was ruled by the Jebusites. He connected it to an old religious custom of making the center of the country a city,[10] which did not belong to Judah or to Israel, the royal city, the capital of his united kingdom (vv. 6–10). Then it was time for him to bring the ark, left in Kiriath-Jearim, to Jerusalem. This event had political and religious significance for a theocracy.

Although no concrete information about exactly when the ark was brought over is provided, this project was probably one of David's first undertakings after he settled in Jerusalem. If the date 930 BC is accepted as the year of the division of the kingdom,[11] then David's reign probably commenced around the period when the Syrian states such as Aram

---

8. "Israel" in the first verse was used to mean "the whole people," apart from the "personal union" theory that each kingdom retained its own character in the united kingdom as suggested by Alt ("Davids," 66–75) and Herrmann ("'Realunion' und 'Charismatisches Königtum,'" 103).

9. It hardly seems reasonable to think that they coveted the conquest of Jerusalem as Aharoni and Eissfeldt held, because there is a direct connection between David's anointing and the attack of the Philistines. Aharoni, *Land*, 260; Eissfeldt, *Hebrew Kingdom*, 44–46; see Ohmann, "Een top bereikt," 137; Bright, *History*, 198.

10. See Holwerda, "De Priester-koning," 60.

11. See Thiele, *Mysterious Numbers*, 79.

Zobah and Damascus had been remarkably strengthened by aligning with other powerful countries in the Old Near East.[12]

C. THE PREPARATION FOR TRANSPORTING THE ARK (2 SAM 6:1–2; 1 CHR 13:1–14)

The attempt to carry the ark to Jerusalem is told in the consecutive events David initiated: "David again gathered all the chosen men in Israel" (6:1) because the adverb "again" indicates that there has already been a large meeting, one that is not reported in the text.[13] The previous group seems to be a military group David had gathered to fight against the Philistines (ch. 5).[14] The people whom David chose would have been regarded as warriors for war.[15] Although such an armed force is not suitable for this peaceful expedition, it is conceivable that he wanted to mobilize them because the initial stages of his reign were strongly militaristic (see 1 Chr 13:1).[16] Thirty thousand[17] men were chosen out of all the tribes, out of the "whole Israel" (1 Chr 13:6), matching a national assemblage.[18] As a

---

12. See Pitard, *Ancient Damascus*, 89.

13. It is generally said that it does not match the "ark narrative." According to Campbell (*Ark Narative*, 39–40), all of v. 1 is not required in order to connect this "ark narrative" with 1 Sam 7:1. However, this word may be able to prove that the hypothesis of the "ark narrative" is groundless; it appears to underline the continuous historical story in 2 Sam.

14. Regarding their army, Goslinga believes they fight against the Jebusites as well as the Philistines, but this military action appears to be undertaken by David's personal troop (*Samuël*, 108). Keil contends this point, stating that the first assemblage must be the people's meeting in Hebron, one that was not brought together by David (*Bücher Samuelis*, 258).

15. Weisman, "Bāḥūr," 443.

16. Noordtzij, *Kronieken*, 117. As regards this military expedition, seeking a Babylonian parallel looks awkward; Miller and Roberts, *Hand*, 16: "Just as Assurbanipal's army participated in the return of Marduk to his new sanctuary, so David's army participated in the return of the ark of Yahweh."

17. The Hebrew word *ʾelef* (thousand) is where some difficulty lies because it has in general been doubtful that *ʾelef* points out exactly one thousand in number. However, it would be acceptable that *ʾelef* in this text means one thousand in consideration of Mendenhall's statement that in the early monarchy the royal army contained units of a thousand men under the command of an officer appointed by the king (Mendenhall, "Census Lists," 60, 66). "The number 3, 30, 300, 3000, 30,000, and 300,000 are above all associated with military forces, and especially warfare between the Israelites and Philistine" (Rezetko, *Source and Revision*, 101).

18. Albright, *Biblical Period*, 56. According to him, the population during the ruling of David and Solomon doubled in number, possibly from 400,000 to 800,000.

military escort, they were to be accompanied by an enthusiastic procession for the ark. According to 1 Chronicles 13:1–3, the plan to carry the ark to Jerusalem was formed by David himself. The reason David undertook this project is clear if we take into consideration the political and spiritual policies he diligently pursued. With respect to David's motive, it appears to be somewhat unreasonable to evaluate David's action simply as a political move (Ps 132:1–7).[19] It is impossible to ignore the fact that a firm and unshakable trust in Yahweh motivated him: faith, thus, appears to take precedence over political concern. It appears that his zeal for the Israelite God drove him to transfer the ark to the new capital city of Israel. With his personal faith coloring this official event, his reign began with the expectation of Yahweh's sovereignty. However, it is also true that David's political interest was closely tied to his theocracy.

They had to bring up the ark from Baalah-Judah (2 Sam 6:2a). "Baalah-Judah" is probably the same place as Kiriath-Jearim in 1 Chronicles 13:6 (see Josh 15:60; 18:14). "Kiriath" as a local name seems to refer to a kind of antiquity, considering that Kiriath-Sepher was the old name of Debir (Josh 15:15; Judg 1:11) and Kiriath-Arba was that of Hebron (Josh 14:15).[20] The city lay on the border of Judah and Benjamin (about eleven kilometers to the west of Jerusalem) and was one of the most prominent cities of the Gibeonites (see Josh 9:17–27).[21] Here the ark appears to have remained for just less than hundred years.[22] There

---

19. Many scholars tend to regard David's motive as political calculation (see Bright, *History*, 200–201; Jagersma, *Geschiedenis van Israël*, 150; Herrmann, *Geschichte Israels*, 200; Brueggemann, *Samuel*, 247–48; Japhet, "King's Sanctuary," 132–39). De Tarragon connects his political intention with a central function of tribes of the new kingdom ("David et l'arche," 521). In contrast with a more general view, van der Toorn and Houtman consider such a notion as "a Deuteronomic phantom, produced by the projection of a late theological ideal upon Israel's prehistory" ("David and the Ark," 231). Yet, this occasion appears far from a deuteronomic character because the ark is repeatedly described simply as "the ark of God" (seven times) but not "the ark of the covenant of the God" or "the ark of the covenant of Yahweh," which are deemed as typically deuteronomistic and the atmosphere of the sacrifice in this chapter is closer to Prather than deuteronomic disposition, according to critical views (ibid.).

20. A. A. Anderson, *2 Samuel*, 101. Schicklberger states that Baalah-Judah and Kiriath-Jearim were two neighboring locations of topographical origin, identified as one and the same by late redactors (*Ladeerzählung*, 139).

21. Now the place passes for "Deir el-'Azar" in Arabic and "Qiryat Ye'arim" in Hebrew (Aharoni, *Land*, 380). See Tsumura, *Samuel*, 228.

22. Brouwer (*De ark*, 160) and Keil (*Bücher Samuelis*, 260) argued fifty and seventy years respectively. It can be calculated as follows: The period of young Samuel's work

are reasons why the ark of Yahweh received little attention from the Israelites for such a long period of time. One reason is that the Israelite people were no longer interested in the ark after the war in Ebenezer (1 Sam 4:10–11) because, perhaps, they thought that the ark's function as a war-palladium fell short of their expectations. A more practical reason is that Kiriath-Jearim, as a member of the Gibeonites union (Josh 9:17), was a predominant Amorite and Canaanite city. It is probable that the city had been under Philistine suzerainty.[23] Thus, the city remained outside the Israelite authorities until David seized power. Another reason is related to the faith of the monarch. Saul, known as an ungodly king of Israel, appeared uninterested in dedications to Yahweh and possibly regarded it as of little importance (1 Sam 22:18, 19; 23:1, 27; 1 Chr 13:3).

The second part of 2 Samuel 6:2 gives a long explanation regarding the name of the ark in relation to the name of God: "the ark of God, which is called by the Name, the name of Yahweh Almighty, who dwells between the cherubim that are on the ark." This expression is a legitimization of a new title given to Yahweh in relation to the ark, the ancient symbol of his presence in the midst of his people.[24] This name shows how the ark is a possession of Yahweh. The name is often connected with Yahweh Zebaoth, commonly believed to have a close association with God's omnipotence (see 1 Sam 4:4). Yahweh Zebaoth as an epithet is reflective of God's ability to redeem, protect, and lead the people of Israel. The connection between the name of the ark and the cherubim symbolizes Yahweh's glorious and majestic presence. David as a theocratic king demonstrates that the ark is still the external sign of the security, preservation, and future of Israel.

D. FIRST ATTEMPT TO TRANSPORT THE ARK (2 SAM 6:3–5)

The Israelites set the ark of God on a new cart (6:3a). In contrast to how the ark had been pulled into battle as if a chariot of war, it was now being pulled along on a cart led by two cows. A new cart (see 1 Sam 6:7), which was not yet contaminated, was deemed suitable to carry the holy object. They tried to place the ark on the cart the same way the Philistines did,

---

(20 years, 1 Sam 7:2) + old Samuel's work before Saul (± 30 years, 1 Sam 7:3; 8:1–2) + the period of the reign of Saul (±40 years, 1 Sam 8–31) + David's reign in Hebron (7.5 years, 2 Sam 2:11; 5:4) = ±97.5 years.

23. Mauchline, *Samuel*, 222; see Goldman, *Samuel*, 220; Gordon, *Samuel*, 230.
24. De Vaux, *Bible et Orient*, 259.

even though this violated the law, because a holy object like the ark must be carried on the shoulders of the designated men of God (see Num 3:29–31; 7:9). It is not reported why David chose such a method to do the job, but he appears to try to carry it with his utmost sincerity regardless of the law. Then the "sons" of Abinadab were possibly superstitious, for they might have heard about a new magical power in the ark when the Philistines returned it on a new cart. "The house of Abinadab" was located "on the hill" (2 Sam 6:3b). It was still the same house as in 1 Sam 7:1. The route taken to transport the ark may have been from the eastern end of the Sorek valley by way of Kiriath-Jearim to Jerusalem.[25]

In this procession, Uzza and Ahio were appointed as escorts.[26] Ahio preceded the ark while Uzza stood next to the cart, near the ark, as they drove along (2 Sam 6:4). Since initially the procession had a festive character, David and all Israel were skipping with joy.[27] The expression "all Israel" reflects the national aspect and implies that the ark is the center of their religion. Unlike the refined motions of a cultic dance, they skipped with gladness before Yahweh to the accompaniment of various musical instruments and songs of gladness (see 1 Chr 13:8). Thus a frenzied rejoicing and religious enthusiasm in the presence of God made the procession an overwhelming experience. The accompaniment by all the

---

25. See Dorsey, *Roads and Highways*, 186.

26. It is held that Uzza was once identified with Eleazar from 1 Sam 7:1. "Uzza" may be a shortened form of Eleazar (Budde, *Samuel*, 228; van der Toorn and Houtman, "David and the Ark," 223). This said, he cannot be the same figure or his brother, for there is a chronological chasm of almost hundred years between Eleazar and Uzza. It may be possible that he is (a son of) a grandchild of Abinadab (see Goslinga, *Samuël*, 111; Hertzberg, *Samuelbücher*, 228). The proper name Ahio is translated as "his brother" in LXX. The word can be translated so, but it seems plausible that the name is a variant of "Ahijah," Yahweh is brother (see Smith, *Commentary*, 293; A. A. Anderson, *2 Samuel*, 103).

27. The verb *śḥq* in pi. means here "to dance," "play," and "skip" (see 1 Sam 18:7; *HALAT* 1226). In particular, "skip" indicates that they moved in a certain direction at the same time: "Die übliche Übersetzung Tanzen ist hier nicht ganz korrekt. Der kultische Tanz, mit Beteiligung der Frauen, heiß *ḥûl* (Stoebe, *Das zweite Buch Samuelis*, 189). The participle used here indicates some kind of continuous motion.

instruments[28] of cypress,[29] with lyres and harps and tambourines and sistra[30] and cymbals, served to give expression to the festive rejoicing and to raise it to a fever pitch. The procession was an enormous celebration with music, dance, and song. It was a special national festival but the rejoicing was short-lived because of Uzza's sudden death.

E. PEREZ-UZZA (2 SAM 6:6–8)

When they reached the threshing floor of Nachon,[31] the festive mood was dampened on account of Uzza's accident. The location of the threshing-floor of Nachon is unknown but probably not far from Baalah-Judah.[32] Here "Uzza stretched out his hand to the ark of God and took hold of it, for the oxen stumbled" (v. 6b).[33] The reason for the oxen's stumble is not mentioned but it may be related to the slippery state of the threshing-floor.[34] Although Uzza's reaction is comprehensible, his deed is sinful

28. The words $b^e \underline{k}ōl$ 'aṣē $\underline{b}^e rōšīm$ form the *lectio difficilior*. Many scholars tried to reconstruct it after the parallel of Chronicles: $b^e \underline{k}ōl$ 'ōz ūḇešīrīm. They believe that the emendation of this text should be allowed following the text of Chronicles. They also believe the latter makes the origin of the MT explicable: changing the place of r and $š$, replacing w with y, and crossing z and $ṣ$. It sounds acceptable to correct the text of Samuel after Chronicles. However, the problem is not solved completely with this correction: it is not certain that the text of Chronicles is its original text. The names of musical instruments in Samuel differ from those of Chronicles.

29. The cypress is *Juniperus Phoenicea* or *Juniperus excels*, an especially durable kind of wood that is identified as a chief tree of Lebanon (Isa 60:13) and is associated with cedar (2 Kgs 19:23; Ps 104:17; Isa 14:8; Zech 11:2). See Walker, "$b^e rōš$," *NIDOTTE* 1:740–41.

30. What instrument $m^e na'an\bar{\imath}m$ (< *nw'*, to shake) refers to is totally uncertain, but most likely it was a shaking instrument, perhaps even a rattle. Vulgata translates it as *sistra*.

31. It is plausible that $nā\underline{k}ōn$ is considered as a common noun, "ruin," "fixed," unlike the LXX. See Rezetko, *Source and Revision*, 121–22. Tur-Sinai supposes that $k\bar{\imath}dōn$ (1 Chr 13:9) should be translated as a synonym of $nā\underline{k}ōn$, ruin, destruction. "Ark," 283.

32. According to Simons, a spot somewhere on the southwestern heel of Jerusalem is probably included in it. *Jerusalem*, 245.

33. The verb *šāmaṭ* (qal, to shake) has almost a transitive meaning in other places (Exod 22:11; Deut 15:2; 2 Kgs 9:33; Jer 17:4). However, it can here better be taken up as intransitive, since it does not have an explicit accusative and "the oxen" should be the subject. The LXX, Tg, and Vg follow the vocalization *šemāṭō* (his shaking), which can be regarded as the result of *šāmeṭū*.

34. "The reader, upon being informed that the oxen had come to a 'permanent threshing floor' would immediately picture a floor either of rock or of very hard earth, on which a slip such as that of Uzzah was quite natural." Marget, "*nkwn gwrn*," 75.

in nature. "Yahweh's anger burned against Uzza and God struck him down because of his imprudence" (v. 7).³⁵ Uzza's action demonstrates his ignorance concerning the holy nature of the ark so he died beside the ark, punished by God.³⁶ He violated the law of God by touching the ark (Num 4:15). In consideration that the ark was to be moved about only with carrying poles (Exod 25:14), 1 Chronicles 15:13 widely explains the reason for the punishment: the infringement arose out of a lack of respect for the prescription God himself gave. In fact, undertaking to carry the ark on a cart from the beginning was a violation. Presumably the Philistines too touched the ark but God did not punish them for their behaviors. However, such is not the case with Israel. Yahweh expected complete observance of the law from his own people. One out of the congregation was punished severely: Uzza is representative of the slovenliness of all the people with regard to the law. God maintains his right and holiness.³⁷ All that happened had to do with David's plan to set up worship in Jerusalem. God treated the king severely so that the service would be organized in accordance with his law.³⁸ This accident

---

35. 'al haššal of the MT is found only in this part of the Old Testament. The origin of šal is not clear. The old versions such as LXX and Vg translate the word with *propeteia* and *temeritas* (rash). There is no reason to remove 'al haššal by replacing it with a parallel text from Chronicles or 4QSamₐ, as some scholars propose. Hertzberg, *Samuelbücher*, 226; Mauchline, *Samuel*, 224; Gordon, *Samuel*, 232. Chronicles offers a plain interpretation for 'al haššal "because he put forth his hand to the ark."

36. Yet it is not necessary to suppose that the ark radiated the enormous power, as Eynikel mentions. "Eli Narrative," 96.

37. As for the smite, Seow is inclined to regard the reference to Yahweh's anger in this text as authentic to the ritual in the light of the Ugaritic parallel (*KTU* 1.6.II.30–37). Primarily it is understandable that he refutes the theory of deuteronomistic editing of this passage with this statement. However it is questionable what the disaster has to do with the ritual even though the Ugaritic document has the cultic *Sitz im Leben*. Moreover he mentions that the element of divine anger understandably belongs with the motif of the divine warrior's advance against the enemies (Hab 3:8; Job 9:13). The Ugaritic literature displays how Anat thoroughly vanquished Mot, the enemy of Baal. Naturally such a mythological description is a deification of nature in the agricultural cycle of the year. Then it appears clumsy that the victory of Anat against Baal's enemy in the mythological combat is compared with Yahweh's wrath against Uzza. It may well state that Yahweh considers Uzza to be not so much an enemy as a member of covenantal people who are responsible for serving him in accordance with his law. In fact it is groundless to hold that God regards creatures such as monsters and the phenomenon of nature, like a great wave, as a rival to be defeated. Thus Seow's explanation with the Ugaritic parallel is hardly applied to the event of Uzza (*Myth, Drama*, 99–101).

38. See Gootjes, "Ons ten voorbeeld geschied," 2; Calvin, *Predigten*, 135.

is an obvious warning to King David that nobody may treat the ark of Yahweh at random. "David was angry" (2 Sam 6:8a):[39] David's anger appears not to be directed against God but against the disaster issued by Yahweh's wrath.[40] First Chronicles 15:13 makes it known that David realized that they did not inquire of God about how to carry the ark in the prescribed way. It is true that David himself was informed later of the legal prescription concerning the treatment of the ark, but it is unimaginable that David did not know the regulation before the first attempt to carry it was made. So he had a right to be angry with himself. The death of Uzza stopped the procession and the festive mood ended abruptly.

The verb *wayyiqrā* (he called) makes David the subject, as in the LXX, but the last words of 2 Sam 6:8, "to this day," do not support it. The appellation "Perez-Uzza" is indirectly derived from David himself; he immortalized the name so that it vividly could remind the Israelites, the covenant people, of the actual event. From generation to generation it was to be narrated that fellowship with God can only be realized in accordance with his law because Yahweh is holy.

F. THE ARK IN THE HOUSE OF OBED-EDOM (2 SAM 6:9–11)

David was fearful when he realized that Yahweh's displeasure was aroused: "David was afraid of Yahweh" (6:9). This "being afraid" is not the same as respectfulness (Gen 22:12; Josh 24:14) but fear and anxiety that come from a guilty conscience (Deut 5:5). At this moment, David saw the risk of association with the ark (i.e., fellowship with God) but his anxiety was not associated with a consciousness of the ark's danger. In addition to blessings (2 Sam 6:11) there is the possibility of curses for those who associate with God. Nevertheless, David still has the desire to place the ark in Zion, the city of David (5:7): "There is no longer any doubt concerning the identification of the city of David with the triangular hill wedged between the valleys of the Tyropoen and the Kidron, and overlooking the gardens and pools of Siloam" (2 Chr 32:30).[41] He

---

39. Another translation of *wayyiḥar* can be offered here: "he was deeply grieved" (see Gen 45:5; 1 Sam 15:11). The next verse is the basis of this translation: "David was afraid of Yahweh" (2 Sam 6:9).

40. The expression "*wayyiḥar... le*" points out the ignition of wrath (Gen 4:5; Jonah 4:9).

41. Barrois, "City of David," *IDB* 1:782.

considers his situation: how can the ark of Yahweh come to me? His fear at God's holiness made David's intention lose momentum.

Since David had to lodge the ark somewhere as soon as possible, it arrived at the neighboring house of Obed-Edom the Gittite, a man from Gath, which appears to be the well-known Philistine city. Thus, Budde and Gordon suppose that he was a Philistine who became a Levite later (1 Chr 15:18).[42] However it is hard to explain how a Philistine was listed in Levite genealogy. In fact, there are many places with the name Gath in the Old Testament, for example Gath Hepher (2 Kgs 14:25), Gath Rimmon (Josh 19:45; 21:24), Gittaim (2 Sam 4:3), and Gath Padalla in Sharon. Some scholars believe Obed-Edom originated from the Levite city Gath Rimmon and identify him with the Levite in 1 Chronicles 15:18, 21, 24, and 16:38.[43] So David ordered that the ark be taken to the house of the Levite.

The benefits of the presence of the ark in the house of Obed-Edom (2 Sam 6:11) are in sharp contrast to the death of Uzza. The ark remained under the shelter of Obed-Edom for three months. During this period he experienced the blessing of Yahweh in all that he had (1 Chr 13:12). Even though there is no further description of these blessings, they probably came in the form of material prosperity (Lev 26:3-13; Deut 18:1-14) because it is a visible blessing (2 Sam 6:12). Yahweh blessed him for the sake of the ark. God's presence itself is a blessing but the service of God can become dangerous when it is not done in accordance with his commandments.

G. FESTIVE ENTRY OF THE ARK INTO DAVID'S CITY (2 SAM 6:12-19)

1. *The Procession around the Ark (2 Sam 6:12-15)*

The report that "Yahweh has blessed the household of Obed-Edom and all that belongs to him, on account of the ark of God" was interpreted as a sign of Yahweh's approval of David's plan to carry the ark to Jerusalem.[44] He reacted immediately, as if he were waiting for it. Without any anxiety

---

42. Budde, *Samuel*, 230; Gordon, *Samuel*, 233. Klein and Krüger proposed that Obed-edom was apparently a Philistine expatriate who was loyal to David. Klein & Krüger, 1 *Chronicles*, 335.

43. Keil, *Bücher Samuelis*, 262; Goldman, *Samuel*, 222; see A. A. Anderson, 2 *Samuel*, 104.

44. See A. A. Anderson, 2 *Samuel*, 105.

he was convinced that the transportation of the ark would not conflict with God's will. While Chronicles does not disclose David's awareness of the blessing of Obed-Edom, the text supplies a broad account of the preparations to carry the ark to David's city (1 Chr 15:2–15), which is identical with the southeastern spur conquered by David.[45] Many things happened before the new procession began: the sons of Aaron and the Levites were gathered, sanctified, and appointed for the task. First Chronicles 15:2 and 13 show us that David checked exactly the correct procedure for transporting the ark; it had to be carried by Levites and priests, not by soldiers (Exod 25:12–15; Num 4:4, 15). He went to bring up the ark of the covenant with the elders of Israel and the commanders of the military units he had assembled (1 Chr 15:3, 25). The festive character of the procession is elevated into something purer than the first procession, for God approves of this transport.

When those who were carrying the ark of Yahweh had taken six steps, David sacrificed a bull and a fattened calf (2 Sam 6:13).[46] The beginning of the undertaking is a pivotal moment, so that the first six steps form a symbolic beginning. The meaning of the number "six" is uncertain here. By this number the hope for a bright future may be intended because the number seven means "perfect" for the Israelites (see Ruth 3:15). Instead of the expression "the first six steps," 1 Chronicles 15:26 gives an explanation: "Because God had helped the Levites who were carrying the ark of the covenant of Yahweh." The offering is an expression of gratitude for the favorable beginning of the undertaking while simultaneously a prayer for successful advancement; Yahweh is recognized as the actual leader and head of the procession. It shows that David had become very cautious, since he did not bring an offering at the first attempt. David is the subject of the verb, "sacrifices" (*wayyizᵉbaḥ*), but it is not necessary that he himself carried out the offering. Another

---

45. Mulder, *I Kings*, 103; Mare, *Archaeology*, 26–27.

46. "Six steps" (*šiššā ṣᵉʿādīm*) does not mean "each six steps." This runs contrary to the interpretation of Miller and Roberts who explain these words in the light of the parallel of the return of Marduk, the god of Babylon (*Hand*, 96). They hold the opinion: "If the Assyrians could offer sacrifices all the way from Assur to Babylon . . . a quite considerable distance . . . why could David not offer sacrifices every six steps from the house of Obed-Edom to Jerusalem?" Here the distinction between Yahweh and Marduk should be considered before making use of parallels with Babylonia. The Assyrians might have to bring offerings all the way from Assur to Babylonia in order to propitiate their god, while Yahweh does not need to be treated in the same manner. See Goldman, *Samuel*, 222–23.

person could have done this under his direction (see Deut 10:1–5; Exod 37:1).[47] The text in Chronicles gives reason to think that others made the sacrifice: "they (probably Levites) sacrificed" (*wayyizbᵉḥū*).[48]

"David was dancing before Yahweh with all his might" (2 Sam 6:14a). "Dancing" indicates that David himself moves continually forward in a rhythmical dance. His dance is evoked by the unspeakable joy that profound solidarity with Yahweh brings. The King of kings enters the city that David chose (2 Chr 6:6; 33:4). David's dance is not seen as a refined, legitimate liturgical dance that points out the qualification of priests, nor political activity as Brueggemann thinks.[49] Rather, David and the whole people did this in the presence of Yahweh. It is plausible that the dance is an expression of David's sheer joy (see 2 Sam 6:5; Pss 149:3; 150:4).[50] During the dance he wore a linen ephod instead of a royal garment. This attire does not imply that David played the role of priest, for priests wear this apparel exclusively (the clothes of the priest described in Exodus 28 is called ephod but not a linen ephod).[51] The young Samuel, who did not belong to the body of priests, wore such clothes as a santuary servant (1 Sam 2:18). The ephod, not worn by children, indicates a certain relationship between the man wearing it and the sanctuary.[52] It symbolizes dedication to God. At this moment David felt himself united with the holy people, the kingdom of priests (Exod 19:6). He humbly served God by the ark and with ordinary men and women who were servants of Yahweh. While his disrobing, leaping, and dancing was for the glory of Yahweh, they were seen as offensive by his wife, Michal.

"David and the entire house of Israel brought up the ark of Yahweh with shouts and the sound of trumpets" (2 Sam 6:15). In the same terms

---

47. This contrasts with Mowinckel's view, "der König ist selbst Opferpriester." *Psalmenstudien*, 116.

48. For the detailed discussion on the role of David and priests in the two texts, see, Rezetko, *Source and Revision*, 196–209.

49. Brueggemann, *Samuel*, 250.

50. It should not be regarded as the prelude to the "holy wedding" with Michal or as a fertility rite, as Porter and Carlson argue. They interpreted it as a Canaanite ecstatic dance. The narrative gives us little clue about David's intention (Porter, "Samuel and Psalm," 166; Carlson, *David*, 87). Wright thinks that the music and dance make the whole rite more pleasurable and more acceptable and agreeable to the deity ("Music and Dance," 224).

51. See Kroeze, *Genesis veertien*, 212.

52. Tedwell, "1 Sam II 18 and 2 Sam VI 14," 507.

the whole earth is exhorted in Psalm 98:6 to shout with joy before Yahweh, the King.53 Trumpets or horns made of ram's horn serve not only to give signals (2 Sam 2:28) but also to assist festivity (Joel 2:15; Pss 47:5; 81:3; 98:6; 150:3). The author of Chronicles mentions other musical instruments as well: trumpets, cymbals, lyres, and harps (1 Chr 15:28). This great event is recorded in several psalms (24; 47; 68; 132): In particular, Psalm 24:7–10 details the glory of this procession. David may have sung this psalm as he entered through the gate of the city. Psalm 24 may have been the song sung in accompaniment when the ark was lifted up and laid down.

David's carrying of the ark in 2 Samuel 6 is a unique event in the history of Israel.[54] Selecting Zion as the earthly throne of the King who reigns eternally (Pss 29:10; 66:7; 146:10; etc.) is not comparable with the ascendancy to a throne. This historical installation of the ark appears to become the ideal model for the restoration of Israelite religion in the post-exilic period because the Chronicler commences his book with this event.[55]

2. The Contempt of Michal (2 Sam 6:16)[56]

The phrase "Michal daughter of Saul looked down through a window . . . she despised him in her heart" seems to notify beforehand what will happen in 2 Samuel 6:20–23. Michal is not called the wife of David but the daughter of Saul. "The reason for these abnormalities is clear; Michal is not behaving as David's wife (contrast 1 Sam 19) but as his opponent;

---

53. See Ollenburger, *Zion*, 36.

54. Mowinckel connected this procession with the so-called annual Thronbesteigungstag Jahwäs: "Jeden Neujahrstag kommt Jahwä wieder und besteigt seinen Tron. Dieser Tag ist sein Tag, der Tag Jahwäs (Neh 8:10; Hos 7:5), an dem er alle die Grosstaten übt, die sein Reich begründen. Man hat den Tag mit einer grossen Prozession begangen, dem Königseizug des siegreichen Gottes, bei dem Jahwä selbst (unsichtbar?) in seinen Palladium, der Lade, zum Tempel hinaufgetragen wurde (Pss 132, 24, 47:6, 2 Sam 6)" (*Psalmenstudien*, 213). He sees a parallel with the festivals dedicated to Marduk: the *Akkitu* festival in Babylonia is correlated to the festive worship of Israel. However, it is doubtful that there was an annual entrance of the ark into the city of David in Israel.

55. See Dempsey, "Ark and Temple," 233–39.

56. The first word is $w^e h\bar{a}y\bar{a}$ (Then it happened so). In this case the combination with w^e and perfect form has a special meaning; it offers a short repetition in order to accentuate the significance of the preceding event. This is probably the event following v. 19. De Boer, "Perfect," 147.

she is acting like a true daughter of Saul."[57] The expressions "King David" and "before Yahweh" seem to reflect the feelings of the author rather than those of Michal because it is doubtful to what extent she acknowledged David as king. She saw him leap and dance in an undignified manner before female slaves. David, on the other hand, was dedicating himself to God during the dance, being aware of the eyes of Yahweh.

The phrase "looked down through a window" often represents looking from "up" to "down" (see Judg 5:28). Some scholars draw this picture, based on Canaanite practices and Ancient Eastern culture (e.g., David's dance is concerned with marriage fertility).[58] However, the text does not allow us to make such an analogy since it is in harmony with the law God prescribed. Furthermore, according to Keel, the reason Michal criticizes David's cultic dance is that Yahweh is not like the old image of the gods who are linked with the weather but is rather the stunning God Yahweh, who governs with justice and righteousness, enthroned upon the powerful cherubim.[59] But such an assessment of Michal is challenged by the narrative in 2 Samuel 6:20–23.

"She despised him in her heart" (6:16). The word "despise" means an actual working of the heart; the redundant expression "in her heart" underlines how deep her despising is. Brouwer directly links her contempt with the "priestly cloth of David and his priestly service."[60] Yet his action has nothing to do with the priestly office, as above mentioned. The exact reason for her despising is not exposed clearly. It is possible that Michal was not interested in the plan of David to realize God's lordship over Israel; there is an obvious contrast between the festive joy at the great moment of the entrance of the ark and Michal's feeling. The contrast is emphasized also by the names "daughter of Saul" and "King David."

---

57. Clines, "X, X *BEN* Y, *BEN* Y," 128.

58. "A frequent theme of ancient pictorial art is the portrayal of a woman at a window, goddess or (sacred) prostitute, and thus this suggests the part Michal should be playing in the ritual. Underlying the narrative here are indications of a ritual eventually held to be too alien for Israel, that of the 'sacred marriage': the ceremonial leading up to a marriage between king and queen as representative of god and goddess, and designed to bring fertility and well-being to the whole community" Ackroyd, *Second Samuel*, 69. See McCarter, 1 *Samuel*, 172; Porter, "Samuel and Psalm," 166; Carlson, *David*, 94–96.

59. Keel, "Davids 'Tanz,'" 11–14.

60. Brouwer, *De ark*, 168.

3. The First Worship on Zion (2 Sam 6:17–19)

Finally the ark found a resting place, being set "in its place" (Ps 132:13–14).[61] The tent that David prepared for the ark seems not to be identified with the tent of meeting because "it would be quite logical to infer that the tabernacle was at Nob at that time, having been taken there after the disaster at Aphek (1 Sam 4)."[62] Instead it was meant as a temporary residence for the ark, until a permanent residence for it could be built. No information on the form and arrangement of the tent in Zion is given. The tent stretched out by David might have been an ordinary tent or house made of cloth, poor in contrast to the distinguished standing residence in which King David was living (2 Sam 7:2). According to 1 Chronicles 16:37–42, singers and gatekeepers ministered regularly before the ark of the covenant of Yahweh in the tent, while Zadok the priest and his fellow priests presented daily burnt offerings before the tabernacle at the high place in Gibeon. Now Yahweh had his resting place in Zion; he would stay there forever (see Pss 68:17; 132:13–14).

"David sacrificed burnt offerings and peace offerings before Yahweh" (2 Sam 6:17b). It was the first worship service for Yahweh on Mount Zion and David appears to be the leader. Here he made positive use of priests for the service as he had with the offerings in verse 13. Concerning David's behavior regarding the offerings, the dance before the ark, and the blessing, most scholars attribute it to his function as priest-king, similar to the behavior of the kings in Egypt, Mesopotamia, and South Arabia, and of the Hittite monarchs.[63] However, the Bible tells us nowhere that David had such a double office: "Israel expected only the priest-king: the Lord Jesus."[64] The transportation of the ark, begun with an offering (v. 13), also closes with one. While for the burnt offering

---

61. Rowley considered this an allusion to an already existing shrine. He seems to assign such passages as 2 Sam 6:17; 7:2, 6; 2 Kgs 8:4, to a later redaction (*Worship*, 125–27). Scholars such as Rupprecht and Brouwer assert that the ark is placed in an old Jebusite temple on the threshing floor of Arauna, but their assertion is unfounded (Rupprecht, *Der Tempel*, 103–5; Brouwer, *De ark*, 169).

62. Pitkänen, *Sanctuary and Centralization*, 64; Ohmann, "Een top bereikt," 148, "When the Philistine rubbed the ark in the defeat of Aphek 1080 BC, Shiloh probably was devastated just after the event. Psalm 78:60–64 may allude to it and Jeremiah 7:12–15 too . . . We read about priests in Nob in 1 Samuel 21. Did the tabernacle stand there then? And was it brought over from there to Gibeon (1 Kings 3:4)?"

63. Ackroyd, *Second Samuel*, 70; Gordon, *Samuel*, 234; Koolhaas, *Theocratie*, 106.

64. Holwerda, "De Priester-koning," 57.

the whole animal is burnt except the skin (Lev 7:8), only specified parts of it are burnt on the altar in a peace offering. The priests take a part of the meat and those who offer it eat the rest. This becomes a festive meal before Yahweh (Lev 3:1; 7:11–18). While the offering shows harmony between God and man, the sacrifices play an important role when the community is confronted with new events and circumstances.[65] The term *šᵉlāmīm* matches this context well to the meaning of maintenance or restoration of the appropriate relationship with God; the well-being of a human being has to do with his right relationship to God.[66] David wanted to lead Israel into a renewed relationship with God so that she might become his own people. Another function of the peace offering (Lev 7:15) is added here: the people wanted to thank God for the successful procession. The expression "before Yahweh" (2 Sam 6:17b) appears to identify Yahweh's presence in David's tent with the ark installed there at David's behest.[67]

After the offerings, "he blessed the people in the name of Yahweh Zebaoth" (6:18b). The blessing of the people by David does not indicate the special priestly right of the king. Indeed the blessing was not exclusively the task of priests but also that of fathers and leaders of the people, such as Moses (Exod 39:43; Deut 33:1) and Joshua (Josh 22:6).[68] As a theocratic king he behaves in place of Yahweh. He may bestow the blessing of Yahweh Zebaoth, who is present at the ark and enthroned in Zion. Concerning the name Yahweh Zebaoth, Brongers illuminates the blessing of David: "this is more than a wish speech. The blessing is to be taken as something exhibitive (e.g., it is an objective, real power)."[69] Brongers gives much attention to the blessing itself, as if the blessing has a certain magical power. In reality, the biblical blessing never has anything to do with invisible powers in the universe, but rather with the covenant:

---

65. See Pedersen, *Israel*, 348.
66. Rowley understands *šᵉlāmīm* as "peace" and "well-being." *Worship*, 122–23.
67. See Murray, *Prerogative and Pretension*, 137–38.
68. Mowinckel regards David's blessing as an ancient royal practice: "Auch im alten Israel galt der König als heilig, als 'Sohn Jahwes,' durch die Salbung mit dem 'Geiste Jahwes' ausgerüstet, ein 'Elohim,' ein Gottwesen, der Kanal für den Segen der Gottheit; . . . Der sakrale König hat aber auch als 'Vertreter' seinen Platz unter den heiligen kultischen Personen." *Religion and Kultus*, 41. However, it is unknown if David used the priestly blessing mentioned in Num 6:24–26.
69. Brongers, "*bᵉsêm jhwh*," 8.

"it matters to the mighty God."⁷⁰ It is significant that the people of Yahweh can keep the blessing in their hearts as they return home.

To the blessing, David added a material gift. Second Samuel 6:19— "He gave a loaf of bread, a cake of dates and a cake of raisins to each person in the whole crowd of Israelites, from men to women"—underscores that "all the participants" received the presents. A cake of dates⁷¹ and a cake of raisins would be proper to take for a trip. Everyone had to receive this royal gift as coming from Yahweh, who now resided on Mount Zion (Ps 132:15).

Now that the ark has been set in Zion, the place comes to have a special meaning. It becomes "the city of God" (Ps 48:7) because God resides there (Isa 8:18). The city becomes the center of the religious life of the Israelites and the world (Ezek 38:12), since Yahweh reigns over the world as its King. Because of the designation Yahweh Zebaoth, Zion is designated as a place of unassailable strength.⁷² At any event, as Rendtorff's allusion, "bringing the ark was the first step with which the foundation for further development is put."⁷³ Namely the people of Israel in the reign of David came to meet another new phase in the progression of redemptive history: realization of the theocracy.

---

70. Greiner, *Segen und Segnen*, 186.

71. While the etymology and meaning of *ʾešpār* are uncertain, it can be translated as "a cake of dates" (*HALAT* 93; *DCH* 1:418). This translation is based on a corresponding root in Arabic which means "a traveler's provisions for a journey"; this could support the meaning here as "date-cake." Using the ancient versions (Tg, Vg), Goslinga thinks of it as a portion of meat on the basis of the numerous slaughters (*Samuël*, 122). This view is not acceptable, in light of the regulation of the peace offering: "The meat of his peace offering of thanksgiving must be eaten on the day it is offered; he must leave none of it till morning" (Lev 7:15). David could not run the risk that certain people might not eat the meat that day.

72. Such utterances in Psalms (46; 48; 76) about Zion do not have to be considered as productions of a "Zion-tradition," maintained to be associated with Jebusite tradition, or developed only after Jerusalem's deliverance from Assyrian aggression in 701 (see Strong, "Zion," *NIDOTTE* 4:1318–22). Rather, they show the redemptive progression of God's revelation in history: "The so-called Zion-theology is a theologoumenon that gains the power of a dogma in the biblical-critical Old Testament studies and that originates from an election tradition, namely, the election of Zion that runs parallel with that of the Davidic house. Particularly the tradition comes to the fore in Psalms and Isaiah." Ohmann, "Een top bereikt," 140.

73. Rendtorff, *Theologie*, 103.

H. THE TENSION BETWEEN DAVID AND MICHAL (2 SAM 6:20-63)

1. The Mockery of Michal (2 Sam 6:20)

It is obvious that the term "to bless" in this verse means more than just "greeting." Most likely, after the massive distribution, David went to the house, still in a festive and thankful mood, to wish the blessing of Yahweh on his family also. For him the joy of the people was also the joy of his family. However, the attitude of Michal, who was absent from the national ceremony, is unexpected: "How the king of Israel has distinguished himself today, disrobing in the sight of the maids of his servants as one of the foolish would shamelessly disrobe!" (v. 20). Ironically she speaks of "honor" (*kbd*), while she sketches its opposite meaning in the subordinate clause; Josephus mitigates the asperity of these insulting words by means of the initial prayer for the king's welfare.[74] It is striking that David does not stand up for himself but is prepared to disgrace himself ("disgrace" *qll*, v. 22)[75] even further in her eyes as long as his God is glorified. She greeted him with sarcastic criticism, accusing him of indecent behavior and disapproving of his actions. In her view David's honor consisted of the applause of female slaves by whom Michal appears to mean all the young women of Israel, even though *'amhōṯ* denotes literally "unfree women." There seems to be excessive scorn in her description of David's appearance, when she compares him with frivolous men (see Judg 9:4). What she may have had in mind was the heroic appearance of her husband as the king of a newly united kingdom rather than that of a godly king.

2. David's Answer (2 Sam 6:21-22)

The core of David's immediate and emphatic answer is the repeated phrase "before Yahweh," which summarizes why he behaved the way he did and how he did so. Michal's behavior identifies her as one who was not a child of God. The subordinate sentence informs us that he was the chosen king of Israel: "to choose" (*bḥr*) is not related with the "eternal election" of salvation. Instead it justifies his kingship. David was not appointed as a *męlęk*, but as a *nāg-īḏ* who stands in front, and is compared

---

74. Josephus, *Antiquities*, 7.87; Begg, "David's transfer," 34.

75. Crüsemann, "Witze," 225: "*qll* bildet nämelich die entscheidende sprachliche und sachliche Opposition zu *kbd*."

with the *praepositus* or *praefectus*. The same author makes it known that *nāgīd* has a stronger theological character.[76] In connection with *nāgīd*, it should be noted that it is doubtful whether it originally describes the charismatic warrior, for the term is not used for figures in the premonarchic period.

We can conclude that David's intention in this dialogue is simply to refute Michal's criticisms. All he does is to offer a reason for his behavior and then points out its validity.[77]

3. The Judgment of God (2 Sam 6:23)

The conflict between David and Michal is more than an ordinary marital quarrel; it has to do with the kingdom and God's redemptive history. The author tells us that God intervened in the debate. The copulative links in verse 23 with the scene described in verses 20–22 point out the result.[78] "Therefore, Michal, daughter of Saul, had no children to the day of her death" (v. 23).[79] It is clear that God punishes Michal; she remains barren. Her barrenness appears to have nothing to do with his intention to build his house. Sterility for women in Israel was a trial, sometimes associated with God's purposes (Gen 30:1; 1 Sam 1:5–6). In the case of Michal it is more severe than other cases because it is a result of unbelief; she despised joy in the presence of God, was not interested in the entrance

---

76. See Ohmann, "Een top bereikt," 134; Koolhaas, *Theocratie*, 65: "The theocratic character that had this naming as a title for the king of Israel especially continues to appear: *nāgīd* over my people Israel. Just in this connection, it puts the special place of Israelite monarch under King Yahweh."

77. It is interesting to note that structurally Brueggemann asserts that the Yahwistic claim is centered on the conversation between the two (*Samuel*, 253). We can see this through the use of a fantastic chiastic structure created by Murray, *Prerogative and Pretension*, 155.

78. White rejects the conjunction as a causal relationship because he regards it as the final statement about her at this point. Thus, her barrenness has not been caused by this incident at all ("Michal," 461–63). In this case the reason why the final statement is placed here and the narrator describes David as a hero may have to be clarified enough.

79. The result of the argument between David and Michal should not be treated as an explicit reflection of the pro-Davidic tradition because the view of redaction criticism is not so helpful to understand God's revelatory history in this text. "Warum hatte König David keine Kinder mit seiner ersten Frau, der Königstochter Michal? Wer diese Frage stelle, ist nicht schwer zu erraten: die Anhänger des Hauses Saul, allgemein die in Davids Reich offenbar nie zufriedenen Nordisraeliten. Wer ihren hier eine Antwort erteilt, ist ebenfalls klar: prodavidische, höfische Kreise." Dietrich and Naumann, *Samuelbücher*, 136.

of the ark, and was indifferent to the notion of being under God's reign. Her childlessness meant that because of her unbelief she lost the opportunity to become the mother of David's heir.[80] Hence, she was excluded from the throne of the great king and a place in the Messianic line. Through the completion of the punishment and rejection of Saul and his house, announced in 1 Samuel 13 and 15, Saul's blood was entirely excluded from the throne of Israel.[81] This is a part of God's judgment on Saul's house (see 2 Sam 21:1–14). This event's bearing on the attitude towards the ark of Yahweh displays that God's redemptive history proceeds through the faith in him.

---

80. See Smelik, "Hidden Messages," 58.

81. See Hertzberg, *Samuelbücher*, 230; Rezetko, *Source and Revision*, 231. Rowe (*Dilemma*, 203) states that "in the absence of male heirs transmission of the patrimony to the grandsons was through daughters."

9

The Ark in the Book of 1 Kings

A. CONTEXT

THE BOOK OF KINGS commences with the problem of Solomon's succession to the throne. Taking advantage of the passive attitude of the old and enfeebled King David (1:1–4) with regard to the succession, Adonijah conspired with Joab and Abiathar to proclaim himself king (1:5–7). However, the intrigue came to nothing because, according to his oath (1:17) and God's word (1 Chr 22:9), David ensured that Solomon was to be king (1 Kgs 1:33–35).

Solomon, acclaimed king of the united monarchy of Israel, began to exercise power by conducting a purge of accomplices and reactionaries, such as Adonijah, Joab, and Abiathar, to tighten official discipline and fulfill David's will. His expurgation cannot be evaluated as entirely political. The death of Abiathar belongs to the fulfillment of God's prophetic words addressed to Samuel (2:27). Solomon's reign, on the whole, was peaceful: there appears to be only one military campaign towards Hamath Zobah (2 Chr 8:3). Instead of serious military operations, he had to strengthen the realm that David built into a small empire. He fortified the major cities such as Jerusalem, Hazor, Megiddo, Gezer, Upper Beth Horon, and Lower Beth Horon (see 1 Kgs 9:15, 17–19; 2 Chr 8:5–6). Although he was already married to Naamah, Rehoboam's mother (1 Kgs 14:21), he made numerous foreign noblewomen his wives to strengthen diplomatic ties with neighboring countries. Most distinguished of Solomon's wives was the daughter of the pharaoh of Egypt, who is probably identified with Siamun, the penultimate pharaoh of the feeble Twenty-first Dynasty.[1] It shows how elevated the international prestige of Solomon's kingdom was.

He ruled the people with outstanding wisdom given in answer to his prayers (1 Kgs 3:12; 4:29; 10:1–4). Furthermore, through vigorous trade with surrounding countries including Arabia (probably related to Sheba's visit), he achieved unprecedented prosperity for Israel.[2] Jesus' reference to "Solomon's glory" verifies that his kingdom attained the heights of prosperity (Matt 6:29). The temple he constructed in Zion, through his amicable relationship with Hiram, must be recognized as his most brilliant feat. This was a significant event in Israelite religion and history. The construction of the temple meant that the "rest" ($m^e n\bar{u}\d{h}\bar{a}$) that Yahweh promised to Moses was accomplished (1 Kgs 8:56).

David had transferred the ark to Jerusalem and so it was placed in the inner sanctuary of the temple, the most holy place. It is most likely that the date of this historical event was September or October (*Ethanim* by the old calendar, that is, Babylonian Tishri) between 961–958 BC when the beginning of Solomon's reign was dated in 973–970 BC and one year after the completion of the building (see 1 Kgs 6:38, 8:2).[3]

B. SOLOMON'S SUMMONS TO ASSEMBLE THE PEOPLE (1 KGS 8:1–3A)

"Then Solomon assembled the elders of Israel, and all the heads of the tribes, the chief of the Israelite families, to King Solomon in Jerusalem, to bring up the ark of the covenant of Yahweh from the city of David, which is Zion. And all the men of Israel were assembled to King Solomon in the month of Ethanim, at the feast which is the seventh month. And all the elders of Israel came" (vv. 1–3a). The centerpiece of Solomon's dedication was the transportation of the ark of the covenant from the tent David had prepared for it (2 Sam 6) into the Holy of Holies of the new temple. After finishing the project of building the temple (1 Kgs 7:51), Solomon assembled (*qhl*) the elders to complete his dedication, by furnishing the temple with the ark. The word "to assemble" (*qhl*), the substantive, was generally translated as *ekklēsiajō* in LXX and was here associated with religious assembly, albeit it was often used to

---

1. Green, "Solomon and Siamun," 66; Bright, *History*, 207–8.
2. See Kitchen, "Sheba and Arabia," 138–39.
3. See Handy, "Dates," 105.

designate persons gathered for a military reason (Gen 49:6; Judg 20:2; 21:5, 8; 1 Sam 17:47; 2 Chr 28:14; etc.). During the mornarchic period, elders chiefly appear as the leaders of their local communities, who are commonly referred to "the elders of the town" (1 Sam 16:4).[4] The elders/heads of all the tribes of Israel were to attend this special cultic manifestation.[5] The heads were the titular "chiefs of the Israelite families," the ones responsible for learning the law and leading their families to obey it.[6] The text seems to stress the single-minded, unanimous participation of the people (note the use of the word "all"): "the elders of Israel, all the heads of the tribes, the chiefs of the fathers of Israelites" (1 Kgs 8:1). This convocation of the leaders throughout the country is enough to display the gravity of the cultic event.

The ark of the covenant of Yahweh was about to be transferred from its old location, the city of David, which is identified as Zion, to the new temple that was built on the summit of Mount Moriah where David sanctified the threshing floor of Araunah.[7] It reminds us that the temple was constructed outside the confines of David's Jerusalem, which consisted of the city of David.[8] With this opportunity, the boundaries of Zion could presumably be expanded to the Temple Mount (see Pss 9:12; 20:3; 48:3; 50:2).

Solomon chose to bring the ark into the temple during the feast in the month of Ethanim,[9] the seventh month, coinciding with our months of September/October. The feast (*ḥag*) points to the Feast of Tabernacles,[10] the most prominent of the three great pilgrim feasts that traditionally took place during this month (Lev 23:34).[11] This date means

---

4. Aitken, "zāqēn," *NIDOTTE* 1:1138.
5. See Mulder, *I Kings*, 378.
6. Hubbard, *Kings*, 52.
7. See E. Mazar and B. Mazar, *Excavations*, 53.
8. Mare, *Archaeology*, 26.
9. "The term 'Ethanim' appears in Phoenician inscriptions as the name for the seventh month, which indicates that it was a Canaanite name employed in Israel much like the names Ziv and Bul (1 Kgs 6:1, 37–38) prior to the introduction of the Babylonian calendar." Sweeney, *Kings*, 131.
10. LXX lacks "at the feast which is the seventh month." "The minus element of G*, which may also be considered a plus of M+, contains the first mention of 'the Feast (of Tabernacles) in the historical books." Tov, *Textual Criticism*, 268.
11. Many scholars believe that the Feast of Tabernacles in Israel was of Canaanite origin, but Moses commanded the Israelites to observe the feast in the wilderness be-

that there is a gap in time between completion of the project and its dedication, as suggested in 1 Kings 6:38: "in the month of Bul, the eighth month, the temple was finished in all its details according to its specifications." Thus, Solomon waited for eleven months at least to transport the ark into the temple after all the work he had done for the temple of Yahweh had been finished.[12]

The Feast of Tabernacles is the only festival event in the Israelite calendar wherein God commands rejoicing (Deut 12:7, 12, 18; 14:26; 16:11, 14; 26:11; 27:7). The Israelites were to celebrate this occasion by living in tents for the week of the feast. That was to commemorate the departure from Egypt and the sojourn in the tents during the long journey through the wilderness to Sinai (Lev 23:43). Moses wrote the Book of the Law for the establishment and the renewal of the covenant with all Israelites and ordered them to read it at the observance of this feast every seven years (Deut 31:9–13). Thus, Solomon's choice of the Feast of Tabernacles for this historic event was strategic in that it was at the traditional time of national gathering and a reminder of three things: 1) Israel's deliverance from Egypt, 2) the gracious guidance of Yahweh through the wilderness, 3) that this was a time of covenantal renewal.[13]

C. TRANSFER OF THE ARK AND SACRIFICES (1 KGS 8:3B–5)

"The priests took up the ark, and they brought up the ark of Yahweh and the tent of meeting and all the sacred vessels in it. The priests and Levites brought them up" (vv. 3b–4). The relationship between the priests and Levites is evident in the process of historical progress. According to Mosaic law (Deut 18:18), the priests appear to be distinguished from

---

fore their entrance to Canaan. Kronholm, "*sākak*," *ThWAT* 5:838–56.

12. Von Ewald holds that Solomon dedicated the temple before it was finished: " . . . the king determined to arrange the festival of the actual consecrating of the new sanctuary in this month, so that the dedication of the temple should take place the week before" (*History*, 245). However, such a statement is directly challenged by the report of completion of the temple's construction in 1 Kgs 7:51. To show the reason why he had to delay the event, Mulder searches in the New Year's festival Canaanite world, by mentioning that de Moor stresses the link between the New Year's festival and the Feast of Dedication of the Baal temple. According to them, Solomon's delaying the function was an act of obedience to an ancient eastern tradition according to which sanctuaries must preferably be dedicated on a New Year's Day that coincides with the feast of the king's own coronation. Yet, this explanation appears not to gain support from the Bible. See Mulder, *I Kings*, 381–82; de Moor, *Seasonal Pattern*, 59–60.

13. See House, *Kings*, 137.

the Levites. As a result, their tasks are different from those of the Levites: carrying the ark was one important duty of the priests (Deut 10:8; 31:9), while the Levites were the guardians of the tabernacle and the protectors of the sanctuary from unlawful entry (see Num 4:15). During the period of Ezekiel, the Levites had a subordinate order of cultic officials,[14] albeit the terms "the Levites" and "the priests" were treated synonymously in the period of Malachi.[15] David also used both terms without any distinction (1 Chr 15:11–15, 26). However, the distinction appears not to be based on hierarchy but on function when their position and duties were treated differently. In this text, with the spiritual assistance of non-Levite leaders, the priests were in charge of carrying the ark, and the Levites were charged with carrying the tent of meeting, along with the sacred vessels, to the temple. To bring up the tent of meeting was not to use it as a revelatory tent because the newly built temple substituted for its function from that moment on. This practice by the priests and Levites, as a whole, coincides with the Mosaic regulations. Solomon was careful not to repeat the blunder David made when he transferred the ark to Jerusalem (2 Sam 6:3).

"And King Solomon and the entire congregation of Israel that were assembled with him were before the ark, sacrificing so many sheep and oxen that they could not be recorded or counted" (1 Kgs 8:5). It was "before the ark" that the whole assembly of the Israelites sacrificed innumerable sheep and oxen: before the visible symbol of the presence of Yahweh. The stem-modification of the verb "sacrificing" ($m^ezabb^eh\bar{\imath}m$, pi. pt. pl) frequently conveys an iterative and successive element.[16] The expression, "they could not be recorded or counted," which demonstrates the splendid scale of the feast sacrifice, implies an unsurpassable dimension in the material sense even though the exact number of the sacrifices is recorded in 1 Kings 8:62–63. It is interesting to note that Josephus describes the superlative degree of this sacrifice "drenching the ground with libations and the blood of numerous victims, and burning

---

14. Gunneweg, *Leviten und Priester*, 185: "Aaroniden und Leviten zusammen bilden den Stamm Levi, die Aaroniden sind die Priester, die Leviten ihnen als Clerus minor unterstellt. Stellung und Aufgabe jeder der beiden Klassen sind genau festgelegt."

15. See O'Brien, *Priest and Levite*, 48.

16. Jenni, *Pi'el*, 205.

so vast a quantity of incense that all the air around was filled with it and carried its sweetness to those who were at a great distance."[17]

D. THE INSTALLATION OF THE ARK (1 KGS 8:6–11)

"The priests then brought the ark of covenant of Yahweh to its place in the inner sanctuary of the temple, the most holy place, beneath the wings of the cherubim. For the cherubim spread their wings over the place of the ark and overshadowed the ark and its poles" (vv. 6–7). The climax of this festive event is when the ark reaches its destination. The ark is placed in the inner sanctuary (*mᵉqōmō ʾel-debīr*) of the temple, the most holy place (6:16) that Solomon had specially prepared (6:19).[18] The text indicates that *māqōm* (place) of the ark is in the *debīr* of the temple. However, the *māqōm* cannot refer to a separate shrine within the *debīr* (see 6:19). Moreover, the fact that the *debīr* already carries the superlative title the most holy place hardly leaves room for an even more special shrine for its principal cultic appurtenance.[19] Actually, the redundant expression consisting of four elements (its place, the inner sanctuary of the temple, the most holy place, beneath the wings of the cherubim) refers to the same position as apposition to emphasize the importance of the place of the ark. The ark comes to rest under the wings of the cherubim that stretch from wall to wall and are different from the cherubim on the ark (6:27). They covered the ark to protect it. The cherubim (see chapter 2C) reflect the glorious and majestic presence of Yahweh at the ark that is positioned in the most holy place of the temple, Yahweh's eternal dwelling place (8:13). This description of bringing up the ark illustrates that the ark was still symbolizing the presence of Yahweh among his people, unlike the tent of meeting. However, Fritz describes it as if the role of the ark is of no consequence after its installation in the temple.[20] But the ark was treated differently from the tent of meeting, which had played a part from the period of the wilderness but is now replaced with the temple.

17. Josephus, *Antiquities*, 8:102.
18. The rendering (the oracle of the house) of KJV for *debīr* does not make sense.
19. Murray, "MQWM and Future," 302–3.
20. "Das Zeltheiligtum wird von Tempel abgelöst, indem die Lade in den Tempel übernommen wird. Im Tempel hat die Lade dann keine besondere Bedeutung mehr besessen, da die Vorstellung der Bindung göttlicher Gegenwart an die Lade durch die Vorstellung vom Wohnen Gottes im Tempel verdrängt worden ist." Fritz, *Könige*, 86.

"These poles were so long that their ends could be seen from the holy place in front of the inner sanctuary, but not from outside the holy place; and they are still there today" (8:8). The long poles were permanently attached to the ark (Exod 25:12–15), but this passage makes it clear that these were attached to the long side of the ark and extended through the curtain in front of the the holy of holies; their ends could be seen from the holy place in front of it. The poles remain in the ark to serve as a visible reminder of the hidden ark's presence. The phrase "still today" (literally, "until this day") refers to a point of time before the ark was lost in the destruction of the temple 586 BC.[21]

"There was nothing in the ark except the two stone tablets that Moses put in it at Horeb, where Yahweh made a covenant with the Israelites when they came out of Egypt" (1 Kgs 8:9). Most exegetes are perplexed over the annotation of this verse. Noth suggests that "explicit emphasis... wants to avert the purely apocryphal idea such as that of Heb 9:4 according to which the jar with Mannah (Exod 16:33) and Aaron's staff (Num 17:25) were stored in the ark."[22] His comment appears not to appreciate the evidence of the New Testament (i.e., the latter two objects never existed). Similarly, Fritz appears to attribute this phrase directly to the character of "Deuteronomistic Theology."[23] Mulder is more emphatic because "a great deal more of the Canaanite religious legacy was incorporated in the new temple without any of the usual polemics."[24] His assumption was derived from the tension between the northern tribes and Jerusalem.[25] He seems to consider the word "only" (*raq*) as a later addition of the redactor. Another solution was provided by House: "This emphatic comment probably is intended to clear up the possible misconceptions that Aaron's rod and a jar of manna were there as well. These items were placed alongside the ark but never in it."[26] His suggestion appears plausible to some extent. However, the remark stressed by the term "only" may still hint that there were only the stone tablets in the ark at the time but there had been other things in it before. Thus the word "only" leads the readers in the period of the New Testament

21. See Cogan, 1 *Kings*, 280.
22. Noth, *Könige* 1, 180.
23. Fritz, *Könige*, 87.
24. Mulder, *I Kings*, 392.
25. Ibid., 388.
26. House, *Kings*, 13.

to be conscious of harmony with the content of Hebrews 9:4. It may be conceivable that the jar of manna and Aaron's staff may have been lost in an unknown disaster before Solomon's temple, which appears consistent with the stories told in the two testaments.

The text makes it clear that there was nothing in the ark except the two stone tablets. It still remains a mystery that the two other items vanished before Solomon's temple was built. However, from the viewpoint of the progress of revelatory history, it seems reasonable that the jar of manna and Aaron's staff disappeared since they were particularly associated with the Israelites' life in the wilderness. Above all, Aaron's priestly succession was broken (see 2 Sam 2:35; 1 Kgs 2:27) and Yahweh, in the resting place, gave the "rest" that he had promised Moses and now would bless the people with abundant provisions (see 1 Kgs 8:56; Ps 132:16). Thus, the jar of manna and Aaron's staff might have played no special role in the period when the temple became a central part of Israelite religion, just as the tent of meeting lost its function at that time.[27]

Adding the supplementary explanation that Moses put the two stone tablets in the ark at Horeb, which is identical to Sinai (see Deut 10:5), the author highlights the Israelite covenantal relationship with Yahweh when they came out of Egypt. The Decalogue inscribed on the tablets still remains the fundamental law of the covenant community. Apart from political notions such as a contract between king and people,[28] the reference to the Decalogue demonstrates that the Solomonic temple is connected with the Sinaitic covenant, and the covenant law of Israel conditions God's presence in the temple. Thus the ark placed in the temple appears to grant legitimacy to the temple as God's residence.

"When the priests came out of the holy place, the cloud filled the house of Yahweh. And the priests could not stand to minister because of the cloud, for the glory of Yahweh filled Yahweh's house" (1 Kgs 8:10–11). These verses correspond in many respects to Exodus 40:34–35. What happened to Moses there as the cloud descended on the tabernacle also happens to the priests in these verses. The cloud is identified with "the

---

27. Calvin implies this possibility of the proposal: "it is hence probable that they were deposited in the ark, together with the tables. But when the Temple was built, these things were arranged in a different order, and certainly history relates it as a thing new that the ark had nothing else but the two tables." *Paul*, 196–97.

28. See J. Maier, *Heiligtum*, 70–71. The whole scene of this narrative suggests that Solomon's project was not simply motivated by a political concern, as Buis supposes (*Le Livre*, 97).

glory of Yahweh," so that "the glory of Yahweh" is present in the cloud (Exod 16:10). Here, "the glory of Yahweh" and "the cloud" signaled that Yahweh approved of his new quarters and had occupied them, as he did so with the cloud filling the tabernacle when Moses dedicated that earlier worship center. The expression "stand to minister" was used as a typical expression for the official work of the priests before Yahweh (Num 16:8–9; Deut 10:8; Ezek 44:11; 2 Chr 29:11). The awesome glory of Yahweh appears to prevent them from serving Yahweh temporarily. As a whole, these verses serve to underscore that after the transfer of the ark the Solomonic temple is the legitimate continuation of the dwelling of Yahweh, who in the time of Moses dwelt in a wilderness sanctuary.[29] Here the ark of Yahweh, which is a revelatory instrument of divine attributes, adds greater glory to Solomonic temple. Yahweh's people are continually able to live before his glorious presence.

---

29. See Mulder, *I Kings*, 396.

10

The Ark in the Poetic and Prophetic Books

A. THE ARK IN PSALM 132

PSALM 132 IS THE only psalm wherein the term "ark" is explicitly mentioned in the Psalter, although there are some allusions to the ark in the Psalms without any consensus of opinion on which passages imply the ark. In fact, it is unnecessary to deal with all psalmic references that appear to refer to the ark because it is sufficient enough to grasp the use and significance of the ark in Israelite worship from the texts in this study. Hence, Psalm 132, which is obviously associated with the ark, will be singled out as the object of exegesis in this chapter.

1. The Psalm's Origin and Form

Psalm 132's origin is fraught with controversy. Gunkel dates the psalm at a later period in the kingdom of Judah by assuming the Davidic monarchy as a contemporary institution.[1] On its definitive content, Jacquet is sure that this psalm is a product of the liturgy of the Second Temple.[2] Seybold classifies this psalm as a pilgrim's psalm, which was derived from the post-exilic situation, by acknowledging that Psalm 132:8–10 quoted old materials such as 2 Chronicles 6:41–42.[3] Pietsch ascribes this psalm to the Persian period because of its unitive and intentional

---

1. "Keine Spur ist in dem Liede davon, daß Jahve Zion inzwischen verlassen hätte, oder daß Davidhaus nicht mehr im Besitz der Krone wäre. Daß schon von den Söhnen der Söhne Davids gesprochen wird, führt in eine spätere Zeit des judäischen Königtums" Gunkel, *Die Psalmen*, 586.
2. Jacquet, *Psaumes et cœur*, 525.
3. Seybold, *Die Psalmen*, 11, 497.

composition.[4] Rogerson and McKay appear to take a compromised view. They believe verses 1–16 comprise a psalm composed before the exile, while verses 17–18 were added after the exile.[5] However, the latter is possible only when their translation of the Hebrew phrase of verse 17a, *šām 'aṣmîᵃḥ qeren lᵉdāwiḏ*, "There will I renew the line of David's house," is justified.

However, many scholars state that the psalm dates from the late pre-exilic period, on the grounds that the quoted material is much more ancient. They believe that the date should be firmly fixed before Solomon's death[6] and the material contains an accumulation of allegedly deuteronomistic features such as "servant" (v. 10), "fruit of womb" (v. 11), and "lamp" (v. 17).[7] Resting upon Mettinger's statement that Psalm 132 exhibits a later development of the basic promise of Nathan in 2 Samuel 7, Allen judges that Psalm 132 is a royal and prophetic liturgy that did not necessarily originate later than the period of Josiah. Allen concludes this by recognizing the possibility that a later form of the tradition of Nathan's promise is echoed in verses 11–12.[8]

However, it seems more important to note that the term "ark" is explicitly mentioned in this psalm, in contrast with the fact that it is hardly mentioned in the rest of the Psalms; the reference to the ark looks like a reflection of the pre-exilic situation of the First Temple.[9] Of course, it is true that this psalm offers a recollection of the past related to David's transportation of the ark to Zion. Yet, before we make the mistake of seeing a clear connection with the cult of the Second Temple, it should be noted that interest in the ark had probably disappeared from the liturgy. Jeremiah's prophecy implies that the ark was obsolete in the service of the temple: "'When you are multiplied and increased in the land, in those days,' Yahweh declares, 'they will no longer say, "the ark of the covenant of Yahweh," it will not enter into mind, and they will not

---

4. "Psalm 132 hat sich eine einheitliche und planvoll gestaltete Komposition aus der persischen Zeit erwiesen, in deren Zentrum eine aktualisierende Neuinterpretation der Nathanverheißung steht." Pietsch, » *Sproß Davids . . .* « 137.

5. Rogerson and McKay, *Psalms*, 136–37.

6. Roberts, "Davidic Origin," 343.

7. Mettinger, *King and Messiah*, 276–78.

8. Allen, *Psalms*, 209.

9. "Da die Heilige Lade erwähnt wird v. 7f . . . kann der Psalm nur aus der vorexilischen Zeit stammen." Weiser, *Die Psalmen*, 538.

remember it, and they will not miss it, and it will not be made again'" (Jer 3:16b). In addition to this, Rendsburg contends that linguistic evidence proves that Psalm 132 has a northern quality and composition; it refers back to earlier Israelite history.[10] Hence, the origin of Psalm 132 appears to match the liturgical features of the pre-exilic state. Yet, the possibility that this psalm was composed to commemorate the dedicatory event of Solomon's temple cannot be entirely dismissed.[11]

As to the form of Psalm 132, it is very intricate. In order to analyze its structure, we need to consider certain clues. A variety of structural forms have been suggested,[12] but there is a general agreement that this psalm can be divided into two major sections: verses 1–10 and 11–18, each introduced by the recall of an oath and its citation (vv. 2–5 and 11–12).[13] The first section concerns David's role in finding a resting place for Yahweh and the second concerns Yahweh's role in maintaining David's throne in Zion. Undoubtedly, it is not intended that there be two independent poems. In fact, the whole psalm is composed as a prayer and an answer according to the respective sections. This is the decisive literary feature of this rather complex composition; the form and the content are harmonized, as šûḇ in verse 10 and šûḇ in verse 11 are interwoven in content. There is no clear evidence that these psalms were collected and selected by a theologian, historian, or literary editor to formulate a supposed historical event.[14]

---

10. Rendsburg, *Linguistic Evidence*, 87–90.

11. See Van Groningen, *Messianic Revelation*, 311–12.

12. Dahood classifies it into three stanzas: 1–5, 6–10, and 11–18 (*Psalms*, 241–42); Seybold divides it into four strophes: 1–5, 6–10, 11–13, and 14–18 (*Die Psalmen*, 496–99); Jacquet divides it into five different literary models: prayer (1, 10), oath (3–5, 11c–12), quotation (2, 11ab, 13), professional song (6–9), and oracle (15–18) (*Psaumes et cœur*, 525); Fretheim makes a litany composed of four parts between priest and choir ("Cultic Use," 129–30).

13. See Gunkel, *Die Psalmen*, 565–67; Weiser, *Die Psalmen*, 538–40.

14. Bentzen, *King and Messiah*, 32. Some recent scholars such as Seow and Starbuck argue that the coalescence of Zion theology and royal (Davidic) theology into a royal/Zion amalgamated theology occurred early in the history of the Israelite monarchy. The section reflecting the historical event (vv. 6–9) may be interpreted eccentrically in prayer but it appears natural to refer these verses to the epochal moment of David's transfer of the ark to Zion and Yahweh's election of it. Seow, *Myth, Drama*, 185–96; Starbuck, *Court Oracles*, 125. For the most detailed analysis of this psalm, consult Auffret, *Là moment*, 96–111.

In attempting to determine its genre, the psalm has been classified as a "Song of Zion,"[15] a "Royal psalm,"[16] and simply a liturgy.[17] Bentzen in particular regards it as a "historified myth," while the story of the ark is a "Davidic version" of the myth.[18] It is true that the various topics proposed as its genre have some value, for they contain some important elements of the Psalms. However, most commentators tend, intentionally or unintentionally, to overlook the title of the psalm, deemed as traditionally conceived by the compiler—a "song of ascents." It seems unnecessary to preclude its title. It appears unreasonable to ignore the possibility that this psalm belongs to the pilgrims' songs, as Seybold suggested above. The reason why this psalm has been included in the sub-collection of ascent psalms is that just as David was faithful in finding the ark and a resting place for Yahweh, so too the pilgrims, as they made their way to that same Zion, shared in David's faithfulness, seeking to prostrate themselves at Yahweh's footstool. The Israelites, who were required to go up to the temple three times a year, would sing this psalm on their way to Zion.

2. David's Role in Finding a Resting Place for Yahweh (Ps 132:1–10)

The psalm begins with a petition, a supplication to Yahweh: "Yahweh, for David, remember all his afflictions" (v. 1). "For David" ($l^e d\bar{a}wi\underline{d}$) is not to be the object of the verb, even if the preposition l^e can be sometimes used to introduce a direct object (see Exod 32:13; Deut 9:27; Pss 25:7; 136:23). Yet, the phrase $l^e d\bar{a}wi\underline{d}$ does not denote that this psalm is a prayer for David who is dead, but rather signifies "on behalf of his merit in the past" (see Ps 132:10). The verb "to remember" (*zkr*) is here used in a specific construction, in which not only what is thought of is mentioned, but also the person for whom this is a remembrance. David's affliction as the object of the verb "remember" should not be understood in the merely mental or physical state but on the level of piety as well.[19] The purpose of the prayer is to recall the pious hardships that David had endured in fulfilling the vow he had made to Yahweh. This seems to have something

---

15. Gunkel, *Die Psalmen*, 568.
16. See Holladay, *Psalms*, 69.
17. See Kraus, *Psalmen*, 1576.
18. Bentzen, *King and Messiah*, 32.
19. LXX's rendering, πραΰτητος, "humility," can help us understand this, although the Akkadian cognate *anāḫu* supports the Hebrew meaning, "toil." *CAD* A2:101.

to do with the transportation of the ark to Jerusalem (vv. 2–5). With respect to the oaths, it is interesting to notice that David's oath to Yahweh (v. 2) is paralleled by Yahweh's oath to David (v. 11) and the content of the oath of David to Yahweh (vv. 3–5, in the first person) corresponds to the content of the oath of Yahweh to David (vv. 11b–12, in the first person).[20] Verses 3–5 describe David's resolution not to allow himself rest until his oath is fulfilled. As for the phrase "I will not climb up into my bed" (v. 3b), Rogerson and McKay apply an ascetic conception to help interpreting this expression: "probably, he abstains from marital intercourse, a self-denial that often accompanied vows."[21] However, it seems more likely to be a reference to sleep, since their interpretation is immediately challenged by the following verse: "I will not allow sleep to my eyes, nor slumber to my eyelids" (v. 4). The verses 3 and 4 appear to consist of progressive parallels in some way. It is natural to maintain that the object of David's fervor is associated with the divine abode by the discovery of the ark and its transfer to the city of David, rather than the tent of meeting or the temple. David was filled with perplexity on account of the ark because he knew of Moses' law, according to which the Israelites would worship Yahweh in the place he chose (Deut 12:5). David's anxiety indicates his affection and desire to be with God.

The divine epithet "the Mighty One of Jacob," which occurs in Psalm 132:2 and 5 (and Gen 49:24; Isa 49:26), seems to reflect the intimacy between Israel and God. "The place of Yahweh" and "dwellings for the Mighty One of Jacob" (Ps 132:5) that David was fervently eager to find are to be conceived as having the same connotations as "his dwellings" and "his footstool" (v. 7). The correct translation of verse 6 is "We heard of it in Ephrathah."[22] But a grammatical difficulty arises in this sentence. What the object *hā* (fem. sg.) "it" indicates is debatable because there is no antecedent for "it" in the previous sentence; "place" (*māqōm*) has a masc. sg. form and "dwellings" (*miškānōṯ*) has fem. pl. form. It appears to be understandable that Mays understood it as the ark in accordance with the content.[23] Yet it is rather forced to refer to the word dwellings. The term "we" appears to be employed as a kind of

---

20. See Fretheim, "Cultic Use," 132; Auffret, *Sagesse*, 506.
21. Rogerson and McKay, *Psalms*, 138.
22. Kön, III§22.
23. Mays, *Psalms*, 411.

foreshadowing.[24] Ephrathah is probably the region where Kiriath-Jearim was located or otherwise a village or town not far from it. Ephrathah in verse 6 is perhaps geographically different from Bethlehem.[25] The phrase that follows, "the fields of Jaar" (v. 6b), is described as a poetic designation of the surroundings of Kiriath-Jearim:[26] in "the fields of Jaar" is the house of Abinadab, on a hill, the place where the ark was housed after it returned from Philistia (see 1 Sam 6:21; 7:1; 2 Sam 6:3).[27]

"Let us go to his dwellings, let us worship at his footstool" (Ps 132:7). The psalmist exhorts the worshipers to go up to the place where the ark is placed in the mount of Zion. In this verse the relation between "his dwellings" and "his footstool" may be regarded as a synonymous parallel. It means that "his footstool" refers to the entire temple or Mount Zion rather than to the ark (see chapter 4E).[28]

God's footstool is a metaphorical expression for a "resting place" (v. 14) for the feet of the enthroned deity, unlike Solomon's actual throne (2 Chr 9:18). In Psalms 99:5 and 132:7, and in Lamentations 2:1, footstool is a metaphor for Zion. While God sits on the heavenly throne as universal and eternal ruler (Pss 11:4; 103:19), he puts his feet on the earth, specifically on Zion. This image matches God's various attributes: greatness (Pss 48:1; 99:2; etc.), glory (Pss 8:1; 19:1; 148:13), majesty (Ps 93:1; 1 Chr 29:1), righteousness (Ps 9:4), lordship (Acts 4:24), supremacy (Ps 119:91; Isa 48:13), and dominion (Col 1:16), etc. The footstool as an earthly counterpart to the heavenly throne stresses divine immanence, although God's intrinsic attributes are transcendent. The fact that Zion is the footstool literally does not mean that God treads it under his feet in some negative way, as Yahweh made David's enemies his footstool.

24. "Zuerst spricht ein Wir, die Suchgruppe Davids (6f.), dann ein Beter, der im Stil der Ladesprüche (Num 10, 35f.) JHWH zum Aufbruch auffordert (8f.)." Seybold, *Die Psalmen*, 498.

25. Referencing 1 Sam 17:12, Briend denotes that Ephrathah was mistakenly identified with Bethlehem, since it was David's city and he was the son of Jesse from the village of Ephrathah. "Bethléem-Ephratha," 29.

26. See Kraus, *Psalmen*, 1063.

27. Rendsburg prefers to interpret Ephrathah in v. 6 as an alternative designation for Ephraim, the connotation of which makes much more sense (*Linguistic Evidence*, 88). After all, the home of the ark for most of Israel's early history was in Shiloh in the territory of Ephraim. However, this argument doesn't fit well with the biblical story of David bringing the ark into the city of David.

28. See Haran, "Ark and Cherubim," 91. Haran believes that "the symbolic significance of the footstool, which is attributed to the ark, is primary, almost archaic."

Instead the royal footstool stands for God's sublime and simultaneously gracious presence. That is why Zion as God's footstool is the center of his people's worship, but they approach it to pay obeisance to God by expecting his righteous judgment (Pss 9:4–7; 45:6; 89:14; 97:2) and gracious reign (Pss 47:8; 93:1–2; 103:19).

In the context of this psalm, the "dwellings" and "footstool" that the psalmist mentioned can really be understood only in connection with the ark, which signifies the invisible presence of Yahweh. The epithet "footstool," which is related to the ark, demonstrates his glorious and majestic presence and at the same time intimates that the sanctuary could never contain the immensity of his essence, as men are prone to imagine. The mere outward temple with all its majesty being no more than his footstool, his people were called upon to look upwards to the heavens and fix their contemplations with due reverence upon God himself.[29] The psalmist exhorts the people to go up to the place, to worship God, who is present at the ark and in the temple where it is placed, even though he is omnipresent throughout the whole universe. In this verse, the steps of the pilgrims reach their climax.[30]

"Arise, Yahweh, to your resting place, you with the ark of your might" (Ps 132:8). The pregnant construction of "arise . . . to" (*qūmā . . . lᵉ*) seems awkward. It should be rendered as "arise and (come) to" in the context. However, Hillers opposes this general rendering. He interprets the preposition *lᵉ* as "from" instead of "to" by appealing to the absence of examples of such a usage.[31] He also translates the preposition as "from" on the basis of Dahood's suggestion (*sub* "*l*, from"). Actually, it seems clumsy that this phrase is put as "arise and rest," since the verb was used mostly as a call for God to intervene vigorously on the people's behalf (see Num 10:35; Pss 3:8; 7:7; 9:20; 10:12; 17:13; 35:2; 76:10, etc.). His suggestion seems reasonable, but raises another question: Does the notion that Yahweh should rise with the ark and leave Zion, his resting place, even exist in the Old Testament?[32] There is nothing that parallels the prayer that Yahweh leave Zion. Furthermore, Dahood himself rejects Hillers's rendering "from," because he believes that this destroys

---

29. Calvin, *Psalms*, 149–50.
30. See Millard, *Komposition*, 220.
31. Hillers, "Ritual Procession," 48–52.
32. Booij, *Godswoorden*, 341.

the parallelism between verse 7 and 8.³³ The reason Hillers tried to translate the preposition *lᵉ* as "from" appears to be his intention to challenge Mowinckel's theory that the ark was in procession during the time when Solomon's temple was standing. Willis, following Hillers, rightly observed that the phrase "arise Yahweh" (*qūmā yahweh*) is basically a military plea or summons.³⁴ Yet, he had to consider the construction of the verb with the preposition *lᵉ*.

As a matter of fact, many other scholars, such as Fretheim, Kraus, Weiser, and Mays, maintain that this verse is the central passage referring to the annual festival of the procession of the ark.³⁵ However, its use seems different when Psalm 132 is classified as a song of pilgrims rather than a liturgical psalm. Allen argues that the psalm most likely used material concerning an "ark procession," but adds that this psalm does not necessarily belong to the cultic milieu of the ark, which did not demand a special annual celebration.³⁶ Rather, this verse invites Yahweh, the God of heaven and earth, who symbolically dwells with the ark, to come into a new place of residence. The pilgrims who climbed to Zion would sing this part of the psalm in remembrance of the pivotal event that David performed at Jerusalem. "The ark of your might" recalls the use of the ark in the holy wars such as the conquest of Jericho; Yahweh, who is invisibly present at the ark, not only leads the people, but also scatters their enemies.³⁷

It is interesting to note that the version of Solomon's dedicatory prayer for the temple in 2 Chronicles 6 closes with a quotation from Psalm 132:8–11; Solomon pled that the temple be a place of efficacious prayer, and the quotation bases the plea on the movement of the ark and David's role in it. The significance of the moving of the ark to Zion is expressed in verse 13: "for Yahweh chose Zion, he desired it for his

---

33. Dahood, *Psalms*, 245.

34. Willis, "QUMAH YHWH," 207–21.

35. Fretheim, "Cultic Use," 136; Kraus, *Psalmen*, 1061; Weiser, *Die Psalmen*, 539; Mays, *Psalms*, 409.

36. Allen, *Psalms*, 209; cf. the Feast of Sukkoth, according to Mitchell, *Message*, 267.

37. As for the phrase "the ark of your might," Calvin comments like this: "Hence it is called the *Ark of his strength*, not a mere dead idle shadow to look upon, but what certainly declared God's nearness to his Church." (*Psalms*, 4:151). It appears insufficient when Kraus notes that "In 8b klingen mit *ʾărōn ʿuzzękā* Erinnerungen an die Zeit auf, in der die Lade Palladium des Heiligen Krieges war (vgl. 1 Sam 4:3; Ps 24:8)" because the ark was not permitted to be used as a war-palladium (Kraus, *Psalmen*, 1063).

dwelling." In fact, David seems to take the initiative and make the vow, which he fulfills (2 Sam 6). Yet, what David did is reported as Yahweh's desire and choice (vv. 13–14). Mysteriously, the human initiative to find a proper resting place for the ark coincides with the divine choice. But, of course, this was no "coincidence." David's choice came about through the sovereign activity of Yahweh.[38] At any event, from the time when the ark is set in Zion, this place comes to have a special meaning as "the city of God" (Ps 48:7), for Yahweh dwells there (Isa 8:18). The city becomes the center of the religious life of the Israelites as well as of the world (Ezek 38:12) because Yahweh reigns over the world as king. Thus, Zion is inviolable (Ps 132:13, 18) and receives the pilgrims' praise.

3. Yahweh's Role in Maintaining David's Throne in Zion (Ps 132:11–18)

The second section of this psalm exhibits the prophetically written counterpart of David's vow and its fulfillment—Yahweh's oath to maintain the line of David. It is generally accepted that verse 11 is Yahweh's response to David's vow. Verses 2 and 13–16 are the counterparts of verses 6–9. Verses 17 and 18 are a summary answer to the petitions of verses 1 and 10. Verse 18 is the answer to the hardship and humility David experiences in verse 1. Verse 17 is the answer to the request for the king to be looked upon favorably in verse 10; the dynasty will continue in strength and prosperity. In particular, the content of verses 15–18 confirms that. With the installation of the ark in Zion, the city of David became a representation and manifestation of the salvation and blessing of Yahweh's reign (see Pss 133; 2:6).[39] However, the oath regarding the permanence of David's throne and the promise of blessing for Israel is conditional; Yahweh's oath in response to David's vow is dependent on his keeping Yahweh's covenant (Ps 132:12). Yahweh's presence at the ark is also conditional. The kings of the Davidic dynasty are to be the servants of the covenant and its directives.[40]

The Israelites who were on a pilgrimage to Zion would praise Yahweh by means of this psalm. They would recall the glorious scene of Yahweh's entrance into Zion through David's transfer of the ark. The

---

38. "Bezeichnenderweise wird auch niemals gesagt, David habe sich die Stadt ausgesucht (*bḥr*). Israels Gott ist es, der die Wahl getroffen hat." Schreiner, *Königssitz*, 56.

39. It is funny that *ṣayid* in v. 15 is translated as *thēran*, "widow" in LXX: it looks like a corruption of *chēran*, "hunt, prey."

40. See Birch et al., *Theological Introduction*, 239.

blessing and prosperity of David's dynasty, prophesied by Nathan, was realized. This psalm demonstrates succinctly that the foundation and history of Israel revolved around the ark, the tangible representation of God's presence. Hence, Mays entitled this psalm "David and Zion," by regarding them as topics of central importance in psalmic theology.[41] The ark links the two poles for Zion and becomes Yahweh's residence as a result of David's choosing Zion and transferring the ark there.

B. THE FATE OF THE ARK (JER 3:16)

"'When you are multiplied and increased in the land, in those days,' Yahweh declares, 'they will no longer say, "the ark of the covenant of Yahweh," it will not enter into mind, and they will not remember it, and they will not miss it, and it will not be made again'" (Jer 3:16).

This verse in Jeremiah refers to the ark for the last time in the books of the Old Testament. It is generally supposed that the reason it is almost never directly mentioned in worship or on other occasions after it was placed in the newly constructed temple of Solomon is that the role it played in Israelite worship became a secondary one. The ark was the most important object at the early stage of Israel's history. However, it is understandable that the significance of the ark was reduced after its installation in the temple because the two together functioned equally as symbols of the presence of God.

Verse 16 belongs to a unit of Jeremiah's preaching that is introduced by the headline ". . . and Yahweh said to me in the days of the King Josiah." In this respect, it is broadly thought that verses 15–18 were inserted into the original unit of verses 14 and 19–22, echoing motifs from Ezekiel.[42] In fact, the promise of a new shepherd is closely linked to Ezekiel 34. The transformation of Israel in Jerusalem sounds like the restoration of Jerusalem in later Ezekiel. The unity of Judah and Israel here articulated is either an echo or anticipation of Ezekiel 37:15–23. Yet, such an assumption of parallels may not offer absolute proof of a later insertion, for the expressions about the restoration of Israel and Judah are frequently propounded in the prophetic books of Isaiah (see 2:2–4), Amos (see 9:11), Micah (see 4:1–4), Zephaniah (see 3:14–17). This study

---

41. Mays, *Psalms*, 409.
42. See Craigie et al., *Jeremiah*, 59–60; Bruggemann, *Commentary*, 46.

pertains to the present shape of the text, even though the canonical form of this unit may look awkward.

The issue of whether or not the ark existed in the time of Jeremiah seems largely to rest on the translation and the object of Jeremiah 3:16.[43] First it is evident that the ark existed in the reign of King Josiah (2 Chr 35:3).[44] Then the ark could have still existed in the days of Jeremiah, even though the text is connected with his preaching before the fall of Jerusalem because this prophecy will be fulfilled in the distant future (Jer 3:16a). Jeremiah sees beyond the catastrophe of his time, in which the chosen people are on the verge of collapse, to a future period in which many of the Israelites will be restored to the true faith. Regardless of the prophetic nature of this verse, Cazelles renders the imperfect verbs in the past tense by regarding this prophecy as being directed to the northern kingdom.[45] This suggestion appears much less likely than translating it as the future tense.

In any case, verse 16 obviously hints at the disappearance of the original ark, the ark that had attracted so much reverence in the past. Needless to say, the ark is still regarded as the holy symbol of the presence of Yahweh in the temple, perhaps until the destruction of the temple. It is not degraded to the role of unimportant cultic object on account of the temple cult. Unlike the past and the present, in the projected future it will be irrelevant. The language implies that it will be destroyed and no attempt will be made to remake it.[46]

Here, the question is raised about the reason Jeremiah prophesied that the ark would lose its relevance. As a possible answer, Jones denotes the perversion at that time of legitimate symbols and cultic objects like the ark and the temple: "in the face of popular loyalty which regarded

---

43. For instance, Soggin suggests three cases: If it is late, as many scholars maintain (i.e., not by Jeremiah), it obviously means that the ark disappeared in 586 BC, although we do not know how; if the text is attributed to Jeremiah, (namely, directed to the north), the ark no longer existed in the earlier years of Josiah's reforms around the third quarter of the seventh century BC; if the verse refers to Judah, it can only mean that in the years 597–586 there was no ark in the temple. This argument can be upheld if we accept the translation of GNB: "Nor will they make another one." "Ark," 219.

44. Thompson indicates that "the original words of v. 16 should be dated either to the days of Zedekiah or shortly after the destruction of Jerusalem and the temple." *Jeremiah*, 203.

45. Cazelles, "Israël du nord," 158: "Par elle ils n'ont plus fait d'appel": "n'ont plus gouverné."

46. Jones, *Jeremiah*, 102.

the ark and the temple with fetish-like devotion, this is like the shaking of the foundation. It is tantamount to the abolition of religion in its folk-character."[47] His elucidation looks persuasive, for it properly reflects the reality of the corrupt religion of Israel. Yet, it is still insufficient to answer the question because Jeremiah's prophecy is not so much linked with contemporary reality as with features of the future. The question about why the ark was disposed of as a symbol can be answered within the context that deals with the restoration and future blessing, not by the people's repentance, but as a result of Yahweh's unilateral grace. The phrases "When you are multiplied and increased" (v. 16a) and "At that time" (v. 17a) form "a picture of eschatological redemptive period" that, on the one hand, is associated with "new order on Zion and the homecoming of Israel and Judah from the diaspora of north"[48] and, further, with the motif of the pentecostal event in which the ancient call to Israel to serve as a nation of priests (Exod 19:5–6) would be fulfilled. On the other hand, they mention that all nations will be assembled to Jerusalem, Yahweh's throne, which is openly accessible to all in the days of salvation because divine presence will be symbolized by the entire city of God.[49] As Woudstra proposed, they point to the *shalom* situation the notion of which stands for man's comprehensive well-being and exists where the covenant comes to its fullest fruition, and the eschatological endtime that will bring about the full fruition of all the cultus ever stood for (see Isa 4:5–6; Zech 14:20–21; Ezek 37:26–27).[50] Then the ark will be of no value as a unique symbol of God's presence at all and there will no longer be any need for an externally specified cultic object such as the ark, when the *shalom* prevails throughout Jerusalem as God's throne. In a final development of this motif, the new Jerusalem to which the nations come has no need of a material temple (Rev 21:22–25).[51] Here, Woudstra suggests a valuable insight into biblical exegesis: "Jeremiah's words must be understood in the light of the progress of God's revelation concerning the relation between cultus and culture. Only then will its full meaning be grasped."[52] From this viewpoint, it is desirable that

47. Ibid., 103.
48. Werner, *Jeremia*, 66.
49. See Martens, *Jeremiah*, 55.
50. Woudstra, "Ark," 125; see Calvin, *Predigten*, 137.
51. Allen, *Jeremiah*, 58.
52. Woudstra, *Ark*, 38. Aalders, similarly, states ("Jeremia," 280) that this verse should be understood in the light of the eschatological redemptive expectation.

the ark is described as a dispensable object in the future because its loss is a signal for the coming of the glorious future toward the era of the new covenant. However, the ark need not be considered a demythologized piece of ancient wood, a demoted sacred object, in view of the allegedly deuteronomistic treatment of the ark, as Carroll argues.[53] The message of this Old Testament text pertaining to the ark implies that the old covenant is in the process of transition towards a new covenant: "Then the law of the Lord will be written on the hearts in the redemptive future (Jer 31:33)."[54] The Israelites had to learn to live without the material symbol of the divine presence, even though they had regarded it as indispensable in maintaining their identity as God's people.[55]

---

53. Carroll, *Jeremiah*, 150.
54. Schreiner, *Jeremia*, 29.
55. See McKeating, *Jeremiah*, 39–40.

11

Some Theological Considerations

IN THIS SECTION a variety of theological themes concerning the ark are treated, mostly on the basis of the outcome of the exegetical explanations in the previous chapters. So, they are of a summary nature to some degree.

A. THE ARK AS A REVELATORY INSTRUMENT OF DIVINE ATTRIBUTES

Through the word, God directly revealed some of his attributes, such as omnipotence (Gen 17:1), holiness (Lev 11:45; 19:12; 20:26; 21:8), and goodness (Ex 22:27; 33:19; 34:6), etc., and simultaneously showed Israel his properties through material representations such as the ark.[1] God's word itself about his attributes is understandable enough but he probably used the ark as a complementary apparatus for the people to confirm the word. In addition to its meaning as a symbol of the special presence of God, the ark of Yahweh has another function as a revelatory tool. Then the ark is to assist Israel to perceive some divine attributes even with their limited cognizance. The Israelites would realize what Yahweh was like when they saw the ark being used in the circumstances that they experienced. Some of God's attributes seen in relation to the ark are:

1. Omnipotence

The idea of omnipotence is applied only to the God, who does not have any limitations of power. Scripture nowhere sets bounds to God's power. Already in the names El, Elohim, El Shaddai, and Adonai the idea of

---

1. Similarly Köhler states that God reveals himself through representations: the ark, the angel, the face and the glory of God. *Theologie*, 107–8.

power comes to the fore.[2] Actually his omnipotence was displayed in all his works: creation, providence, redemption, etc. God can do whatever he wills (Pss 115:3; 135:6).

With respect to the ark, God revealed his omnipotence to the people of Israel. God performed miracles in association with the ark to lead his people safely when Israel was confronted with difficulties.

When the Israelites crossed the Jordan, they experienced God's supernatural power. While the priests carrying the ark of Yahweh stood in the riverbed, they were able to pass over the Jordan on dry ground, as the waters of the river were cut off at a time when it was in full flood: "The Jordan overflows all its banks all the time of harvest" (Josh 3:15b). Yahweh performed this miracle, so that all the people of the earth might know that the hand of Yahweh is mighty and so that the Israelites might be encouraged to serve their God forever (4:24).

Another example of God's omnipotence in action in conjunction with the ark is the collapse of Jericho's walls (Josh 6). It was impossible for the Israelites militarily to conquer the city because they were not a well-trained regular army. In the event, Israel had nothing to do but follow God's instructions to march around the city in procession for seven days: God gave Jericho into Israel's hand. Nobody would believe that it happened by chance, because Yahweh, symbolically dwelling at the ark, was there and led them. The demolition of the walls of Jericho underscores the primary role of the ark as the prominent symbol of Yahweh's powerful presence.

In these two historical events that Israel experienced, the ark functioned as an instrument revealing God's omnipotence.

2. Omnipresence

Infinity in the sense of not being confined by space is synonymous with God's omnipresence. This attribute too is most evidently represented in Scripture.[3] Omnipresence means simply that God is present everywhere, which is not only an infinite idea about space but includes God's immanence. It is a spiritual manifestation of God. The contents of Psalm 139:7–10 express his omnipresence in a most vivid way.

---

2. Bavinck, *Reformed Dogmatics*, 245–46.
3. Ibid., 164.

This concept appears not to match the basic purpose of the ark to symbolize Yahweh's special presence.[4] However, the feature of the stretched wings of the cherubim would suggest God's omnipresence to his servants' mind. In addition, if we consider that the ark with the atonement place and the cherubim is regarded as God's royal footstool (1 Chr 28:2), it may be coupled with the idea of Yahweh's omnipresence because the expression "Heaven is my throne and the earth is my footstool" (Isa 66:1) indicates God's universal existence.

God's footstool is a metaphorical expression for a resting place for the feet of the enthroned deity. In Psalms 99:5 and 132:7, and in Lamentations 2:1, footstool is a metaphor for Zion. Thus "the ark unit" as God's footstool points out God's presence and simultaneously reflects his transcendence. These two concepts formulate the divine attribute in terms of omnipresence.

3. Goodness

The goodness (*tōḇ, ḥesed*) of God is a broad concept including benevolence, love, mercy, and grace. Yahweh himself revealed his goodness (*ḥesed*) to Moses: "Yahweh, Yahweh, a God merciful and gracious, slow to anger, and abundant in goodness and truth" (Exod 34:6).[5] The psalmists praised this quality of God by juxtaposing the two words, *tōḇ, ḥesed* (Pss 23:6; 107:1; 118:1, 29; 136:1). In general, the goodness of God contains grace, love exercised towards the unworthy, and mercy, kindness exercised towards those worthy of punishment.

God's goodness is first seen in the behest that Moses should make the ark (Ex 25:10). Yahweh had initiative of the fabrication of the ark. It means that God, who met his people at Sinai, manifests the divine volition that he wants to keep holding the communion with them from that time. Yahweh is invisibly present at the ark in the midst of his people. He wanted to give them the visible pledge of his dwelling among them.[6]

---

4. Grudem explains the meaning of God's presence at the ark: "It is not that God was not present elsewhere, but rather that here he especially made his presence known and here he especially manifested his character and brought blessing to his people." *Systematic Theology*, 176.

5. ESV reads *ḥesed* as "steadfast love" in Exod 34:6: "The Lord, the Lord, a God merciful and gracious, slow to anger, and abounding in steadfast love and faithfulness."

6. Calvin, *Psalms*, 2:212.

Thus, we can say that Yahweh's instruction to make the ark itself attests his goodness.

The first chapters of the book of Samuel show us how corrupt Israel was spiritually, by describing the sin of the priests Hophni and Phinehas at Shiloh. Apparently, their serious transgression spiritually contaminated the sanctuary at Shiloh and the people of Israel. It was into this spiritual background that Samuel was called as a prophet. However, the ark of God was in the defiled sanctuary (1 Sam 3:3), which means that Yahweh was with Israel even though Israel had abandoned him. The ark represents Yahweh's goodness to and steadfast love for his people.

Another case is concerned with the event when the Philistines tested the cause of their calamity, and let the ark return to Israel. However, contrary to natural maternal instincts, the cows pulling the cart went straight in the direction of Beth-Shemesh along one highway (1 Sam 6:12). God was showing them his supernatural power and durable love for his own people with the ark of Yahweh.

4. Holiness

Holiness is one of God's fundamental attributes. In general, the term, *qōdęš* means "separateness," but its etymological definition does not help much in understanding it properly. One of the cogent explanations of holiness is that the phrase "God is holy" expresses that he is totally different from others (Isa 40:25).[7] Some biblical texts used holiness as an attribute to lead human beings to fear, worship, and glorify God (Pss 99:9; 111:9; Rev 15:4). God is the fearful One, who deserves to be worshiped and glorified because he is holy.

There are several arguments to support the belief that the ark, as a cultic object, is designed to show God's holiness: 1) The fact that the ark was overlaid with pure gold to enhance its dignity may point to holiness because gold is, at times, associated with God's holiness (see Exod 28:36; 39:30). 2) The ark is always linked with the cherubim of glory (Heb 9:5) and the atonement place. Such configurations of the ark figuratively reflect God's holiness. 3) The place where the ark was kept was called the Most Holy Place. Both are holy because they are symbols of the presence of the holy God. Solomon mentioned that "the places where the ark of Yahweh had come are holy" (2 Chr 8:11). 4) The ark

---

7. See Peels, *Shadow Sides*, 127.

was only to be carried by designated persons: the Levites, especially the sons of Kohath (Num 4:4, 15), because of its sanctity. 5) The deuteronomic phrase "in the presence of Yahweh," which implies that the ark is a symbol of the divine presence of Yahweh, tells us that Deuteronomy uses language attaching sanctity to the ark. 6) The distance between the ark and the Israelites near the Jordan River (Josh 3:4) appears to indicate the holiness of the ark. 7) Uzza's death beside the ark shows that God was jealous for his holiness (Num 4:15). 8) The people of Beth-Shemesh who looked into the ark with curiosity were killed because they violated God's holiness (1 Sam 6).

All of these references confirm that the ark is clearly related to God's holiness. The ark in and of itself is nothing divine, but the ark as a symbol of God's presence reflects God's holiness.

5. Sovereignty

Strictly speaking, sovereignty is not a property of the divine nature, but a prerogative arising out of the perfections of the Supreme Being.[8] However God's sovereignty is at times classified as God's personal attribute.[9] God's sovereignty is his exercise of rule over his creation. The Bible everywhere asserts the sovereignty and supremacy of God (Pss 24:1; 115:3; 1 Chr 29:11; Rom 11:36; etc.). His dominion reaches out to nations (1 Sam 28:17), the earth (Ps 8:2), and even individuals (Ezek 18:4). The NIV rendering of "O Sovereign Lord" for the Hebrew phrase *yahwê ʾᵃdōnāy* appears to accentuate God's lordship and supremacy over his creation (Gen 15:2, 8; Deut 3:24; 2 Sam 7:18–20; Pss 68:20; 71:5, 16; 73:28; 109:21; 140:7; etc.).

God's sovereignty is also seen in the ark passages. Primarily we can refer to the cherubim whose permanent place is above the ark. The figures of the cherubim on the ark indicate God's transcendent sovereignty. In addition, several events that are concerned with the ark of Yahweh demonstrate his sovereignty. During the period of the detention of the ark in Philistia, Yahweh demonstrated his superiority and sovereignty over the territorial supreme deity by desecrating Dagon and by bringing plagues against the people of the Philistine cities (1 Sam 4–6), and his

---

8. See Hodge, *Systematic Theology*, 440. Bavinck mentioned (*Reformed Dogmatics*, 136) that "these are the attributes in which God appears before us as Lord, king, and sovereign: his will, freedom, and omnipotence."

9. Bray, *Doctrine of God*, 218.

sovereignty over natural laws is seen in the incident with the cows when the ark is returned to Israel.

B. THE CONTENTS OF THE ARK

Regardless of biblical information on this topic, some scholars have different opinions about the contents of the ark. Vatke assumes that the ark originally contained a holy stone from Sinai to represent Yahweh's presence since the stone sets forth the deity and might of God and radiates his holiness in the container (Gen 28:10–22).[10] Gressman argues that the ark originally contained a golden calf, Yahweh's image.[11] May presumes that there were Urim and Thummim in the ark according to the Arabian analogy of Betyls, found in the *qubba* of pre-Islamic times.[12] Maier assumes that the ark was made as a container for "the document of the covenant" or "the symbol of the covenant" of tribal organization, which appears to be based on Noth's hypothesis of amphictyony.[13] These interesting parallels seem to satisfy our curiosity to some extent but hardly provide a proper solution to the subject in question.

According to biblical materials, Hebrews 9:4 of the New Testament testifies that there were three objects in the ark, although Schroer denies their historicity: "The Old Testamental information about the content of the ark (Manna, the tablets of the law) is not reliable historically."[14] As to their historical provenances, the intact narrative in the Pentateuch affirms that from the beginning the ark served as a container for the tables of the law (Exod 25:16; 40:20; Deut 10:5; see 1 Kgs 8:9). Two additional objects within the ark were a jar of manna (Exod 16:33–34) and Aaron's rod (MT, Num 17:25).

The fact that the stone tablets of the Ten Commandments were deposited in the ark appears to imply the essential importance of the law document. At times the tablets, named as Testimony, indicate the ark (Exod 16:34; 26:33, 34; 30:6, 26). In comparative religion's view, the idea of "kingly protocol" has been quite widely circulated. This idea concerned the tablets of the Decalogue housed in the ark. It empha-

10. Vatke, *biblische Theologie*, 321.
11. Gressmann, *Jahwes und Allerheiligste*, 25.
12. May, "Ark," 220, 226.
13. J. Maier, *Heiligtum*, 59.
14. Schroer, *Samuelbücher*, 50.

sized that the document of the pact or treaty was often placed beneath the feet of a god who served as witness to it in the ancient Near East.[15] However, a dilemma resides in the question: Is there a bridge to connect the religious and political customs of ancient society with God's revelation? Rather, it reminds Israel of God's gracious action to reestablish an intimate relationship with a contaminated people who were guilty of worshiping a golden calf in the Sinai wilderness. Indeed, the tablets of the testimony preach that Yahweh, as the redeeming Savior, demands the obedience and faith of the covenantal people in accordance with the commandment; only on this basis can their communion with God be sustained. Thus, the Israelites constantly had to learn from the content of the testimony rather than be interested in the tablets as such (Deut 31:26–28).[16]

According to Exodus 16:33-34, Aaron had to take an omer of manna and keep it "before" Yahweh for the generations to come. Then, he placed a jar of manna "in front of the testimony," which could only refer to the law, which was probably given later. An omer is equal to an individual's daily bread. It is to serve future generations as a vivid reminder of Yahweh's providential care of Israel throughout the wilderness period. This jar with manna sample ensures God's gracious sustenance of his people, albeit manna was bestowed as Yahweh's response to the rebellion of the Israelites in the wilderness (Exod 16:3). According to the psalmist, they could be satisfied with "the grain of heaven" and "the bread of angels" (Ps 78:24–25). In the New Testament, Jesus indicated that he is the true manna from heaven, the bread of life, and whoever feeds on this bread will have eternal life (John 6:32–35, 58).

As for Aaron's staff, the difficulty lies in whether it was placed in the ark or not because Aaron's staff was to be put *before* the testimony, according to Numbers 17:25. The phrase does not indicate that it was put in the ark, but the New Testament furnishes evidence that Aaron's rod was placed in the ark with other objects (Heb 9:4). Aaron's sprouted staff, as an admonitory sign, refers to God's punishment in order for the rebellious to cease the grumblings against Yahweh and the priesthood of Aaron and his descendants and to not die (Num 17:5, 10). The staff shows that Yahweh himself will clear the way for reconciliation through

---

15. See de Vaux, *Bible et Orient*, 256.

16. "Wichtiger als die deponierten Tafeln werden die Lehren des Gesetzes, die es periodisch vorzulesen gilt." Loretz, "Steinernen Gesetzestafeln," 161.

the intermediary role of the priesthood; it portends restoration and life through the high priesthood of Jesus Christ.

The significance of these three contents of the ark is essential for Israel to be a theocratic community. They show that Yahweh led his people to faith using different sacred objects in the progression of redemptive history.

C. THE ARK, TABERNACLE, AND TEMPLE

Tabernacle has a variety of names: the tent (Exod 26:9), the tent of meeting, the tent of the testimony (Num 9:15), the house of the tent (1 Chr 9:23), the tabernacle of the testimony (Exod 38:21), and the house of God (Judg 18:31). Above all, tabernacle (*miškān*) is differentiated from the tent of meeting (*ʾōhēl mōēḏ*), which is a most frequently used synonym; the former refers to structure and the latter to its religious use.[17] The tabernacle of Yahweh, built in Sinai, refers only to the tent structure inside the court, not to the sanctuary complex as a whole. This is true for most relevant texts in the Old Testament (see Exod 26:1). It is the central place of worship, the sanctuary that houses the ark of the covenant. Frequently it is the location of revelation. It is presented in the biblical narrative as the visible sign of Yahweh's presence among the people of Israel: a reminder of the immanence of the transcendent Creator.

However, as to the origin of the tabernacle and its relationship with the ark, Wellhausen takes a negative position. According to him, the biblical account about the existence of the tabernacle is just a myth, P's pious fraud.[18] The tabernacle could not have been in the wilderness because, he speculates, its splendid materials could not have been found in the destitute circumstances of the wilderness. Fairly recently Gunneweg also adopted this classical criticism: "Tabernacle, as it is described here in detail and should correspond to the celestial model (Exod 25:40; 26:30), is certainly retrojection of people of the Jerusalem's temple in Moses' time."[19] Wellhausen argues that the ark was broken up with the tabernacle at the end of the Judges' period, while the inseparable link between them had existed previously.[20] Alluding to the abolition of

---

17. See Jacob, *Second Book*, 880.
18. Wellhausen, *Prolegomena*, 39–40.
19. Gunneweg, *Biblische Theologie*, 99.
20. "Von dem Vorhandensein der Lade Jahve's allerdings finden sich gegen Ende der Richterzeit deutliche Spuren (1 Sam. Kap. 4-6). Bürgt nun die Lade für das Tabernakel?" Wellhausen, *Prolegomena*, 43.

the Shiloh tabernacle, he appears to want to draw up this scheme: "the tabernacle-the ark-the temple" as sanctuaries that stand for God's presence. In fact, in the chapter "The place of religion" of his *Prolegomena*, he attempts to prove that the Israelite religion evolved from a low to a high point and from a primitive to a cultured condition. He bases this theory on Hegel's historical philosophy.[21] However, the tabernacle was found at Gibeon during the period of David and Solomon (1 Kgs 3:4; 1 Chr 21:29; 2 Chr 1:3, 4). It appears to have been transferred with the ark (1 Kgs 8:4; 2 Chr 5:2–5).

Through the impact of archaeology, skeptical supposition of the historicity of biblical documents was fairly rooted out. Nevertheless, scholars continue to maintain that the "priestly" account is schematized and idealized and that the "priestly" writers read the theological interpretations and historical developments of later ages into their system. Modified Wellhausenists now point to such things as the lists and genealogies of P as containing information that cannot be passed over lightly.[22] According to von Rad, who belongs to the traditio-historical circle, the tabernacle and the ark radically diverged in origin as well as in theological significance. "There is no exaggeration: between the idea of Jahweh's coming in the camp (1 Sam 4) and that of his coming in the clouds over the Tabernacle, there is no bridge originally."[23] As to their distinction, the tabernacle was from the south and represented a theology of glory and dwelling in P, whereas the ark was from the north and represented a theology of covenant and presence in D. Yet, he is of the opinion that there was a late, priestly coalescence of polarized ark and tent traditions in the history of Israel's theology.[24] In regard to von Rad's assumption about the theological combination, Hague rightly observes that a close examination of the texts in question reveals the impossibility of isolating theological polarization along these traditio-historical lines.[25] In addition, the complete lack of consensus in identifying the

---

21. Wellhausen also confessed that he was mostly influenced by Vatke, the Hegelian, in his study: "Meine Untersuchung ist . . . nähert sich der Art Vatkes, von welchem letzteren ich auch das meiste und das beste gelernt zu haben bekenne." Ibid., 14.

22. See Woudstra, "Tabernacle," 89–90.

23. Von Rad, "Zelt und Lade," 123.

24. Ibid., 125: "Und jetzt erst war die Stunde gekommen, daß Lade und Zeltvorstellung verbunden werden konnten. Das war die theologische Tat des Priesterkodex, der selbst von Haus aus in der Zelttradition steht."

25. Hague, *'ărōn*, *NIDOTTE* 1:505.

proposed synthesis of a theological dialectic in P (which is itself seen in flux) has brought the historico-traditional methodology itself into question.

From the beginning, the tabernacle was not used merely as a covering for the ark but as a tent-like sanctuary that symbolized that Yahweh resided among the Israelites (see Judg 18:31) and met them in glory. In particular, Rendtorff connects the notion that in the tabernacle God represents the glory of his presence (Exod 40:36–37) with his glorious presence in Sinai (Exod 24:16–17).[26] From this perspective, the function of the tabernacle is not clearly set apart from that of the ark because the glory associated with God's presence on Mount Sinai is also inextricably associated with the ark within the tabernacle in the camp: the glorious epiphany of Yahweh occurs by the ark. Furthermore, the idea that the tabernacle is to reveal the divine intention to be present with, and for, the believing community in a tangible way, in both the ritual of liturgy and the commonality of daily life, is precisely tantamount to the significance of the ark.[27] Thus, the tight connection between the tabernacle and the ark demonstrates a feature of Yahweh's foremost sanctuary, even though the tabernacle was dismantled during the journey and its appurtenances played no part in that case.

The ceremony of Solomon's transfer of the ark into the temple in 1 Kings 8 explicitly displays the intimate association between the ark and the temple. The ark of the covenant of Yahweh was brought to its place in the inner sanctuary of the temple, the most holy place, and put beneath the wings of the cherubim. Buis evaluates Solomon's ceremony to carry the ark into the temple from a political view.[28] Yet, the response of God was positive (8:10), although it is unknown to what extent Solomon took advantage of the ark politically. Rather, it appears to mean not so much political succession as that of the tradition of the historical faith based on the exodus and Sinai's lawgiving, since the ark itself has irrefutable connections with the history of the exodus (vv. 9b, 10b). Linville also underpins such a historical liaison between the ark and temple: "The

26. Rendtorff, *Theologie*, 61.

27. See Klein, "Back to the Future," 275.

28. "Salomon achève ce transfert en le rendant definitive. Ainsi les anciennes traditions qui définissaient l'identité d'Israël passent sous le contrôle et la protection de la dynastie davidique: le document de l'alliance est enfermé dans un bâtiment qui est l'oeuvre et la propriété du roi. Il faudra donc faire une synthèse entre ces traditions et l'idéologie royale, plus l'idéologie de la ville de Jérusalem." Buis, *Le Livre*, 97.

whole scene in 1 Kings 8:1–13 seems infused with a sense that the dedication of the temple is not so much a singular event, but rather marks the ultimate end to the exodus itself."[29]

Similar to the ark, the temple symbolizes God's presence as "the house of God" (which occurs twenty-two times throughout Kings). In particular, the cherubim fabricated by Solomon, which differ from those of the ark, seem to multiply the meaning of the glorious presence of God with the ark; the transcendental Creator and King is immanent. It is no exaggeration to say that the author of the Books of Kings views the ark and the temple as the place where God has deigned to dwell among the people (1 Kgs 6:13, 23–27; 8:6, 7, 10–13; 2 Kgs 19:15; see Pss 11:4; 65:5; 138:2). Nevertheless, it also reminds them that God's presence, associated with the cultic objects, is thoroughly conditional on the covenantal faith of the people. In this regard, Fretheim's comment is instructive: "The temple and God's dwelling therein is most fundamentally for the people . . . The emphasis is not for the sake of the temple *per se*, but for the sake of the people for whom the temple is integral to their faith and life and for the sake of God who desires to be present among them."[30] Practically, faithful psalmists comprehended dwelling in the temple as staying before Yahweh, so that they always longed to climb up to the temple, especially when they were in difficulties (see Pss 5:8; 26:8; 27:4; 42:3; 43:3; 65:4; 84:5; 116:26; 122:1).

Although the ark, the tabernacle, and the temple are separate and independent cultic objects, they have inseparable connections to one another in the functional sense. Together they were the paramount sanctuaries of the glorious presence of Yahweh among the covenantal people. However, the ark with the atonement place and the cherubim was not only at the heart of the sanctuary but was also highlighted as God's royal footstool (1 Chr 28:2).

D. THE ARK AND WORSHIP OF YAHWEH

From the perspective of religious science, cultic worship is generally defined as a "designated and arranged form of communion with the divine being," so that its concept contains the dedication of a ritualized offering and the congregation of worshipers whose purpose is to pay homage to

---

29. Linville, *Israel*, 279.
30. Fretheim, *Kings*, 54.

God.³¹ This definition is composed of two components: a material one, because of the stress that the cultus puts on sacred places, seasons, and rites, and a sociological one because in the cultus the determining factor is the community as a whole. While the cultus of the Old Testament apparently seems to have a similar structure, above all it arises from the fact that God wants to dwell among his people. The essence of the cultus is spiritual intercourse between God and men, both individually and in community (see Ps 22:3). In this regard, it is comprehensible that Brueggemann delineates the cult as a mediator: "the cult, in its many forms and expressions mediates Yahweh's 'real presence.'"³² Yahweh, who is pleased to have communion with his people, exhibits his presence in the ritual practice. In the Old Testament period, the priests, authorized office-bearers who were caring for symbolical cultic objects just like the ark and the tabernacle, oversaw the presence of God in public worship. So too, the ark, the palpable emblem of Yahweh's presence, played a tremendously momentous part in the cultic practice of Israel.

Notwithstanding, it is unknown how the ark was actually utilized in cultic worship. Thus, many scholars have attempted to extract conjectures concerning the ark's use from Near East parallels. Particularly, Mowinckel argued that Israel annually carried the ark in procession at "Royal Zion festival," by establishing the theory of the New Year festival of Yahweh's enthronement on the basis of 2 Samuel 6, 1 Kings 8, Psalm 132, and the like. He found at least twenty-two ideological continuities between Israel's kingship theology and that of the general ancient Near East.³³ Furthermore, he contended that nowhere in the Old Testament do we meet with the "metaphysical" unity of Yahweh and the king, or a really "mythological" idea of the king's relation to Yahweh.³⁴ Yet, in his opinion, the basic conceptions have been fundamentally altered under the influence of the Yahweh religion, although Israel adopted a number of ideas, functions, and style forms from such oriental monarchies. Royal concepts, which in Mesopotamia or Egypt took on mythological force, have been taken out of the mythical-literal context and reinterpreted. For him, the king was "adopted," not "born," in Israel.³⁵

31. Diebner, "Gottesdienst," *TRE* 14:5–28.
32. Brueggemann, *Theology*, 650.
33. Mowinckel, *Psalmenstudien*, 1:297–99; 2:93–94, 111–17.
34. Mowinckel, *Psalms*, 52–60.
35. See Starbuck, *Court Oracles*, 42.

As a matter of fact, concerning Yahweh's kingship, it is generally assumed that the nomads of the wilderness would not have used the analogy of kingship prior to the establishment of the monarchy. However the idea of Yahweh's kingship is presumed in several archaic, premonarchial poems (Exod 15:18; Num 23:21; Deut 33:5). Apparently, Yahweh was king from the outset: Mowinckel's translation of "Yahweh became king" for *yahweh męlęk*, which is offered as his firm argument for the annual enthronement ceremony, should be corrected as "Yahweh is King."[36] Yahweh does not need to be ratified as a king on an annual basis.

Instead of the New Year festival promoted by Mowinckel, Kraus proposes the "Royal Zion Festival," according to which, during the Davidic monarchy on the first day of Tabernacles, an annual festival was held with a procession and a cult-dramatic performance of the *hieros logos* (sacred word) by which Zion and David's dynasty had been "chosen" by Yahweh.[37] The heart of the festival was the carrying of the ark into the temple in remembrance of the first transfer of the ark from Kiriath-Jearim to Jerusalem under David, or from the tent to the temple under Solomon. However, the biblical evidence for such an annual festival remains obscure, even if an evident reference to the procession with the ark appears to be provided in Psalm 68:25–26, which seems to be regarded as a song for the festive event of 2 Samuel 6 rather than an annual procession. In reference to the procession with the ark, Maier concludes that "because of deuteronomistic reformation and the covenantal renewal the ark did not have to leave its place in the Holy of Holies, even one time."[38]

The Israelites expected Yahweh's blessing encompassing the conception of protection, grace, and peace in the cult. This is to be found in the priestly benediction, which is performed in front of the tabernacle that housed the ark, at the end of public worship (Num 6:24–26; see Lev 9:22). In that blessing, proclaimed before God's presence, they could always anticipate all that they would need to survive and even to enjoy prosperity physically and spiritually. In the promised land as well as in the wilderness, the cultus of Israel could not dispense with the ark. The ark of the covenant was positioned at the center of the solemn cult of

---

36. Mowinckel, *Religion und Kultus*, 72; see H. Schmidt, "Kerubenthron und Lade," 131.

37. Kraus, *Psalmen*, 1059.

38. J. Maier, *Heiligtum*, 80.

the covenantal renewal near Shechem (Josh 8:30–35), signifying that Yahweh, who is symbolically present at or with the ark, led Israel to the center of the land of Canaan; the ark seems to conduct her through the region, as if it is identified with Yahweh. The ark as a symbol of Yahweh's invisible presence functions as a reaffirmation that Yahweh is with his people and requires their observance of his law to maintain the covenantal relationship, in order for them to be blessed. Even in emergency circumstances, the ark was regarded as the center of the designated cultus (see Judg 20:27; 21:2). The ark sustained the significance of Shiloh as a cultic place because the site lost its cultic function after the capture of the ark (1 Sam 1–4).

Moreover, the installation of the ark led to Zion being brought into prominence as the central location for the Israelite cult (see Ps 132:13–14), where Yahweh bestows on the people blessing and eternal life (Ps 133). In particular, the work of the priests in the cult exhibits the intimate connection with the ark. We see this in the fact that David appointed Levites to minister *before* the ark of Yahweh, to invoke, give thanks, and praise him (1 Chr 16:4, 37). This is proof that cultic practice revolved around the ark during the monarchical period, although it naturally was a cultic center during the wilderness period, and during the conquest and settlement of the land. Therefore, it was unthinkable for the Israelites to practice public worship apart from the ark. However, the ark is regarded as dispensable in the process of redemptive history (Jer 3:16).

E. THE LOCATION OF THE ARK

Several places are mentioned in connection with the ark including Shiloh in Ephraim, and a series of cities at the borders of the Benjamite territory: Gilgal and Jericho towards the east, Kiriath-Jearim towards the west, Jerusalem at the southern border, and Bethel (see Judg 20:27) at the northern border, even if the ark might temporarily be stationed in some other places as well. The ark also appears in some Philistine cities, as in Judaean Beth-Shemesh, causing great disasters in each of these cities. In this section, locations that were sanctuaries of the ark will be treated.

1. The Ark Near Shechem

There is no evidence that the ark was located at Shechem, but the covenant ritual revolving around the ark was maintained by Joshua on the slopes of Mount Gerizim and Mount Ebal in the vicinity of Shechem (Josh 8:30–35). The ark of the covenant of Yahweh was located in the narrow valley between Ebal and Gerizim. With its position settled, Joshua read all the words of the law, the blessings and the curses, in the presence of the whole assembly of Israel, including the women and children and the aliens who lived among them (vv. 34–35). Joshua's actions concerning the construction of the altar and the offerings followed precisely the Mosaic instruction (Deut 27:1–8). Verse 33 describes how the ark forms the center of the ceremony, the law's blessings and curses. It is remarkable that the movement of the ark comes at the command of Joshua but according to the Law of Moses. This event shows that Yahweh's law was to be kept from generation to generation (Deut 6:2). Yahweh's own people surrounded the ark on both sides.

The ark of the covenant is positioned at the center of the ceremony of the covenantal renewal near Shechem, which signifies that Yahweh, who is symbolically present with the ark, had the initiative at the conquest of the land of Canaan. The Israelites expected a life in the promised land blessed by Yahweh through their covenantal relationship with him.

However, the thesis that this event established Shechem as the tribal league shrine and that the tribal league organizations constituted by the covenant and sanctioned at and by the central shrine at Shechem became especially meaningful for the northern tribes seems too hypothetical.[39] For example, it is said that the phrase "under the terebinth in the holy place of Yahweh" (Josh 24:26) suggests that the tabernacle was at Shechem, housing the ark.[40] It seems unlikely to interpret the term *miqdaš* (holy place) as a sanctuary, such as renderings in many English versions (KJV, RSV, NASB and ESV), in the light of chapter 22 and the centralization requirement expressed therein.[41] At that time the holy place in Shechem was a place with its old associations, where Abraham built an altar for the first time when he entered the land of Canaan (Gen 12:7) and Jacob renewed the covenant with Yahweh by burying all the

---

39. Kelm, *Escape*, 196.
40. See Howard, *Joshua*, 440.
41. Pitkänen, *Joshua*, 397.

foreign gods (Gen 35:4). This tree was so conspicuous and so famous that it served as a landmark to identify other sites.[42] Thus, it is hard to say that the ark was at Shechem.

2. The Ark at Shiloh

The ark was present in Shiloh (1 Samuel 3:3; 4:3). Shiloh became a prominent place as the political and religious center of Israel after the tent of meeting was set up there in the days of Joshua (Josh 18:1a). It is unclear why it was singled out as an important cultic locus, although Schley reminds us that before Shiloh became an Israelite shrine it had been the site of an old Canaanite cultic center.[43] He bases this hypothesis on archaeological evidence and his individual interpretation of Judges 21:16-24. Yet it was a legitimate place chosen by Yahweh, where God made his name dwell at first (Deut 12:11; Jer 7:12, 14), although there is no reference that Shiloh was chosen by Yahweh as Zion was. During these early years, the Aaronite priesthood of Eleazar (Josh 21:1-3) and his son Phinehas (Josh 22:9-34) administered Shiloh. At one time, Shiloh may have claimed exclusive rights over the other sanctuaries of the land (see Josh 22:9-34). Therefore Brouwer's proposition that Shiloh was not the central sanctuary is not convincing.[44] The location is said to have a "house of God" (Judg 18:31) and an annual festival was held there (Judg 21:19) but it is rash to assume from this verse that "the early Israelite tribes may have worshipped together with non-Israelites at the shrine at Shiloh, before the Ephraimite hills fell totally into Israelite hands."[45] The elaborate description of the verse appears to indicate that the annual festival taking place at Shiloh is a local festival rather than a national one.[46] Moreover, it would not be desirable for the elders to suggest men of Benjamin to marry them, if the daughters of Shiloh were Canaanites. The fact that the vineyard festival of dancing women is called a "festival of Yahweh" seems to reflect intention that the elders try to sanctify their strategy.[47]

42. Sarna, *Genesis*, 91.
43. Schley, *Shiloh*, 191.
44. Brouwer, *De ark*, 190.
45. Schley, *Shiloh*, 191.
46. Butler, *Judges*, 463.
47. Block, *Judges, Ruth*, 580.

Apparently some Israelites made their pilgrimages to Shiloh during an annual festival (1 Sam 1:3), albeit it is natural to suppose that very few people would attend the annual occasion in view of the spiritual state of the nation in the period of the judges. It was "before Yahweh" that Hannah prayed in earnest to God for a child and vowed the dedication of such a child to the service of Yahweh (1 Sam 1:11–12). Through Yahweh's remembrance of her, she conceived and bore a child whom she named Samuel. When the child was weaned he was brought to the priest Eli to be raised in the service of Yahweh at Shiloh. This event, along with the calling of Samuel at the sanctuary where the ark was housed (1 Sam 3:1–14) implies the commencement of a hopeful situation in Israel. On the contrary, the Elide house would be demolished on account of the unfaithful implementation of the office. This event changed the fate of the sanctuary of Shiloh.[48]

In any event, Shiloh was the cultic center of the Israelite tribes after the conquest and until the capture of the ark by the Philistines: the significance of Shiloh as the sanctuary depended on whether or not the ark was present there.

3. The Ark at Bethel

Judges 20:27 testifies that the ark was stationed in Bethel, which was located in Ephraim, probably at modern Beitin, about seventeen kilometers north of Jerusalem on the border of Benjamin.[49] Under normal circumstances, the ark was supposed to be in the inner sanctuary of the tabernacle at Shiloh. It appears that the ark was temporarily established at Bethel in uncommon circumstances. The phrase "in those days" probably denotes that it was there during the entire campaign against Benjamin. It seems to have been moved there from Shiloh (see Judg 18:31) in order to facilitate inquiries of God by the high priest for the

---

48. Incidentally, the slightly perplexing expression $m^e z \bar{u} z a \underline{t}\ h \bar{e} \underline{k} a l\ yhwh$, "the doorpost of Yahweh's temple" (1 Sam 1:9; 3:3, 15) should first of all be considered as an interchangeable term with $\bar{o} h \underline{e} l$, "tent" (Ps 27:4). Concretely, it appears to indicate that the tabernacle had apparently become part of a compound that included auxiliary structures made of stone (Youngblood, "Shiloh," NIDOTTE 4:1220–24). Thus it is not necessary to assume that the ark was in the pagan temple, alongside which the tabernacle stood, as Brouwer insists: "The ark was safely stored in the heathen templebuilding" (De ark, 120).

49. See Southwell, "Bethel," NIDOTTE 4:440–41.

campaign against Benjamin.⁵⁰ In consideration of Israel's battle against the Benjamites, Block suggests that the Israelites brought the ark to Bethel from Shiloh presumably to function as a palladium, a symbol of God's "good luck," in the battle against the Benjamites. Yet, he fails to observe the actual combat situation and the use of the war-palladium;⁵¹ the Israelite camp was in Mizpah, whereas the ark was at Bethel. This biblical document provides another argument against the idea of the ark's habitual use as a war-palladium.

It is apparent that in the very least, the Israelites understood the ark as the place of God's revelation (see Judg 20:18, 23, 27). They had to inquire of Yahweh whether they should go up into battle against Benjamin, even though the ark itself was not the information source to provide God's will. Incidentally, van Dam assumes that "It thus seems highly likely that this inquiry took place by the use of *Urim* and *Thummim*, with the ark meeting the condition *lipnê* YHWH."⁵² Whether this is correct or not, they wanted to receive God's direction at the historic place that had once played an enormously important role in the religion of the patriarchs (Gen 28:11–22; 31:13; 35:7) and that was in the vicinity of Gibeah, the enemy's camp. In particular, the scene where they presented burnt offerings and peace offerings to Yahweh (Judg 20:26) suggests that there was a fully-fledged sacrificial cult with priests, probably at the tabernacle.⁵³ Actually, it was not necessary for them to go as far as Bethel, located further away than Gibeah from Mizpah, if only the ark was at Bethel without the tabernacle. This may be an answer for Amit's question as to the reason "why the army abandoned the battlefield, went north to Bethel, and returned from there in order to make war in the area of Mizpah and Gibeah";⁵⁴ the answer is probably because of the tabernacle. Later, the ark might be moved to Shiloh. At any rate, the ark, the important emblem of Yahweh's presence at Bethel, played a cardinal part as the place of Yahweh's revelation and as a cultic center.

---

50. Van Dam, *Urim and Thummim*, 184.
51. Block, *Judges, Ruth*, 561.
52. Van Dam, *Urim and Thummim*, 184.
53. See Woudstra, *Ark*, 129
54. Amit, *Judges*, 356.

4. The Ark in Kiriath-Jearim

Willis supposes that the ark would have been carried into Ramah after Shiloh was overrun and ceased to be the place where the ark was housed.[55] However his assertion is unfounded because the biblical report admits of no argument about that (1 Sam 6:21). Furthermore the reference to the ark in Kiriath-Jearim (7:1) seems not to function simply as a literary juncture between 1 Samuel 4–6 and 2 Samuel 6 to compose the complete "ark narrative," as many scholars hold,[56] but to demonstrate the historical continuity of the event when David carries it to Jerusalem.

The return of the ark from the Philistine district to Israel signifies the importance of the physical symbols of God's ongoing redemption of the people. Yet for nearly a hundred years, the ark was housed under the protection of Eleazar at the Judahite site of Kiriath-Jearim, which was located on the border of Judah and Benjamin and was one of the most prominent cities of the Gibeonites (see Josh 9:17–27) but probably had been under Philistine suzerainty after the Israelite defeat. This city was also known as Baalah (Josh 15:9) or Baale-Judah (2 Sam 6:2). As for Eleazar, it is possible that the man was a member of the Levitical tribe. Miller and Roberts argue that Eleazar was Eli's successor because it is apparent that he was consecrated to have charge of the ark.[57]

The reason why the ark remained concealed for such a long time appears to be associated with the indifference of the Israelite leader to the ark (1 Sam 22:18, 19; 23:1, 27; 1 Chr 13:3). Israel would have to wait for a lengthy period, until David restored ideal worship of Yahweh with the ark. The ark's installation and protection at Kiriath-Jearim demonstrate how important it is that suitable service for Yahweh is in accord with the law. The provisional concealment of the ark appears to be indicative of a period of time that God used to prepare for a new future and simultaneously to demonstrate that God's activity was not determined by the ark as he continued to watch over Israel (see 1 Sam 7:5–12).

5. The Ark in Zion

In the reign of David, Zion is identified with the city of David (2 Sam 5:7; 1 Kgs 8:1). After Solomon constructed the temple, the realm of Zion

---

55. Willis, "Samuel Versus Eli," 211.
56. See Eynikel, "Eli Narrative," 88–106.
57. Miller and Roberts, *Hand*, 20, 25–26.

appears to have been expanded to the summit of the Temple Mount (see Pss 9:12; 20:3; 48:3; 50:2).

The ark's travels, which began after the receiving of the covenant at Mount Sinai, would climax in the entrance of the ark into Jerusalem. Accordingly, Dempsey states that the Chronicler thought that the history of the ark's entrance to Zion and its installation in the temple was the model for the restoration of proper worship in the post-exilic period.[58]

The destination of the ark's journey was Zion, Yahweh's permanent dwelling. The ark provided Zion with significant status, as the city would play an immensely important part in the religious life of Israel. After the installation of the ark it was called the city of God (Ps 48:7) and his footstool, for God resides there (Ps 9:11; Isa 8:18) and reigns over the universe. Zion as God's dwelling place and as a center of Israelite life attracted regular pilgrimages. Pilgrims could expect physical as well as spiritual blessing in Zion because everything they needed came from God (Pss 128:5; 132:15–17; 133; 134).

In their songs the psalmists exalted Zion as the city of God (48:1), the city of the Great King (48:2), the dwelling place (76:2), the holy mountain (48:1; 99:9) and footstool (99:5; 132:7). They praised Yahweh's reign in Zion (99:1–2; 110:2; 146:10). The significance of Zion remained, even after the ark disappeared, and it is from Mount Zion that Yahweh will rule over men forever (Mic 4:7). The Israelites believed that deliverance would come out of Zion (Pss 14:7; 53:6). During the exilic period, the interest of the Israelite remnants was in Zion. They never gave up the expectation of its restoration, even though some lived as captives in Babylonia (Ps 137). It is from Zion that a redeemer would come (see Ps 2:6; Isa 59:20). For them, it remained the navel of the earth (Ezek 38:12).

Thus, the ark was used as a substantial object that represented how Yahweh chose Zion as his eternal resting place. Indeed, it is on account of the ark that Zion was entitled to play such a cardinal role in the history of Israelite faith.

F. THE ARK AND ISRAEL

This is a theological conclusion regarding the ark of Yahweh in Israelite history. The ark as God's very presence on earth accompanied Israel at the outset of the nation, if she is considered to have been formed as a

---

58. Dempsey, "Ark and Temple," 233–39.

nation after the exodus. By manufacturing the ark at Sinai, in accordance with Yahweh's instruction, Israel could meet her God at the ark. The localization of his epiphany was focused there, whereas previously he had appeared only in tongues of fire from within a bush (Exod 3:1–4) and at the peak of Mount Sinai (19:20; 24:10–18). The ark was to be managed by the priests appointed in service of Yahweh, guaranteeing the sanctity of the ark. When the Israelites committed idolatry, the ark containing the two tablets of the Ten Commandments was employed to restore their covenantal relationship with God. This shows us that Yahweh wanted to keep gracious communion with his people in accordance with the law. During the wilderness wanderings, when the people of Israel were on the march, the ark led the way, representing Yahweh's leadership over the people as they made their way toward the promised land (Num 10:35–36). By using the ark, Yahweh introduced a significant epoch in the process of redemptive history—crossing the Jordan River and the conquest of Jericho.

Even in the land of Canaan, the ark as a marvelous emblem of Yahweh's invisible presence was the center of the covenantal life and cultus of Israel (see Josh 8:30–35). They could experience Yahweh's glorious and majestic presence before the ark in the tabernacle. Thus, they used it as a place of God's revelation and received his directions in urgent military situations (Judg 20:27). However, they were punished when they mistreated or broke the covenantal law (see 1 Sam 6:19; 2 Sam 6:6–8). In a normative relationship with God, the Israelite tribes, scattered in the different districts over the whole area of Canaan, could live by the power of Yahweh, who inhabited the ark. Accordingly, the capture of the ark by the Philistines signified distress for Israel since the ark's deportation stands for *Ichabod* "no glory" (see 1 Sam 4:21–22). But Yahweh brought about his sovereign will among the Philistines as well. While the ark remained at Kiriath-Jearim the complete official cultus was not restored and the people of Israel mourned and sought after Yahweh (see 1 Sam 7:2).

The ark's journeyings, which began after the giving of the covenant at Mount Sinai, would reach their peak in the arrival of the ark at Jerusalem (2 Sam 6). After the installation of the ark in Zion, Yahweh's dwelling place, the city of Zion played an enormously important role in the religious history of Israel.

The fate of the ark was equal to that of the people of Israel (see Jer 3:16). It may have disappeared during the destruction of the temple, but its significance for Yahweh's presence sustained the Israelites until their return from Babylonian captivity. Yahweh resided with them in a different way until that time. However, it is justifiable to say that it is difficult to explain the religion and history of Israel without reckoning with the ark that symbolized the holy presence of God in the daily lives of Old Testament Israelites.

G. THE DISAPPEARANCE OF THE ARK

In his preaching, Jeremiah obviously hinted at the disappearance of the original ark, which had attracted honor and reverence in the past (Jer 3:16). However, it is not certain when and how the ark was lost because Scripture itself is silent on this matter. As a result, assumptions on the disappearance of the ark have grown.

Second Maccabees 2:4–7 says that Jeremiah was told to climb up Mount Nebo and to take a tent, the ark, and the altar of incense, and to seal them in a cave, where they would remain undiscovered until God again gathers his people: "It is recorded also that, in obedience to a divine command, the prophet gave orders for the tent of meeting and the Ark to accompany him, and he went off to the mountain from the top of which Moses had seen God's promised land. Arriving at the mountain, Jeremiah found a cave-dwelling into which he carried the Tent, the Ark, and the altar of incense; he then blocked up the entrance. Some of his companions went to mark out the way, but were unable to find it. Jeremiah heard of this and took them to task. 'The place is to remain unknown', he said, 'until God finally gathers his people together and shows them his favour'" (REB). However, this document is clearly a later legend dependent on the passage of Jer 3:16. In contrast to this, 2 Esdras 10:20–22 claims that the sanctuary was destroyed and the ark was taken as spoil: "'Do not do that', I urged; 'let yourself be persuaded because of Zion's misfortunes, and take comfort from the sorrow of Jerusalem. You see how our sanctuary has been laid waste, our altar demolished, our temple destroyed . . . and the Ark of our covenant has been plundered" (REB).

According to Ethiopian tradition, the biblical account of the Queen of Sheba's visit to Solomon is significantly incomplete. What is missing is the story that Sheba came to marry Solomon, but failed to meet his requirement that she should not take anything from his palace without his permission. This tradition states that Menelik, the son of Makeda, the biblical Queen, met Solomon and took the ark of the covenant back to the Axumite kingdom. The Orthodox Church believes that the ark is still resting in a small chapel in the city of Axum, but no one can see it.[59]

Haran contends that under the kingship of Manasseh of Judah the ark was removed from the inner sanctuary of the temple to make room for an image of Asherah (2 Kgs 21:3, 7; 2 Chr 33:3, 7).[60] In this regard, Ezekiel describes the glorious throne-chariot of God in great detail, while nowhere does he mention the ark. Haran's argument that this omission of the ark in Ezekiel's prophecy can be explained by the fact that the ark no longer existed in his time was irrelevantly applied because the contents Ezekiel saw were a mere vision, and had nothing to do with the existence of the ark.[61] The cherubim and temple described in his prophecy do not mean that they existed in his time. Certainly, the biblical document testifies that the ark was in the temple in the reign of Josiah after the time of Manasseh (2 Chr 35:3).

Agreeing with Jewish tradition, Price is convinced that Josiah hid the ark in a secret room beneath the Temple Mount.[62] He did this to prevent its being captured by the Babylonians. This place is now the location of the Dome of the Rock and is controlled by Muslims. Nevertheless, it remains uncertain whether the ark has in fact survived.

In a recent study on the fate of the ark of the covenant where Day researched twelve different views, he concluded that the ark disappeared about the time of the exile and the most likely explanation is that it was simply destroyed along with the temple in 586 BC.[63] However, the Old Testament nowhere obviously mentions the fate of the ark, not even its possible destruction. Yet, it states clearly that the ark was a disposable object in the process of the redemptive historical progression. Thus, it

59. See Taws, "Guardian?" 10.
60. Haran, "Disappearance," 46–58.
61. Haran, "Ark and Cherubim," 34.
62. Price, *Search*, 323.
63. Day, "Ark?" 250–70. 1) Ark hidden on Mt Gerizim in the time of Eli or Moses, 2) ark taken to Ethiopia in the time of Somomon, 3) ark removed by Shashak, 4) ark removed by deliberate internal action soon after disruption of the united monarchy, 5) ark removed by Jehoash, 6) ark removed by Ahaz, 7) ark removed by Hezekiah, 8) ark removed by Manasseh, 9) ark removed or hidden by Josiah, 10) ark hidden by Jeremiah, 11) ark carried away by the Babylonians under Nebuchadnezzar, 12) ark destroyed by the Babylonians under Nebuchadnezzar.

is biblically insignificant whether or not the ark has survived all these years, because God resides among his people in a different way: through his Holy Spirit. Therefore the disappearance of the ark may have been a part of God's sovereign plan.

Bibliography

Aalders, G. Ch. "Jeremia en de ark." *Gereformeerd Theologisch Tijdschrift* 21 (1921) 276–86.
Ackroyd, P. R. *The Second Book of Samuel*. CBC. Cambridge: Cambridge University Press, 1977.
Aharoni, Y. *The Land of the Bible*. London: Burns & Oates, 1974.
Ahlström, G. W. "The Travels of the Ark: A Religio-Political Composition." *JNES* 43:2 (1984) 141–49.
Aitken, K. T. "zāqēn." In *NIDOTTE*, 1137–39. Vol. 1.
Albright, W. F. *The Biblical Period from Abraham to Ezra*. New York: Harper Torchbooks, 1963.
Alexandere, Monique. "L'Épée de flamme (Gen. 3, 24): Textes Chrétiens et traditions Juives." In *Hellenica et Judaica*, 403–41. Leuven: Peeters, 1986.
Allen, Leslie C. *Jeremiah, a Commentary*. The Old Testament library. Louisville, KY: John Knox, 2008.
Allen, L. C. *Psalms 101–150*. WBC 21. Dallas: Word Books, 1983.
Alt, A. "Das Grossreich Davids." In *Kleine Schriften zur Geschichte des Volkes Israel*, 66–75. Vol. 2. Munich: C. H. Becksche Verlagsbuchhandlung, 1953.
Amit, Y. *The Book of Judges: The Art of Editing*. Leiden: Brill, 1999.
Amsler, S. "Loi orale et loi écrite dans le Deutéronome." In *Das Deuteronomium: Entstehung, Geschtalt und Botschaft*, edited by N. Lohfink, 51–54. Leuven: Peeters, 1985.
Anderson, A. A. *2 Samuel*. WBC 11. Dallas: Word Books, 1989.
Anderson, G. W. "Israel: Amphictyony; `am; kāhāl; `ēdâh." In *Translating & Understanding the Old Testament*, edited by H. T. Frank and W. L. Reed, 135–51. Nashville: Abingdon, 1970.
Arnold, R. W. *Ephod and Ark: A Study in the Records and Religion of the Ancient Hebrews*. Harvard Theological Studies 3. Cambridge: Harvard University Press, 1917.
Auffret, P. *Làmoment des tribus*. BZAW 289. Berlin: De Gruyter, 1999.
———. *La Sagesse a bati la maison*. OBO 49. Fribourg: Éditions universitaires Fribourg, 1982.
Augustine. *De Civitate Dei contra Paganos*. Vol. 1. London: SPCK, 1924.
Averbeck, R. E. "ʾāšām." In *NIDOTTE*, 553–66. Vol. 1.
Ballhorn, Egbert. *Israel am Jordan: narrative Topographie im Buch Josua, Bonner biblische Beiträge*. Bonn: Bonn University Press (V & R Unipress), 2011.
Bavinck, H. *Reformed Dogmatics*. Vol 2, *God and Creation*. Translated by J. Bolt and J. Vriend. Grand Rapids: Baker Academic, 2004.
Beal, R. H. *The Organization of the Hittite Military*. Heidelberg: Carl Winter, 1992.
Begg, C. T. "David's Transfer of the Ark According to Josephus." *BBR* 7 (1997) 11–35.
Bentzen, A. *King and Messiah*. London: Lutterworth, 1955.

Bergen, R. D. 1, 2 Samuel. NAC 7. Nashville: Broadman & Holman, 1996.
Bergsträsser, G. *Hebräische Grammatik*. Vol. 2. Hildesheim: Georg Olms Verlag, 1986.
Berlejung, A. *Die Theologie der Bilder*. OBO162. Freiburg: Universitätverlag Freiburg Schweiz, 1998.
Besters, A. "Israël et Fils d'Israël dans les livres historiques (Genèse–IIRois)." *RB* 74 (1967) 5–23.
Bimson, J. J. *Illustrated Encyclopedia of Bible Places*. Leicester: IVP, 1995.
Birch, B. C., et al. *A Theological Introduction to the Old Testament*. Nashville: Abingdon, 1999.
Bishop, R. E. "Shiloh." *Biblical Illustrator* 15 (1988) 62–64.
Block, D. I. *Judges, Ruth*. NAC 6. Nashville: Broadman & Holman, 1999.
Bock, S. *Kleine Geschichte Israels*. Freiburg: Herder, 1998.
Boling, R. G. *Joshua*. AB. New York: Doubleday, 1982.
Booij, Thijs. *Godswoorden in de Psalmen hun funktie en achtergronden*. Amsterdam: Rodopi, 1978.
Borowski, Elie. "Cherubim: God's Throne?" *BAR* 21:4 (1995) 36–41.
Bray, G. *The Doctrine of God*. Leicester: IVP, 1993.
Briend, Jaques. "Bethléem-Ephratha." *Monde de la Bible* 30 (Aug–Oct 1983) 29.
Bright, J. *History of Israel*. Philadelphia: Westminster, 1991.
Brockelmann, Carl. *Hebräische Syntax*. Neukirchen-Vluyn: Erziehungsvereins, 1956.
Broekhuis, J. "De ark." In *Verkenningen in Exodus*, edited by W. van Benthem, 149–55. Kampen, the Netherlands: Kok, 1986.
Brongers, H. A. "Die Wendung *besêm jhwh* in Alten Testament." *ZAW* 77 (1965) 1–20.
Brouwer, C. *De ark*. Baarn, the Netherlands: Bosh & Keuning, 1955.
Brueggemann, W. *A Commentary on Jeremiah: Exile & Homecoming*. Grand Rapids: Eerdmans, 1998.
———. *First and Second Samuel: Interpretation*. Louisville, KY: John Knox, 1990.
———. *Theology of the Old Testament: Testimony, Dispute, Advocacy*. Minneapolis: Fortress, 1997.
Budd, P. J. *Numbers*. WBC 4. Dallas: Word Books, 1984.
Budde, K. *Samuel*. KHC. Tübingen: J. C. B. Mohr, 1902.
Buis, P. *Le Livre des Rois*. Sources Bibliques. Paris: Gabalda, 1997.
Butler, T. C. *Joshua*. WBC 7. Dallas: Word Books, 1983.
———. *Judges*. WBC 8. Nashville: Thomas Nelson, 2009.
Calvin, J. *Commentaries on the Book of Joshua*. Grand Rapids: Eerdmans, 1979.
———. *Commentaries on the Book of Psalms*. Vol. 4. Grand Rapids: Eerdmans, 1993.
———. *Commentaries on the Epistle of Paul the Apostle to the Hebrews*, Grand Rapids: Baker, 1993.
———. *Commentaries on the Four Last Books of Moses*. Translated by C. W. Bingham. Vol. 2–3. Grand Rapids: Baker, 1993.
———. *Predigten über das 2 Buch Samuelis*, Neuchirchen: Neuchircher Verlag, 1961,
Campbell, A. F. *The Ark Narrative (1 Samuel 4–6; 2 Samuel 6): A Form-Critical and Traditio-Historical Study*. Missoula, MT: Society of Biblical Literature, 1975.
———. "Yahweh and the Ark: A Case Study in Narrative." *JBL* 98:1 (1979) 31–43.
Caquot, A., and P. de Robert. *Les Livres de Samuel*. Geneva: Labor et Fides, 1994.
Carlson, R. A. *David: The Chosen King*. Uppsala, Sweden: Almqvist & Wiksells, 1964.
Carroll, R. P. *Jeremiah*. OTL. London: SCM, 1986.
Cassuto, U. *A Commentary on the Book of Exodus*. Jerusalem: Magnes, 1967.

Cazelles, H. *Écriture Parole et Esprit: trois aspects de l'hermeneutique biblique.* Paris: Descle, 1971.

———. "Israël du nord et arche d'alliance (Jér. III16)." *VT* 18 (1968) 147–58.

Christensen, D. L. *Deuteronomy 1–11.* WBC 6A. Dallas: Word Books, 1991.

Clements, R. E. *Deuteronomy.* Old Testament Guides. Sheffield: Sheffield Academic, 1989.

Clines, David J. A. "X, X *BEN Y, BEN Y*: Personal Names in Hebrew Narrative Style." In *Telling Queen Michal's Story,* edited by David J. A. Clines and Tamara C. Eskenazi, 124–28. JSOTSup 119. Sheffield: Sheffield Academic, 1991.

Coats, G. W. "The Ark of the Covenant in Joshua: A Probe into the History of a Tradition." *HAR* 9 (1985) 137–57.

Cogan, M. *1 Kings.* AB. New York: Doubleday, 2001.

Cohen, A. *Joshua, Judges.* Soncino, Italy: Soncino, 1970.

Cole, R. D. *Numbers.* NAC 3B. Nashville: Broadman & Holman, 2000.

Collon, D. *First Impressions: Cylinder Seals in the Ancient Near East.* Chicago: University of Chicago Press, 1987.

Craigie, P. C., et al. *Jeremiah 1–25.* WBC 26. Dallas: Word Books, 1991.

Crüsemann, F. "Zwei alttestamentliche Witze, ISam 21:11–15 und IISam 6:16, 20–23 als Beispiele einer biblischen Gattung." *ZAW* 92 (1980) 215–27.

Cullmann, O. *Christus und Zeit.* Zürich: Evangelischer Verlag A. G, 1948.

Dahood, M. "Hebrew Ugaritic Lexicography II." *Biblica* 45 (1964) 393–417.

———. *Psalms 101–150.* AB. New York: Doubleday, 1970.

Day, John. "Whatever Happened to the Ark of the Covenant?" In *Temple and Worship in Biblical Israel,* edited by John Day, 250–70. London: T & T Clark, 2005.

De Boer, P. A. H. "The Perfect with waw in 2 Samuel 6:16." In *Selected Studies in Old Testament Exegesis,* edited by C. van Duin, 142–49. Leiden: Brill, 1991.

———. "Research into the Text of 1 Samuel I–XVI: A Contribution to the Study of the Books of Samuel." PhD diss., Leiden University, Amsterdam, 1938.

Delcor, M. "Jahweh et Dagon ou le Jahwisme face àla religion des Philistins, d'après 1 Sam. V." *VT* 14 (1964) 136–54.

De Moor, J. C. *The Seasonal Pattern in the Ugaritic Myth of Ba'lu.* AOAT 16. Neukirchen-Vluyn: Neukirchener Verlag, 1971.

Dempsey, D. A. "The Ark and the Temple in 1 and 2 Chronicles." *Bible Today* 36 (1998) 233–39.

De Robert, Philippe. "Arche et Guerre Sainte." *ÉTR* 56:1 (1981) 51–53.

Derousseaux, L. *La crainte de Dieu dans l'Ancien Testament.* Paris: Les éditions du Cerf, 1970.

De Tarragon, J. M. "David et l'arche: 2 Samuel 6." *RB* 86 (1979) 514–23.

———. "La kapporet est-elle une fiction ou un élément du culte tardif?" *RB* 88 (1981) 5–12.

De Vaulx, J. *Les Nombres.* Sources Bibliques. Paris: Gabalda, 1972.

De Vaux, Roland. "Arche d'alliance et Tente de réunion." In *Àla rencontre de Dieu,* edited by A. Gelin, 55–70. Le Puy, France: Éditions Xavier Mappess, 1961.

———. *Bible et Orient.* Paris: Les éditions du Cerf, 1967.

De Wolff, I., and W. H. de Boer. *De geschiedenis der Godsopenbaring.* Vol. 4. Enschede, the Netherlands: Boersma, 1975.

Dibelius, M. *Die Lade Jahves: Eine religionsgeschichtliche Untersuchung.* FRLANT 98. Göttingen: Vandenhoeck & Ruprecht, 1906.

Diebner, B. J. "Gottesdienst II." In *TRE*, edited by G. Krause and G. Muller. Vol. 14, 5–28. Berlin: Gruyter, 1977.

Dietrich, Walter. *Samuel, 1Sam 1–12.* BKAT. Neukirchen-Vluyn: Neukirchener Verlag, 2010.

Dietrich, W., and T. Naumann. *Die Samuelbücher*. EdF287. Darmstadt: Wissenschaftliche Buchgesellschaft, 1995.

Dorsey, David A. *The Roads and Highways of Ancient Israel*. Baltimore: Johns Hopkins University Press, 1991.

Dothan, T. *The Philistines and their Material Culture*. Jerusalem: Israel Exploration Society, 1982.

Dreytza, M. "yād." In *NIDOTTE*, 402–5. Vol. 2.

Driver, S. R. *An Introduction to the Literature of the Old Testament*. Edinburgh: T & T Clark, 1913.

Eichhorn, W. *Die Religionen Chinas*. Stuttgart: Kohlhammer, 1973.

Eichrodt, W. *Theologie des Alte Testament*. Vol. 1. Stuttgart: Ehrenfried Klotz Verlag, 1933.

Eissfeldt, O. *Einleitung in das Alte Testament*. Tübingen: J. C. B. Mohr, 1976.

———. "The Hebrew Kingdom." In *History of the Middle East and the Aegean Region c. 1380–1000 BC*, edited by I. E. S. Edwards et al. Rev. ed. Vol. 2. Cambridge Ancient History. Cambridge: Cambridge University Press, 1965.

———. "Jahweh Zebaoth." *Kleine Schriften*, 3:103–23. Tübingen: J. C. B. Mohr, 1966.

———. "Die Lade und Gesetzestafeln." *TZ* 16 (1960) 281–84.

———. "Lade und Stierbild." *ZAW* 58 (1940–1941) 190–215.

Eynikel, Erik. "Relation between the Eli Narrative (1 Sam 1–4) and the Ark Narrative (1 Sam 1–6; 2 Sam 6:1–19)." In *Past, Present, Future: The Deuteronomistic History and the Prophets*, edited by J. C. de Moor and H. E. van Rooy, 88–106. Leiden: Brill, 2000.

Fee, Gordon D. "History as Context for Interpretation." In *The Act of Bible Reading*, edited by Elmer Dyck, 10–32. Downers Grove: IVP, 1996.

Firth, David G. *1 & 2 Samuel*, Apollos Old Testament commentary. Nottingham: Apollos Press; Downers Grove: IVP, 2009.

Fohrer, G. *Theologische Grungdstrukturen des Alten Testaments*. Berlin: Töpelmann, 1972

Freedman, D. N., and P. O'Connor. "kerūb." *ThWAT*, 322–34. Vol. 4.

Freeman, C. *Egypt, Greece and Rome: Civilization of the Ancient Mediterranean*. Oxford: Oxford University Press, 1996.

Fretheim, T. E. "The Ark in Deuteronomy." *CBQ* 30 (1968) 1–14.

———. "The Cultic Use of the Ark of the Covenant in the Monarchical Period." PhD diss., Princeton University, Princeton, NJ, 1967.

———. *First and Second Kings*. Westminster Bible Companion. Louisville, KY: John Knox, 1999.

Fritz, Volkmar. *Das erste Buch der Könige*. Zürcher Bibelkommentare. Zürich: TVZ, 1996.

Fuller, Daniel P. *The Unity of the Bible*. Grand Rapids: Zondervan, 1992.

Garsiel, M. *The First Book of Samuel*. Jerusalem: Rubin Mass, 1990.

Geyer, J. B. "Mice and Rites in 1 Samuel V–VI." *VT* 31: 3 (1981) 293–304.

Geoghegan, J. C. "'Until This Day' and the Preexilic Redaction of the Deuteronomistic History." *JBL* 122 (2003) 201–27.

Gispen, W. H. *Numeri 1*. COT. Kampen, the Netherlands: Kok, 1959.

Glueck, N. *The River Jordan*. London: Lutterworth, 1946.
Goldingay, J. *Psalms 90-150*. Vol. 3 of *Psalms*. Baker Commentary on the Old Testament: Wisdom and Psalms. Grand Rapids: Baker, 2008.
Goldman, S. *Samuel*. Soncino Books of the Bible. London: Soncino, 1986.
Gootjes, N. H. "De Geest in Bezaleël (Exodus 31:3)." In *Ambt en aktualiteit: Opstellen aangeboden aan Prof. Dr. C. Trimp*, edited by F. H. Folkerts et al., 25-35. Haarlem, the Netherlands: Vijlbrief, 1992.
———. "Ons ten voorbeeld geschied." Parts 1-4. *De Reformatie* (Sept. 19-Oct. 10, 1987) 62:48, 977-79; 62:49, 997-98; 63:1, 1-3; 63:2, 21-23.
Gordon, R. P. *I and II Samuel: A Commentary*. Exeter: Paternoster, 1986.
Goslinga, C. J. *Het tweede boek Samuël*. COT. Kampen, the Netherlands: Kok, 1962.
Gottwald, N. K. *The Tribes of Yahweh: A Sociology of the Religion of Liberated Israel 1250-1050 BCE*. Maryknoll, NY: Orbis, 1979.
Gray, G. B. *Joshua, Judges and Ruth*. CB. London: Thomas Nelson, 1967.
Green, A. R. "Solomon and Siamun: A Synchronism Between Dynastic Israel and the Twenty-First Dynasty of Egypt." *JBL* 97 (1978) 353-67.
Greiner, D. *Segen und Segnen: Eine systematisch-theologische Grundlegung*. Stuttgart: Kohlhammer, 1999.
Gressmann, H. *Die Lade Jahwes und das Allerheiligste der Salomonischen Tempels*. Berlin: Kohlammer, 1920.
———. *Mose und sein Zeit*. Göttingen: Vandenhoeck & Ruprecht, 1913.
Grudem, W. A. *Systematic Theology: An Introduction to Biblical Doctrine*. Grand Rapids: Zondervan, 1994.
Gunkel, H. *Genesis*. Göttingen: Vandenhoeck & Ruprecht, 1977.
———. "Die Lade Jahves ein Thronsitz." *ZMR* 21 (1906) 33-42.
———. *Das Märchen im Alten Testament*. Frankfurt am Main: Athenäum, 1987.
———. *Die Psalmen*. HAT 2. Göttingen: Vandenhoeck & Ruprecht, 1926.
Gunneweg, A. H. J. *Biblische Theologie des Alten Testaments*. Stuttgart: Kohlhammer, 1993.
———. *Leviten und Priester*. Göttingen: Vandenhoeck & Ruprecht, 1965.
Guthe, H. *Geschichte des Volkes Israel*. Freiburg: J. C. B. Mohr, 1899.
Hamlin, E. J. *Joshua: Inheriting the Land*. International Theological Commentary. Grand Rapids: Eerdmans, 1983.
Handy, L. K. "On the Dating and Dates of Solomon's Reign." In *The Age of Solomon*, edited by L. K. Handy, 96-105. Leiden: Brill, 1997.
Haran, M. "The Ark and the Cherubim: Their Symbolic Significance in Biblical Ritual." *IEJ* 9 (1959) 30-38, 89-94.
———. "The Bas-Reliefs on the Sarcophagus of Ahiram King of Byblos in the Light of Archaeological and Literary Parallels from the Ancient Near East." *IEJ* 8 (1958) 14-25.
———. "The Disappearance of the Ark." *IEJ* 13 (1963) 46-58.
Harman, Allan. *Psalms*. A Mentor Commentary. Ross-shire, Scotland: Christian Focus, 1998.
Harrison, R. K. *Introduction to the Old Testament*. Grand Rapids: Eerdmans, 1985.
Hartmann, R. "Zelt und Lade." *ZAW* 37 (1917-1918) 209-44.
Hasel, G. F. *Old Testament Theology: Basic Issues in the Current Debate*. Grand Rapids: Eerdmans, 1995.

Hegel, G. W. F. *Hegels Religionsphilosophie: in gekürzter Form, mit Einführung, Anmerkungen und Erlänterungen.* Edited by Arthur Drews. Leipzig: Eugen Diederichs, 1905.

———. *Phänomenologie des Geistes.* Edited by Georg Lasson. Leipzig: Felix Meiner, 1921.

Heinemann, O. "Die 'Lade' aus Akazienholz: ägyptische Wurzeln eines israelitischen Kultobjekts?" *BN* 80 (1995) 32–40.

Herrmann, S. *Geschichte Israels in alttestamentlicher Zeit.* Munich: Kaiser, 1980.

———. "'Realunion' und 'Charismatisches Königtum' zu Zwei Offenen Fargen der Verfassungen in Juda und Israel." *ErIsrl* 24 (1993) 97–103.

Hertzberg, H. W. *Die Samuelbücher.* ATD 9, 10. Göttingen: Vandenhoeck & Ruprecht, 1965.

Hess, R.S. *Joshua.* Tyndale Old Testament Commentaries 6. Downers Grove: IVP, 1996.

Hillers, D. R. "Ritual Procession of the Ark and Psalm 132." *CBQ* 30 (1968) 48–55.

Hodge, C. *Systematic Theology.* Vol. 1. London: Thomas Nelson, 1878.

Hoftijzer, J. *The Function and Use of the Imperfect Forms with Nun Paragogicum in Classical Hebrew.* Assen, the Netherlands: Van Gorcum, 1985.

Holladay, W. L. *Jeremiah.* Vol. 1. Philadelphia: Fortress, 1986.

———. *The Psalms through Three Thousand Years.* Minneapolis: Fortress, 1993.

Holwerda, B. *Bijzondere Canoniek.* Kampen, the Netherlands: Van den Berg, 1972.

———. "De Priester-koning in het Oude Testament." In *Begonnen hebbende van Mozes,* 49–77. Terneuzen, the Netherlands: Littooij, 1953.

Hostetter, E. C. *Nations Mightier and More Numerous: The Biblical View of Palestine's Pre-Israelite People.* Richland Hills: BIBAL, 1995.

House, P. R. *1, 2 Kings.* NAC 8. Nashville: Broadman & Holman, 1995.

Houtman,␣C. *Exodus* 3. COT. Kampen, the Netherland: Kok, 1996.

Howard, D. M. *Joshua.* NAC 5. Nashville: Broadman & Holman, 1998.

Hubbard, R. L. Jr. *First and Second Kings.* Chicago: Moody, 1991.

Jacob, B. *The Second Book of the Bible: Exodus.* Hoboken: KTAV, 1992.

Jacquet, L. *Les Psaumes et le coeur de l'homme.* Gembloux, Belgium: Duculot, 1979.

Jagersma, H. *Geschiedenis van Israël in het oudtestamentische tijdvak.* Kampen, the Netherlands: Kok, 1979.

Janowski, B. *Rettungsgewißheit und Epiphanie des Heils: Das Motiv der Hilfe Gottes »am Morgen« im Alten Orient und im Alten Testament.* Vol. 1. WMANT 59. Neuchirchen-Vluyn: Neuchirchener Verlag, 1989.

———. *Sühne als Heilsgeschehen: studien zur Sühnetheologie der Priesterschift und zur Wurzel KPR im Alten Orient und im Alten Testament.* WMANT 55. Neuchirchen-Vluyn: Neuchirchener Verlag, 1982.

Janzen, W. *Exodus.* Waterloo, ON: Herald Press, 2000.

Japhet, S. "From King's Sanctuary to the Chosen City." *Judaism* 46 (1997) 132–39.

Jenni, E. *Das hebräische Pi'el.* Zurich: EVZ-Verlag, 1968.

Jenson, P. P. "ṣebaʾ." In *NIDOTTE,* 34–37. Vol. 4.

Jones, D. R. *Jeremiah.* NCBC. Grand Rapids: Eerdmans, 1992.

Josephus, F. *Jewish Antiquities.* Translated by H. St. J. Thackeray and R. Marcus. Cambridge: Harvard University Press, 1988.

Joüon, Paul. *A Grammar of Biblical Hebrew.* Translated and revised by T. Muraoka. 2 vols. Subsidia biblica 14/1–2. Rome: Pontifical Biblical Institute, 1991.

Kaufman, A. S. "Determining the Length of the Medium Cubit." *PEQ* 116 (1984) 120–32.

Keel, O. "Davids 'Tanz' vor der Lade." *Buk* 51 (1996) 11–14.
Keel, O., and C. Uehlinger. *Göttinnen, Götter und Gottessymbole: Neue Erkenntnisse zur Religionsgeschichte Kanaans und Israels aufgrund bislang unerschlossener ikonographischer Quellen*. QD 134. Freiburg: Herder, 1992.
Keil, C. F. *Biblischer Commentar über die Bücher Samuelis*. Leipzig: Dörffling und Franke, 1875.
Kelm, G. L. *Escape to Conflict*. Fort Worth: IAR Publications, 1991.
Kio, S. H. "What did Saul ask for: ark or ephod?" *The Bilbe Translator* 47:2 (1996) 240–46.
Kitchen, K. A. "Egypt, Ugarit, Qatna and Covenant." *UF* 11 (1979) 452–64.
———. *On the Reliability of the Old Testament*. Grand Rapids: Eerdmans, 2003.
———. "Sheba and Arabia." In *The Age of Solomon*, edited by L. K. Handy, 125–53. Leiden: Brill, 1997.
Klein, R. W. "Back to the Future: The Tabernacle in the Book of Exodus." *Interpretation* 50 (1996) 264–76.
———. *1 Samuel*. WBC 10. Dallas: Word Books, 1983.
Klein, R. W., and T. Krüger. *1 Chronicles*. Hermeneia. Minneapolis: Fortress Press, 2006.
Klement, H. H. *II Samuel 21–24: Context, Structure and Meaning in the Samuel Conclusion*. Frankfurt am Main: Peter Lang, 2000.
Koch, Klaus. "Some Considerations on the Translation of kappret in the Septuagint." In *Pomegranates Golden Bells: Studies in Biblical, Jewish and Near Eastern Ritual, Law, and Literature in Honor of Jacob Milgrom*, edited by David P. Wright, et al., 65–75. Winona Lake, IN: Eisenbrauns, 1995.
Köhler, Ludwig. *Theologie des Alten Testaments*. Neue theologische Grundrisse. Vierte, überarbeitete auflage. Tübingen: J. C. B. Mohr (P. Siebeck), 1966.
Koolhaas, A. A. *Theocratie en monarch in Israël*. Wageningen, the Netherlands: H. Veenman en zonen, 1957.
Körtner, Ulrich H. J. *Der inspirierte Leser*. Göttingen: Vandenhoeck & Ruprecht, 1994.
Kraus, H. J. *Psalmen 60–150*. BKAT 15:2. Neukirchen-Vluyn: Neukirchener Verlag, 1978.
Kristensen, W. B. "De ark van Jahwe." In *Verzamelde Bijdragen tot Kennis der antieke godsdiensten*, 169–99. Amsterdam: Noord-Hollandsche Uitgevers, 1947.
Kroeze, J. H. *Het Boek Jozua*. COT. Kampen, the Netherlands: Kok, 1968.
———. *Genesis veertien: een exegetisch-historische studie*. PhD diss., Vrije Universiteit Amsterdam, Hilversum: Schipper, 1937.
Kronholm, T. "*sākak*." *ThWAT*, 838–56. Vol. 5.
Külling, S. R. *Zur Datierung der 'Genesis-P-Stücke.'* Kampen, the Netherlands: Kok, 1964.
Labuschagne, C. J. *Deuteronomium. IB*. POut. Nijkerk, the Netherlands: Callenbach, 1987.
Lang, B. "Kapper." *ThWAT*, 303–18. Vol. 4.
Langlamet, F. *Gilgal et les récits de la traversée du Jourdain*. Paris: Gabalda, 1969.
Leiman, Sid Z. "The Inverted nuns at Numbers 10:35–36 and the Book of Eldad and Medad." *JBL* 93 (1974) 348–55.
Lettinga, J. P. *Grammatica van het Bijbels Hebreeuws*. Leiden: E. J. Brill, 1976.
Levine, B. A. "More on the Inverted nuns of Num 10:35–36." *JBL* 95 (1976) 122–24.
———. *Numbers 1–20*. AB. New York: Doubleday, 1993.
Lewis, Joe O. "The Ark and the Tent." *Review and Expositor* 74 (Fall 1977) 531–48.
Lieberman, S. *Hellenism in Jewish Palestine*. New York: Jewish Theological Seminary of America, 1950.

Linville, J. R. *Israel in the Book of Kings: The Past as a Project of Social Identity.* JSOTSup 272. Sheffield: Sheffield Academic, 1998.
Lion-Cachet, F. N. *So het dit begin: Gods boodskap in die raamwerk van die historiese boeke van die Ouestament.* Potchefstroom, South Africa: DSP, PU vir CHO, 1989.
Long, V. Philips. *The Art of Biblical History.* Grand Rapids: Zondervan, 1994.
Loretz, O. "Die Steinernen Gesetzestafeln in der Lade: Probleme der Deuteronomium-Forschung zwischen Geschichte und Utopie." *UF* 9 (1977) 159–61.
Lotz, W. "Die Bundeslade." In *Festschrift Seiner Königlichen Hoheit dem Prinzregenten Luitpold von Bayern zum 80. Geburtstage dargebracht von der Universität Erlangen,* 143–86. Vol. 1. Erlangen, Germany: Deichert, 1901.
Lurker, M. *Wörterbuch biblischer Bilder und Symbol.* Munich: Kösel Verlag, 1973.
Maier, Gerhard. *Biblische Hermeneutik.* Wuppertal, Germany: Brockhaus, 1990.
Maier, Johann. *Altisraelitisch Heiligtum.* BZAW 93. Berlin: Töpelmann, 1965.
Mare, W. H. *The Archaeology of the Jerusalem Area.* Grand Rapids: Baker, 1987.
Marget, A. W. "*nkwn gwrn* in 2 Sam 6:6," *JBL* 39 (1920) 70–76.
Martens, E. A. *Jeremiah.* Believers Church Bible Commentary. Scottsdale, PA: Herald Press, 1986.
Matthews, Victor H., and Don C. Benjamin. *Old Testament Parallels: Laws and Stories from the Ancient Near East.* New York: Paulist Press, 1997.
Mauchline, J. *1 and 2 Samuel.* NCB. London: Oliphants, 1971.
May, H. G. "The Ark: a Miniature Temple." *AJSL* 52 (1935/1936) 215–34.
Mays, J. L. *Psalms: Interpretation.* Louisville, KY: John Knox, 1994.
Mazar, A. *Archaeology of the Land of the Bible: 10,000–586 B.C.E.* New York: Doubleday, 1990.
Mazar, E., and B. Mazar. *Excavations in the South of the Temple Mount: The Ophel of Biblical Jerusalem.* QEDEM 29. Jerusalem: Hebrew University, 1989.
McCarter, P. K. Jr. *1 Samuel.* AB 8. Garden City, NY: Doubleday, 1980.
McConville, J. G. *Deuteronomy.* AOTC 5. Leicester: Apollos, 2002.
———. *Law and Theology in Deuteronomy.* JSOTSup 33. Sheffield: JSOT, 1984.
McKeating, H. *The Book of Jeremiah.* Peterborough, UK: Epworth, 1999.
Meinhold, J. *Die "Lade Jahwes."* Tübingen: J. C. B. Mohr, 1900.
Meir, S. Ben. *Rashbam's Commentary on Exodus.* Annotated and translated by Martin I. Lockshin. BJS 310. Atlanta: Scholar, 1997.
Mendenhall, G. E. "The Census Lists of Numbers 1 and 26." *JBL* 77 (1958) 52–66.
Merrill, E. H. *Deuteronomy.* NAC 4. Nashville: Broadman & Holman, 1994.
Mettinger, T. N. D. "Israelite Aniconism: Developments and Origins." In *The Image and the Book,* edited by K. van der Toorn, 173–204. Leuven: Peeters, 1997.
———. *King and Messiah.* Lund, Sweden: Wallin & Dalholm, 1976.
Metzger, M. "Jahwe, der Kerubenthroner: die von Keruben flankierte Palmette und Sphingenthrone aus dem Libanon." In *Ingo Kottsieper,* edited by Jürgen van Oorschot, et al., 75–90. Göttingen: Vandenhoeck & Ruprecht, 1994.
———. *Königsthron und Gottesthron.* AOAT 15:1. Neukirchen-Vluyn: Neukirchener Verlag, 1985.
Michaeli, F. *Le Livre de L'Exode.* Paris: Delachaux & Niestlé, 1974.
Milgrom, J. *Numbers.* JPS Commentary. Philadelphia: Jewish Publication Society, 1990.
Millard, M. *Die Komposition des Psalters.* Tübingen: J. C. B. Mohr, 1994.
Miller, P. D., Jr., and J. J. M. Roberts. *The Hand of the Lord: A Reassessment of the "Ark Narrative" of 1 Samuel.* Baltimore: Johns Hopkins University Press, 1977.

Mitchell, D. C. *The Message of the Psalter: An Eschatological Programme in the Book of Psalms*. JSOTSup 252. Sheffield: Sheffield Academic, 1997.
Moran, W. L. "The End of the Unholy War and the Anti-Exodus." *Biblica* 44 (1963) 333–42.
Mowinckel, Sigmund. *Psalmenstudien 1–2*. Amsterdam: P. Schippers, 1966.
———. *The Psalms in Israel's Worship*. Vol. 1. Oxford: Basil Blackwell, 1962.
———. *Religion und Kultus*. Göttingen: Vandenhoeck & Ruprecht, 1953.
———. *Tetrateuch–Pentateuch–Hexateuch*. BZAW 90. Berlin: Töpelmann, 1964.
Mulder, M. J. *I Kings*. HCOT. Leuven: Peeters, 1998.
Murray, D. F. *Divine Prerogative and Royal Pretension: Pragmatics, Poetics and Polemics in a Narrative Sequence about David (2 Samuel 5.17–7.29)*. JSOTSup 264. Sheffield: Sheffield Academic, 1998.
———. "MQWM and the Future of Israel in 2 Samuel VII 10." *VT* 40 (1990) 298–320.
Naʾaman, N. "The Law of the Altar in Deuteronomy and the Cultic Site Near Shechem." In *Rethinking the Foundations*, edited by S. L. McKenzie and T. Römer, 141–61. Berlin: De Gruyter, 2000.
Noort, Ed. *Das Buch Josua*. EdF 292. Darmstadt: Wissenschaftliche Buchgesellschaft, 1998.
———. "De val van de grote stad Jericho: Kanttekeningen bij synchronische en diachronische benaderingen." *NedTT* 50 (1996) 265–79.
Noordtzij, A. *Kronieken*. Korte Verklaring 1. Kampen, the Netherlands: Kok, 1977.
Noth, M. *Das Buch Josua*. Tübingen: J. C. B. Mohr, 1953.
———. *Geschichte Israels*. Göttingen: Vandenhoeck & Ruprecht, 1954.
———. *Könige 1*. BKAT 9:1. Neukirchen-Vluyn: Neukirchener Verlag, 1968.
———. *Das System der Zwölf Stämme Israels*. BWANT 52. Darmstadt: Wissenschaftliche Buchgesellschaft, 1966.
O'Brien, J. M. *Priest and Levite in Malachi*. SBLDS 121. Atlanta: Scholar, 1990.
Ohmann, H. M. *Tellingen in de woestijn*. Groningen, the Netherlands: Bond van Mannen verenigingen op Gereformeerde Grondslag, 1983.
———. "Een top bereikt: David wordt koning." In *Een verzamelde levendige opstellen voorstelling*, 130–56. Kampen, the Netherlands: Van den Berg, 1993.
Ollenburger, Ben C. *Zion, the City of the Great King*. Sheffield: JSOT, 1987.
Owczarek, S. *Die Vorstellung vom Wohnen Gottes inmitten seines Volkes in der Priesterschrift: Zur Heiligtumstheologie der priesterschriftlichen Grundschrift*. EH 625. Frankfurt am Main: Peter Lang, 1998.
Pedersen, J. *Israel*. Vols. 3–4. Copenhagen: Branner og Korch, 1953.
Peels, E. *Shadow Sides: God in the Old Testament*. Translated by H. Lalleman. Waynesboro, GA: Paternoster, 2003.
Pietsch, M. *»Dieser ist der Sproß Davids . . . «*. WMANT 100. Neukirchen-Vluyn: Neukirchener Verlag, 2003.
Pitard, W. T. *Ancient Damascus*. Winona Lake, IN: Eisenbrauns, 1987.
Pitkänen, Pekka. *Central Sanctuary and Centralization of Worship in Ancient Israel: From the Settlement to the Building of Solomon's Temple*. Gorgias Dissertations—Near Eastern Studies. Piscataway, N.J: Gorgias Press, 2003.
———. *Joshua*. Apollos Old Testament commentary. Nottingham: Apollos; Downers Grove: IVP, 2010.
Porter, J. R. "2 Samuel VI and Psalm CXXXII." *JTS* 5 (1954) 161–73.

Price, R. In *Search of Temple Treasure: The Lost Ark and the Last Days*. Eugene, OR: Harvest, 1994.

Rashi, S. *Pentateuch with Targum Onkelos, Haphtaroth and Prayers for Sabbath and Rashi's Commentary: Exodus*. Translated by M. Rosenbaum and A. M. Silbermann. London: Shapiro, Vallentine, 1930.

Reimpell, W. "Der Ursprung der Lade Jahwes." *OLZ* 11 (1916) 326–31.

Rendsburg, G. A. *Linguistic Evidence for the Northern Origin of Selected Psalms*. Atlanta: Scholar, 1990.

Rendtorff, Rolf. *Theologie des Alten Testaments: Ein kanonischer Entwurf*. Vol. 1. Neukirchen-Vluyn: Neukirchener Verlag, 1999.

Reuss, E. *L'histoire sainte et la loi*. Paris: Librairie Sandoz et Fischbacher, 1879.

Rezetko, Robert. *Source and Revision in the Narratives of David's Transfer of the Ark: Text, Language and Story in 2 Samuel 6 and 1 Chronicles 13, 15–16*, Library of the Hebrew Bible / Old Testament studies. New York: T & T Clark, 2007.

Roberts, J. J. "The Davidic Origin of the Zion Tradition." *JBL* 92 (1973) 329–44.

Robinson, G. *1 and 2 Samuel*. Grand Rapids: Eerdmans, 1993.

Rogerson, J. W., and J. W. McKay. *Psalms 101–150*. CBC. Cambridge: Cambridge University Press, 1977.

Rose, Martin. *5: Mose 1–11/26–34*. ZB. Zürich: TVZ, 1994.

Ross, J. P. "Jahweh ṣᵉḇāōṯ in Samuel and Psalms." *VT* 17 (1967) 76–92.

Rost, L. *Die Überlieferung von der Thronnachfolge Davids*. BWAT 3:6. Stuttgart: Kohlhammer, 1926.

Rowe, Jonathan Y. *Michal's Moral Dilemma: A Literary, Anthropological and Ethical Interpretation*. Library of Hebrew Bible / Old Testament studies LH. New York: T & T Clark, 2011.

Rowley, H. H. *Worship in Ancient Israel: Its Forms and Meaning*. London: Camelot Press, 1939.

Rupprecht, K. *Der Tempel von Jerusalem*. BZAW 144. Berlin: Gruyter, 1977.

Ryken, Leland, et al., eds. *Dictionary of Biblical Imagery: An encyclopaedic exploration of the images, symbols, motifs, metaphors, figures of speech and literary patterns of the Bible*. 1st ed. Downers Grove: IVP, 1998.

Sarna, Nahum M. *Exodus*. The JPS Torah Commentary. Philadelphia: Jewish Publication Society, 1991.

———. *Genesis*. The JPS Torah Commentary. Philadelphia: Jewish Publication Society, 1989.

Schäfer-Lichtenberger, C. "»Sie wird nicht wieder hergestellt werden«." In *Mincha: Festgabe für Rolf Rendtorff zum 75. Geburtstag*, edited by Erhard Blum, 229–41. Neukirchen-Vluyn: Neukirchener, 2000.

Schicklberger, F. *Die Ladeerzählung des ersten Samuel-Buches: Eine literaturwissenschaftliche und theologiegeschichtliche Untersuchung*. Würzburg, Germany: Echter Verlag, 1973.

Schmidt, H. "Kerubenthron und Lade." In *Eucharisterion: Studien zur Religion und Literatur des Alten und Neuen Testament*, edited by H. Schmidt and H. Gunkel I, 121–44. Göttingen: Vandenhoeck & Ruprecht, 1923.

Schmidt, Werner H. *Einführung in das Alte Testament*. Berlin: Gruyter, 1982.

Schley, D. G. *Shiloh: A Biblical City in Tradition and History*. JSOTSup 63. Sheffield: JSOT, 1989.

Schreiner, J. *Jeremia 1–25*. NEB. Würzburg, Germany: Echter Verlag, 1993.

———. *Sion-Jerusalem Jahwes Königssitz: Theologie der Heiligen Stadt im Alten Testament.* Munich: Kösel Verlag, 1963.
Schroer, Silva. *Die Samuelbücher. NSKAT* 7. Stuttgart: Verlag Katholisches Bibelwerk, 1992.
Schwienhorst, L. *Die Eroberung Jerichos: Exegetische Untersuchung zu Josua* 6. SB 122. Stuttgart: Verlag Katholisches Bibelwerk, 1986.
Seebaas, H. *Numeri.* BKAT 4/1. Neuchirchen-Vlyun: Neuchirchener Verlag, 1993.
Seow, C. L. "Ark of the Covenant," *ABD* 1: 386-93.
———. "The Designation of the Ark in Priestly Theology." *HAR* 8 (1984) 185-98.
———. *Myth, Drama, and the Politics of David's Dance.* Atlanta: Scholar, 1989.
Seybold, K. *Die Psalmen.* HAT 1/15. Tübingen: J. C. B. Mohr, 1996.
Settgast, J. *Tutanchamun.* Mainz am Rhein: Philipp von Zabern, 1980.
Sevensma, T. P. *De ark Gods.* Amsterdam: Clausen, 1908.
Shea, W. H. "The Travels of the Ark of the Covenant." *Archaeology and Biblical Research* 3:3 (1990) 73-79.
Simons, J. *Jerusalem in the Old Testament.* Leiden: Brill, 1952.
Smelik, K. A. D. "Hidden Messages in the Ark Narrative." In *Converting the Past: Studies in Ancient Israelite and Moabite Historiography.* Oudtestamentische Studiën 28, 35-58. Leiden: Brill, 1992.
Smith, H. P. *A Critical and Exegetical Commentary on the Books of Samuel.* ICC. Edinburgh: T & T Clark, 1899.
Sœbø, M. "paʿam."In *ThWAT,* 703-8. Vol. 6.
Soggin, J. A. "The Ark of the Covenant: Jeremiah 3:16." In *Le livre de Jérémie,* edited by P. Bogaert, 215-21. Leuven: Leuven University Press, 19972.
———. *Introduction to the Old Testament.* Translated by John Bowden from the Italian. London: SCM, 1989.
———. *Josué.* CAT 5a. Paris: De la chaux & Niestlé, 1970.
Southwell, P. J. M. "Bethel." *NIDOTTE,* 440-41. Vol. 4.
Starbuck, S.R.A. *Court Oracles in the Psalms: The So-Called Royal Psalms in their Ancient Near Eastern Context.* SBLDS 172. Atlanta: Society of Biblical Literature, 1999.
Stoebe, H. J. *Das erste Buch Samuelis.* KAT 8:1. Gütersloh, Germany: Gütersloher Verlagshaus, 1973.
———. *Das zweite Buch Samuelis.* KAT 8:2. Gütersloh, Germany: Gütersloher Verlagshaus, 1994.
Stolz, Fritz. *Das erste und zweite Buch Samuel.* Zürcher Bibelkommentare. Zürich: TVZ, 1981.
Straus, S. A. "Schilder on the Covenant." In *Always Obedient: Essays on the Teaching of Dr. Klaas Schilder,* edited by J. Geertsema, 19-33. Phillipsburg, NJ: P&R, 1995.
Sweeney, Marvin A. *1 and 2 Kings: A Commentary.* OTL. Louisville, KY: John Knox, 2007.
Tate, M.E. *Psalms 51-100.* WBC 20. Dallas: Word Books, 1990.
Taws, Donald H. "Guardian of the Ark?" *New Horizons* (July 1994) 10-11.
Tedwell, N.L. "1 Sam. II 18 and 2 Sam VI 14." *VT* 24 (1974) 505-7.
Thiele, E. R. *The Mysterious Numbers of the Hebrew Kings.* Grand Rapids: Zondervan, 1984.
Thompson, J. A. *The Book of Jeremiah.* The New International Commentary on the Old Testament. Grand Rapids: Eerdmans, 1980.

Tigay, J. H. *Deuteronomy*. The JPS Commentary. Philadelphia: Jewish Publication Society, 1996.
Timm, Hermann. "Die Ladeerzählung (1 Sam 4–6; 2 Sam 6): Und das Kerygma des deuteronomistischen Geschichtswerks." *EvTh* 26 (1966) 509–26.
Tov, Emanuel. *Textual Criticism of the Hebrew Bible (3rd ed. rev.)*. Minneapolis: Fortress, 2012.
Trimp, C. *Heilsgeschiedenis en prediking*. Kampen, the Netherlands: Van den Berg, 1986.
Tsumura, David Toshio. *The First Book of Samuel*, The New International Commentary on the Old Testament. Grand Rapids: Eerdmans, 2007.
Tur-Sinai, N. H. "The Ark of God at Beit Shemesh (1 Sam. VI) and Peres 'Uzza (2 Sam. VI; 1 Chron. XIII)." *VT* 1 (1951) 275–86.
Ungnad, A. *Akkadian Grammar*. Translated by Harry A. Hoffner, Jr. Atlanta: Scholar, 1992.
Van Dam, C. *The Urim and Thummim*. Winona Lake, IN: Eisenbrauns, 1997.
Van der Toorn, K. "The Iconic Book Analogies between the Babylonian Cult of Images and the Veneration of the Torah." In *The Image and the Book*, edited by K. van der Toorn, 229–48. Leuven: Peeters, 1997.
Van der Toorn, K., and Cees Houtman. "David and the Ark." *JBL* 113 (1994) 209–31.
Van Duin, C., ed. *Selected Studies in Old Testament Exegesis*. Leiden: Brill, 1991.
Van Groningen, G. *Messianic Revelation in the Old Testament*. Grand Rapids: Baker, 1990.
Van Seters, J. *In Search of History*. New Haven: Yale University Press, 1983.
Van Zyle, A. H. *1 Samuël*. POut. Nijkerk, the Netherlands: Callenbach, 1989.
Vatke, W. *Die biblische Theologie wissenschaftlich dargestellt*. Vol. 1. Berlin: Bethge, 1835.
Volkwein, Von Bruno. "Masoretisches `ēdūt, `ēdwūt, `ēdōt—«Zeugnis» oder «Bundesbestimmungen»?" *BZ* 13 (1969) 18–40.
Von Ewald, G. H. A. *The History of Israel*. Vol. 3. London: Longmans, Green & Co., 1878.
Von Rad, G. *Deuteronomium=Studien*. Göttingen: Vandenhoeck & Ruprecht, 1947.
———. *Das fünfte Buch Mose: Deuteronomium*. Göttingen: Vandenhoeck & Ruprecht, 1983.
———. "Das judäische Königsritual." In *Gesammelte Studien zum Alten Testament*. ThB 8 (1958) 203–13.
———. "Zelt und Lade." In *Gesammelte Studien zum Alten Testament*. TB 8 (1958) 109–29.
Von Sodon, Wolfram. *Grundriss der Akkadischen Grammatik*. Rome: Pontificium Institutum Biblicum, 1995.
Weippert, Manfred. "Fargen des israelitischen Geschichtsbewusstseins." *VT* 23 (1973) 415–42.
Weiser, Artur. *Die Psalmen*. ATD 14. Göttingen: Vandenhoeck & Ruprecht, 1987.
Weisman, Z. "The Nature and Background of Bāḥūr in the Old Testament." *VT* 31 (1981) 441–50.
Wellhausen, J. *Prolegomena zur Geschichte Israels*. 6th ed. Berlin: Georg Reimer, 1927.
———. *Der Text der Bücher Samuelis*. Göttingen: Vandenhoeck & Ruprecht, 1871.
Werner, W. *Das Buch Jeremia (1–25)*. NSKAT 19:1. Stuttgart: Verlag Katholisches Bibelwerk, 1997.
Wevers, J. W. *Notes on the Greek Text of Exodus*. SCSS 30. Atlanta: Scholar, 1990.
Willis, John T. "QUMAH YHWH." *JNSL* 16 (1990) 207–21.
———. "Samuel Versus Eli, 1 Sam. 1–77." *TZ* 35 (1979) 201–12.

Wilson, I. "Merely a Container? The Ark in Deuteronomy." In *Temple and Worship in Biblical Israel*, edited by John Day, 212–49. London: T & T Clark, 2005.

Wood, B. G. "Did the Israelites Conquer Jericho? A New Look at the Archaeological Evidence." *BAR* 16, 2 (1990) 44–58.

Woudstra, M. H. *The Ark of the Covenant from Conquest to Kingship*. Philadelphia: Presbyterian and Reformed Publishing, 1965.

———. "The Ark of the Covenant in Jeremiah 3:16–18." In *Grace Upon Grace: Essays in Honor of Lester J. Kuyper*, edited by James I. Cook, 117–26. Grand Rapids: Eerdmans, 1975.

———. *The Book of Joshua*. Grand Rapids: Eerdmans, 1981.

———. "The Tabernacle in Biblical Theological Perspective." In *New Perspectives on the Old Testament*, edited by B. Payne, 88–103. London: Waco, 1970.

Wright, David P., et al., eds. *Pomegranates Golden Bells: Studies in Biblical, Jewish, and Near Eastern Ritual, Law, and Literature in Honor of Jacob Milgrom*. Winona Lake, IN: Eisenbrauns, 1995.

———. "Music and Dance in 2 Samuel 6." *JBL* 12:2 (2002) 201–25.

Wright, G. E. *The Old Testament and Theology*. New York: Harper & Row, 1969.

Wright, G. R. H. *Ancient Building in South Syria and Palestine*. Leiden: Brill, 1985.

Yadin, Y. "Some Aspects of the Strategy of Ahab and David." *Biblica* 36 (1955) 332–51.

Zobel, H. J. "$s^e\underline{b}\bar{a}\bar{o}\underline{t}$." *ThWAT*, 876–92. Vol. 6.

Zohary, M. *Plants of the Bible*. Cambridge: Cambridge University Press, 1982.

Zwickel, W. "Dagons abgeschlagener Kopf [1 Samuel v 3–4]." *VT* 44 (1994) 239–49.

Scripture Index

OLD TESTAMENT

Genesis

Ref	Page
1:1—2:3	65
3:24	22, 26
4:5	93
4:20	42
4:26	29
6:14	16
12:7	141
12:8	42
13:7	55n15
15:2	131
15:8	131
15:16	56n14
15:16–21	65
15:18	55
15:19–21	55
17	30
17:1	127
17:8	71
19:25	30
22:12	93
22:14	46n3
23:1–3	55n15
24:35	68
26:12	68
26:34	55n15
28:3	68
28:10–22	132
28:11–22	144
30:1	103
31:13	144
31:48	15
31:50	15
35:2	53
35:4	142
35:7	144
35:12	68
36:2–3	55n15
45:5	93n39
49:6	107
49:24	34, 118

Exodus

Ref	Page
3:1–4	147
3:8	55
3:20	53n6
7:20—12:30	74n15
12:12	77, 78
12:29	25
12:35–36	3
13	8n32
13:5	55
14:6	54n9
14:21	66n51
15:18	139
16:3	133
16:10	23, 113
16:33	111
16:33–34	132
16:34	132
17:16	37
19:2	58n24
19:5	30
19:5–6	125
19:6	31, 96
19:10	53

Exodus (cont.)

Reference	Pages
19:10–15	53
19:14–15	53
19:20	147
20:16	15
22:11	91n33
22:27	127
23:16	42
23:23	55
23:28	55
24	8n32
24:10–18	147
24:16	23
24:16–17	136
25	4n17, 5, 49, 50
25:10	28
25:10–15	5–13
25:10–22	50
25:11	8
25:12	9
25:12–15	95, 111
25:13–15	9
25:14	92
25:15	10
25:16	10, 12, 15, 132
25:16–21	14
25:17	10, 16
25:17–22	2
25:18	17
25:18–19	20
25:18–20	11, 19
25:18–22	22
25:20a	21
25:20b	26
25:21	12, 15, 52
25:21–22	12
25:22	11, 12, 18, 24, 28, 31, 35
25:25	9n33
25:40	134
26:1	22, 134
26:9	134
26:29	8n32
26:30	134
26:31	22
26:33	31, 32, 132
26:33–34	28
26:34	31, 32, 132
26:36	22
26:37	8n32
27:26	8n32
28	8n32, 96
28:36	130
30:3	8n32
30:5	8n32
30:6	2, 18, 31, 35, 132
30:26	31, 132
32:13	117
33:2	55, 55
33:5–6	3
33:19	127
34:1	50
34:6	127
34:10	53n6
34:11	55
34:22	42
34:28–29	10, 15
35:12	2
35:31–33	7
37	5, 10
37:1	7, 28, 96
37:1–5	5–13
37:1–9	50
37:3	9
37:6	10, 16
37:7–9	19
38:21	134
39:27	22
39:30	130
39:35	2, 31
39:43	100
40:3	31
40:5	31
40:20	2, 10, 15, 132
40:21	31
40:34	23
40:34–35	112
40:36–37	136

Leviticus

1:3	81
3:1	100
7:8	100
7:11–18	100
7:15	100, 101n71
9:22	139
9:23	23
10:10	79
11:45	127
16:2	2, 12
16	18
16:2	2, 11, 12, 17, 18
16:13	12, 18
16:13–15	2, 17
16:14–15	18
17:11	17
19:12	127
20:26	127
21:8	127
22:9	81
23:34	107
23:42	42
23:43	42, 108
26:3–13	94
26:21	79
26:24	79
26:28	79

Numbers

1:3	72n11
1:53	52
2:17	46
3:28	52
3:29–31	90
3:32	52
4:4	52, 95, 131
4:5	31
4:15	33, 52, 92, 109, 131
6:24–26	100n68, 139
7:9	90
7:89	2, 11, 12, 18, 24, 31, 36
10:9	63
10:12	46
10:21	46
10:29	45
10:31	45
10:32	45
10:33	46, 61
10:33–36	45–49
10:33a	46
10:33b	46
10:34	47
10:35	47, 120
10:35–36	36, 39, 47n9, 147
10:36	49
11:3	46
11:18	53
11:26	47n9
12:4	47
12:5	47
12:6–8	13
13:2	56
13:29	55
14:10	23
14:14b	47
14:44	46
16:8–9	113
16:19	23
17:5	133
17:10	133
17:25	111, 132, 133
21:26	55n15
23:21	139
34:2–12	56n15
34:18	56
35:30	15

Deuteronomy

1:10	49
1:16	66n51
1:30	48n12
3:11	7
3:24	131
4:19	49
4:31	68
4:46	55n15
5:5	93

Deuteronomy (*cont.*)

5:14	66n51
6:2	66, 141
6:13	61
7:1	55
7:6	30
7:12–16	68
8:15–19	70
9:9	46
9:11	46
9:15	46
9:25–29	49
9:27	117
10	4n17, 5, 10, 40
10:1	52
10:1–5	3, 28, 40, 49, 96
10:1a	50
10:3	7, 50
10:4	50
10:5	50, 112, 132
10:8	40, 109, 113
11:26	68
12:5	118
12:7	108
12:9	47n7
12:11	142
12:12	108
12:18	108
14:21	66n51
14:26	108
14:29	66n51
15:2	91n33
16:11	66n51, 108
16:14	66n51, 108
17:9	52n2
17:14–20	70
17:15	66n51
17:18	25
18:1	52n2
18:1–14	94
18:18	108
20:17	55
24:8	52n2
24:19–21	66n51
26:11	108
26:12–13	66n51
27	67
27:1–7	66n49
27:1–8	141
27:2	67
27:7	108
27:9	52n2, 67
27:9–14	52n2
27:12–13	66
27:14	67
27:15–26	67
27:19	66n51
30:1	68
31:9	31, 109
31:9–13	108
31:25	31
31:26	31, 40, 49–51
31:26–28	133
33:1	100
33:5	139

Joshua

1:1–9	54
1:10	54
2:11	30
2:8–11	62
3	59
3:1—4:24	52–62
3:2–4	54
3:3	31, 52, 60
3:4	53, 131
3:5	53, 53n6, 72
3:5–6	54
3:6	31, 57, 57n19, 60
3:7	54, 61
3:7–13	57n19
3:8	31, 55, 61
3:9	54
3:9–13	54
3:10	55, 61
3:10a	55
3:10b	55
3:11	56, 61

Joshua (cont.)

3:12	56, 60
3:13	30, 55, 56, 58, 60
3:14	57, 60
3:14–15	57n20
3:14–16	57n20
3:15	28
3:15a	57
3:15b	58, 128
3:16	57n20, 58
3:16–17	58
3:16a	57
3:17	58, 61
4:2	56
4:2–5	60
4:3	59
4:5	59
4:7	59, 60
4:8	59
4:9	59–60
4:10	28
4:11	60
4:16	31, 60
4:19	58
4:20	59
4:22	59
4:23	60
4:24	30, 61, 128
5:1	55n15, 62
5:14–15	49
6	62n34, 85n7, 128
6:1	62n37
6:1–21	62–65
6:1b	62n37
6:2	62
6:2–5	61
6:4	28
6:5	65
6:6–7	61
6:7-9	64
6:8–9	61
6:9	28
6:10	61
6:11	64n44
6:11–15	61
6:12	64
6:13	64
6:14	64
6:15	64
6:16	65
6:16–19	61
6:20	65
6:20–21	61
6:20a	65
6:20b	65
7:6	46
7:13	53
8	67
8:30–35	140, 141, 147
8:33	52n2, 66–68, 141
8:33–35	67n55
8:34–35	66, 141
9:1	55
9:17	82, 89
9:17–27	88, 145
11:3	55
12:8	55
13:10	55n15
13:21	55n15
14:15	88
15:8	55n15
15:9	82, 145
15:15	88
15:60	88
17:15	55n15
18:14	88
18:28	55n15
19:45	94
21:1–3	142
21:24	94
22:6	100
22:9–34	142
24	42
24:11	55
24:14	61, 93
24:15	55n15
24:22	15
24:26	141

Judges

1:11	88
1:22–26	55n15
1:34–35	55n15
3:3	55n15
3:5	55
5:12	48
5:28	98
7:9–25	64n45
8:27	41
9:4	102
11:5–11	71n7
16:23	77
18:31	134, 136, 142, 143
19:22	69
20:2	107
20:18	42, 144
20:23	144
20:23–28	42
20:26	144
20:27	140, 143, 144, 147
21:2	140
21:5	107
21:8	107
21:16–24	142
21:19–21	42

Ruth

1:9	47n7
3:15	95
4:1–12	71n7
4:7	15

1 Samuel

1:3	69
1–4	42, 85, 140
1–6	84
1:11–12	143
1:3	69, 143
1:5–6	103
1:9	143n48
1:11	69
1:13–17	69
1:15	143n48
2:1–10	69
2:12	69
2:18	96
2:22	69
2:25	70, 74
2:27–36	70, 75
2:34	74
3:1	70
3:1–14	143
3:3	35, 130, 143n48
3:5	72
3:11–14	70
3:13	75
3:15	143n48
4	33, 37, 41, 42, 135
4–6	2, 84–86, 131, 134n20, 145
4:1—7:1	70
4:1b–22	70–76
4:1b—7:1	84
4:2	71
4:3	29, 121n37, 142
4:3a	71
4:3b	71
4:4	30, 39, 72, 73, 89
4:5	74
4:5–6	63
4:7–8	74
4:8	78
4:10–11	74, 89
4:17	75
4:18	75
4:21–22	147
4:22	29
5:1—6:1	76–79
5:2	29
5:3	76–79
5:3a	77
5:3b	77
5:5	77
5:6	80n38
5:7	78
5:8	78, 85

1 Samuel (cont.)

5:8b	64n44
5:9–10	64n44
5:9a	78
5:11	79
5:12	79
6	131
6:1	79
6:2—7:1	79–83
6:3	79
6:4	78n31
6:5	79
6:7	80, 89
6:9	80
6:12	81, 130
6:13	28, 81
6:17–18	81
6:19	82, 147
6:20	82, 85
6:21	82, 119, 145
6:26	72n11
7:1	82, 85n7, 87n13, 90, 90n26, 119, 145
7:2	147
7:4	72n11
7:5–12	145
10:5	75
12:14	61
12:17	72n11
12:24	61
12:41	72n11
12:51	72n11
13	104
13:3–4	75
13:12–22	75
13:19–22	71, 75
13:20–22	76
13:21–22	76
13:23	75
14:18	421
15	104
15:11	93
16:4	107
17:12	119n12
17:45	72
17:47	107
17:51	77
18:7	90n27
21	99n62
22:18	89, 145
22:19	89, 145
23:1	89, 145
23:27	89, 145
28:17	131
31:8–10	78n31
31:9	77

2 Samuel

2:28	97
2:35	112
3:31–39	86
4:3	94
4:9–12	86
4:12	77
5	8987
5:1	86
5:17–25	86
5:6–10	86
5:7	93, 145
6	33, 41, 84–86, 97, 97n54, 106, 122, 138–39, 145, 147
6:1	87, 108
6:1–2	87–90
6:1–19	85, 87
6:1–20	84
6:2	30, 73, 74, 82, 89
6:2a	88
6:2–19	85
6:3	109, 119
6:3–5	89–91
6:3a	89
6:3b	90
6:4	90
6:5	96
6:6–8	91–93, 147
6:6b	91
6:7	85, 92

2 Samuel (cont.)

6:8	93
6:8a	93
6:9	85n7, 93, 93n39
6:9–11	93–94
6:11	94
6:12	94
6:12–15	94–97
6:12–19	94–101
6:13	95
6:14a	96
6:15	96
6:16	97
6:17	29, 42
6:17–19	99–101
6:17b	99–100, 99n61
6:18b	100
6:19	101
6:20	102
6:20–22	103
6:20–23	97, 88, 102–4
6:21–22	102
6:22	102
6:23	103
7	115
7:2	99, 99n61
7:6	99n61
7:8	72n11
7:18–20	131
7:26	72n11
11:11	42
16:22	42
21:1–14	104
22:11	21

1 Kings

1	25
1:1–4	105
1:5–7	105
1:17	105
1:33–35	105
2	25
2:27	112, 105
3:4	99n62, 135
3:12	106
4:29	106
6:1	107n9
6:9	6
6:13	137
6:15–18	6
6:16	110
6:19	110
6:23–27	137
6:27	110
6:37–38	107n9
6:38	106
7:30	9
7:51	106, 108n12
8	22, 136, 138
8:1	107, 145
8:1–3a	106–8
8:1–13	137
8:1	106
8:3b–4	108
8:3b–5	108–10
8:4	135
8:5	109
8:6	137
8:6–7	110
8:6–11	110–13
8:7	137
8:8	10, 111
8:9	10, 39n30, 110, 132
8:9b	136
8:10	136
8:10–11	112
8:10–13	137
8:10b	136
8:11	23
8:13	23, 110
8:22	58n24
8:56	106, 112
8:62–63	109
9:15	105
9:17–19	105
10:1–4	106
14:21	105
22:19	37

2 Kings

8:4	99n61
9:33	91n33
10:3	25
10:30	25
11:19	25
12:10	1
12:11	1
14:25	94
17:15	14, 31
17:33	61
17:36	61
19:15	137
19:23	91n29
21:3	149
21:7	149

1 Chronicles

9:23	134
10:10	78n31
13:1	87
13:1–3	88
13:1–14	87–89
13:3	41, 64n44, 89, 145
13:6	30, 87, 88
13:8	90
13:9	91n31
13:12	33, 94
15:2	95
15:2–15	95
15:3	95
15:11–15	109
15:13	92–3, 95
15:18	94
15:21	94
15:24	94
15:25	95
15:26	109
15:28	97
16:1	29
16:4	140
16:37	140
16:37–42	99
16:38	94
16:39	75
21:29	135
22:9	105
28:2	16, 39, 129, 137
29:1	119
29:11	131

2 Chronicles

1:3	75, 135
1:4	135
5:2–5	135
6	121
6:6	96
6:41–42	114
8:3	105
8:5–6	105
8:11	130
9:18	119
24:8	1
24:10	1
24:11	1
28:14	107
29:11	113
32:30	93
33:3	149
33:4	96
33:7	149
35:3	149
35:3	124, 149

Nehemiah

8:10	97n54
8:14	42
8:17	42
13:21	58n24

Job

9:13	92n37
16:19	15
22:25–26	8

Psalms

2:6	122, 146

Psalms (cont.)

3:8	120
5:8	137
7:7	120
8:1	119
8:2	131
9:4	119
9:4–7	120
9:11	146
9:12	107, 146
9:20	120
10:12	120
11:4	119, 137
14:7	146
17:13	120
18:5	69
18:9–10	23
18:10	21
18:11	21
19:1	119
20:3	107, 146
22:3	64n45, 138
23:6	129
24	72n12, 97
24:1	30, 97, 131
24:3	46
24:7–10	97
24:8	72n12, 121n37
24:8–10	72n11
25:7	117
26:8	137
27:4	137, 143n48
29:10	25, 97
35:2	120
42:3	137
42:9	64n45
43:3	137
45:6	120
46:6–7	64n45
46:7–11	72n11
47	49, 97
47:5	99
47:6	97n54
47:8	25, 120
48:1	119
48:2	146
48:3	107, 146
48:7	101, 122, 146
50:2	107, 146
53:6	146
65:4	137
65:5	137
66:7	97
68	97
68:17	99
68:20	131
68:25–26	139
69:7	72
71:5	131
71:16	131
73:28	131
76:2	146
76:10	120
77:3	64n45
77:7	64n45
78:12–20	53n6
78:14	64n45
78:24–25	133
78:59–61	75
78:60–64	99n62
78:65–66	79n35
80:1	21
81:3	97
84:2	72
84:4	72
84:5	137
84:9	72
89:14	120
93:1	119
93:1–2	120
95:6	81
97:2	120
98:1	53n6
98:6	97
99:1	21
99:1–2	146
99:2	119
99:5	16, 38, 119, 129, 146

Psalms (cont.)

99:9	38, 130, 146
103:19	119, 120
104:17	91n29
105:39	47
107:1	129
109:21	131
110:2	146
111:9	130
115:3	128, 131
115:4–7	77
116:26	129
118:1	129
118:29	129
119:91	119
122:1	137
128:5	146
132	97, 113–23, 115n4, 116, 138
132:1	116n12, 117, 122
132:1–5	116n12
132:1–7	88
132:1–10	116, 117–22
132:1–16	115
132:2	33–4, 116n12, 118, 122
132:2–5	116, 118
132:3–5	116, 118
132:3b	118
132:4	118
132:5	33–4, 118
132:5–7	10
132:6–9	116n12, 14, 122
132:6–10	116n12
132:6b	119
132:7	38, 117, 119, 121, 129, 146
132:8	120, 121
132:8–10	114
132:8–11	121
132:10	116, 117, 122
132:11	25, 116, 118, 122
132:11–12	116, 115
132:11–13	116n12
132:11–18	116, 116n12, 122–23
132:11ab	116n12
132:11b–12	118
132:11c–12	116n12
132:12	14, 31, 122
132:13	99, 116n12, 122
132:13–14	99, 122, 140
132:13–16	122
132:14	38, 99, 119
132:14–18	116n12
132:15	101, 122n39
132:15–17	146
132:15–18	122, 116n12
132:16	112
132:17	115, 122
132:17–18	115
132:17a	116
132:18	122
133	140, 146
134	146
135:15–17	77
135:6	128
136:1	29
136:23	117
137	146
138:2	137
140:7	131
146:10	97, 146
148:13	119
149:3	96
150:3	97
150:4	96

Proverbs

20:8	25

Ecclesiastes

12:13	61

Isaiah

2:2–4	123
2:3	46

Isaiah (cont.)

6:1	38
6:3	72n11
8:18	101, 122, 146
13:4	72n11
14:8	91n8
30:29	46
37:16	21, 30, 73
40:25	130
44:9–20	77
48:13	119
49:26	34, 118
59:20	146
60:13	91n29
60:17	8
66:1	16, 38, 39, 40, 129

Jeremiah

2:27	37
3:14	123
3:15–18	123
3:16	35, 123–26, 140, 148
3:16–17	36–37, 39
3:16a	124–25
3:16b	116
3:17	37
3:17a	37, 125
3:19–22	123
7	77
7:12	142
7:12–15	99n62
7:14	142
10:10–11	55
17:4	91n33
31:33	126
32:17	128
45:3	47n7

Lamentations

2:1	39, 119, 129

Ezekiel

1	22, 36
1:6–11	20
1:9–11	23
1:26	23
9:3	21, 23
10	22
10:4	21, 23
10:14–22	20
10:18	23
11:22	23
16:3	55n15
16:45	55n15
18:4	131
28:14	22
28:16	22
34	123
37:15–23	123
38:12	101, 122, 146
41:18	22
41:25	22
44:11	113

Daniel

9:1–2	79

Hosea

7:5	97n54

Joel

2:15	97

Amos

3:6	63
9:11	123

Jonah

1:5	61
1:9	61
1:10	61
1:16	61
3:3	46
4:5	57n19
4:9	93n40

Micah

4:1–4	123
4:2	46
4:7	146
7:15	53n6

Habakkuk

3:8	92n37

Zephaniah

3:14–17	123

Zechariah

11:2	91n29

~

NEW TESTAMENT

Matthew

6:29	106

John

6:32–35	133
6:58	133

Acts

3:24	70
4:24	119

Romans

11:36	131

1 Corinthians

15:25–28	81

2 Corinthians

6:15	69

Ephesians

1:22	81

Colossians

1:16	119

Hebrews

1:1	xvii
9:4	111–12, 132–33
9:5	24, 130
11:30	63, 65

1 Peter

1:7	8

Revelation

4	36
15:4	130

~

APOCRYPHA AND SEPTUAGINT

2 Esdras

10:20–22	148

2 Maccabees

2:4–7	148

~

MISHNAH, TALMUD, AND RELATED LITERATURE

Midrash Yadayim

3:5	47n9

Yoma

72a	9n42
72b	8n37

Author Index

Ackroyd, P. R., 98n58, 99n63
Aharoni, Y., 57n22, 86n9, 88n21
Ahlström, G. W., 82n46
Albright, W. F., 87n18
Allen, L. C., 115, 121
Alt, A., 86n8
Amit, Y., 144
Amsler, S., 51
Anderson, G., 44n47
Arnold, R.W., xvn1, 41
Auffret, P., 116n14

Bavinck, H., 131n8
Bentzen, A., 117
Berlejung, A., 80n38
Bergen, R. D., 77n26
Besters, A., 62n36
Block, D. I., 144
Bock, S., 44n47
Briend, Jaques, 119n25
Broekhuis, J., 5n20
Brongers, H. A., 100
Brouwer, C., xv, xviii3, 53n3, 88n2, 98, 119, 142, 143n48
Brueggemann, W., 75, 96, 138, 103n77
Budde, K., 94
Buis, P., 112n28, 136

Calvin, J., 25n48, 48n12, 112n27, 121n37
Campbell, A. F., 5n21, 76n22, 87n13
Carroll, R. P., 126
Carlson, R. A., 96n50
Cassuto, U., 18n24

Cazelles, H., 124
Coats, G. W., 54n9, 59, 63, 65n48
Crüsemann, F., 102n75

Dahood, M., 116n12, 120
Day, John, 149
de Moor, J. C., 108n12
Dempsey, D. A., 146
De Tarragon, J. M., 88n99,
De Vaulx, J., 47n9
De Vaux, Roland, 12, 16n9, 39
Dibelius, M., xv, 2, 4, 36–37
Dietrich, W., 103n79

Eichrodt, W., 48n12
Eissfeldt, O., 3, 73n12, 86n9
Eynikel, Erik, 84, 85n7, 92n36

Fohrer, G., xvii
Fretheim, T. E., 116, 121, 137
Fritz, Volkmar, 110–11

Geyer, J. B., 80n38
Gootjes, N. H., 7n31
Gordon, R. P., 94
Goslinga, C. J., 87n14, 101
Gottwald, N. K., 44n47
Graf, K. H., 2n8
Gressmann, H., 3, 33–34,
Gunkel, H., xvn2, 33, 35–36, 114
Gunneweg, A. H., 109n14, 134
Guthe, H., 3, 33–34

Hague, S. T., 135
Haran, M., 21, 119n28, 149
Harman, Allan, 23

Harrison, R. K., 78n29
Hartmann, R., 4
Hegel, G. W. F., 32, 135
Heinemann, O., 6
Herrmann, S., 44n47, 86n8
Hillers, D. R., 120–21
Hoftijzer, J., 54n8
Hostetter, E. C., 55n15
House, P. R., 111
Houtman, 14n1, 28–29, 85n7, 88n19, 90n26
Howard, D. M., 59

Jacob, B., 9, 11n47, 14
Jacquet, L., 114, 116n12
Janowski, B., 18n21, 25, 14n1, 64n44
Jones, D. R., 37, 124
Josephus, 25n49, 26, 82n43, 102, 109
Joüon, Paul, 64n44

Kaufman, A. S., 7
Keel, O., 98
Keil, C. F., 87n14, 88n22
Klein, R. W., 94n42
Koch, Klaus, 17
Koolhaas, A. A., 103n76
Kraus, H. J., 39n24, 121, 121n37, 139
Kristensen, W. B., 36
Krüger, T., 94n42
Külling, S. R., 30n11

Leiman, Sid Z., 47n9
Levine, B. A., 47n9
Lewis, Joe O., 5n21
Lieberman, S., 47n9
Linville, J. R., 136
Loretz, O., 133n16
Lotz, W., 2, 32

Maag, V., 73n12
Maier, Johann, xv, xvin2, 2, 5n21, 27, 132, 139

Mauchline, J., 92n35
May, H. G., 34–35, 132
Mays, J. L., 118, 121, 123
McKay, J. W., 115, 118
Meinhold, J., 36
Mendenhall, G. E., 87n17
Mettinger, T. N. D., 19, 115
Milgrom, J., 47n9, 80n38
Miller, P. D., 84, 87n16, 95n46, 145
Mitchell, D. C., 126n36
Mowinckel, Sigmund, 96n47, 121, 138–39
Mulder, M.J., 108n12, 111
Murray, D. F., 24n46, 103n77

Na'aman, N., 67n55
Naumann, T., 103n79
Noort, Ed, 62n34
Noth, M., 4, 43–44, 113, 132

Ohmann, H. M., 99n62, 101n72, 103n76

Pietsch, M., 114, 115n4
Porter, J. R., 96n50
Powell, M., 7
Price, R., 149

Rashbam, 11n47
Rashi, S., 9n41
Reimpell, W., 4, 36
Rendsburg, G. A., 116, 119n27
Rendtorff, Rolf, 101, 136
Roberts, J. J., 82n48, 84, 87n16, 95n46, 145
Rogerson, J. W., 115, 118
Ross, J. P., 72n12
Rost, L., 84
Rowe, J. Y., 104
Rowley, H. H., 99n61, 100n66
Rupprecht, K., 99n61

Sarna, Nahum M., 21
Schicklberger, F., 73n22, 88n20
Schley, D. G., 142

Schmidt, Werner H., 29n8
Schreiner, J., 122n38
Schroer, Silva, 132
Schwienhorst, L., 64n44
Seow, C. L., 27, 27n2, 28–29, 92n37, 116n14
Sevensma, T. P., xv, xvin2, 2
Seybold, K., 114, 116–17, 119n24
Simons, J., 91n32
Smelik, K. A. D., 84
Soggin, J. A., 29n8, 59, 124n43
Starbuck, S. R. A., 116n14
Stoebe, H. J., 24n46, 73n13, 90n27
Stolz, Fritz, 24n46

Timm, Hermann, 74n16
Tur-Sinai, N. H., 91n31

van Dam, C., 144
Van der Toorn, K., 85n7, 88n19
Van Seters, J., 84, 85n6
Van Zyle, A. H., 78n31
Vatke, W., 132
Von Ewald, G. H. A., 108n12
Von Rad, G., 5, 16, 28, 39–40, 135

Weiser, Artur, 115n9, 121
Wellhausen, J., xvin2, 1–2, 2n8, 134–35
Wevers, J. W., 17
Willis, John T., 82n48, 121, 145
Wilson, I., 40
Woudstra, M. H., ix, xv, xvin3, 24, 42, 125
Wright, David P., 96n50
Wright, G. E., 44n47

Yadin, Y., 42
Youngblood, R. F., 143n48

Zobel, H. J., 73n12
Zohary, M., 6
Zwickel, W., 77n26

www.ingramcontent.com/pod-product-compliance
Lightning Source LLC
Chambersburg PA
CBHW071515150426
43191CB00009B/1533